PERSONAL FINANCE FOR CONSUMERS

PERSONAL FINANCE FOR CONSUMERS

Benjamin M. Trooboff

Atlanta University

Fannie Lee Boyd

University of Georgia

GENERAL LEARNING PRESS
250 James Street
Morristown, New Jersey 07960

ILLUSTRATIONS BY RICH BERRY

Photo credits: All photos by Victoria Beller-Smith except pp. 98–99, Chris Reeberg from D.P.I.; pp. 154–155, Grant Heilman; pp. 174–175, DeWys, Inc.; p. 199, Grant Heilman (top), Mimi Forsyth from Monkmeyer (middle), and Rocky Weldon from DeWys, Inc. (bottom); pp. 220–221, Culver Pictures, Inc.; pp. 238–239, Environmental Protection Agency; p. 247, DeWys, Inc.; pp. 260–261, Bruce Anspach/EPA; p. 263, Culver Pictures, Inc.; pp. 278–279, Mimi Forsyth from Monkmeyer.

Manufactured in the United States of America

Published simultaneously in Canada

Library of Congress Catalog Card Number 75–46172

ISBN 0–382–18183–2

Preface

Although as much as two-thirds of a person's life is devoted to making a living, too little emphasis has been placed on helping people acquire the knowledge and skills they will need to manage their earnings. Students ought to be given the means to cope with the complexities of our modern marketplace. Moreover, there is a pressing need to look at consumer education and consumer economics from the point of view of the individual rather than the total society. What this book presents is a practical, "micro" view of consumer economics; rather than encouraging blind reliance on the opinions of experts, it tries to help each student make his or her own decisions about personal money management.

We use a "systems" approach to the subject; that is, we stress the interrelationships of spending, planning, values, goals, and resources. We try not to let the student lose sight of the fact that what he or she spends for the basics of food, shelter, and clothing influences what can be spent on recreation, transportation, and insurance. To increase the reader's involvement in the subject, the text presents case problems or critical incidents that concern particular people faced with particular financial decisions. These brief narratives should stimulate class discussion and motivate students to learn how the principles of consumer economics apply to everyday life.

The book is designed so that students can use some of the material in independent work-study programs. Instructors can enrich the presentation by making assignments from the annotated bibliographies and the suggested activities. There are also questions for discussion and glossaries of new terms at the ends of the chapters.

We believe that instructors in community and junior colleges, vocational-technical schools, and universities will find this book suitable for courses in personal finance, consumer economics, and consumer education. It may also fit the needs of adult seminars in consumer problems and advanced secondary-school courses in consumer education and family living.

Benjamin M. Trooboff
Fannie Lee Boyd

Contents

PERSONAL FINANCE FOR CONSUMERS

1

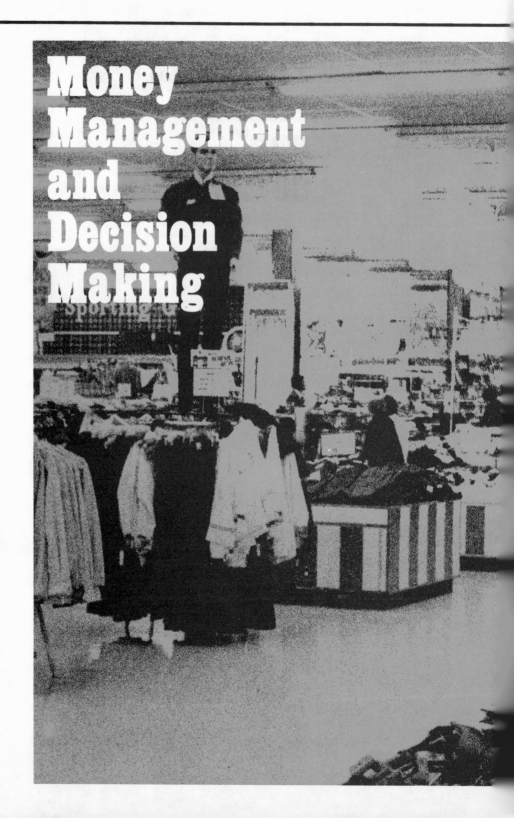

Money
Management
and
Decision
Making

1

Most people believe that there is nothing wrong with the way they manage their money; their only problem, they say, is that they don't have enough. High-salaried executives as well as low-income hourly workers are equally convinced that they could do better with their personal finances if only they had more.

This belief seems to assume that at some level of earnings a person should have enough money to get the satisfaction he or she seeks. Yet at virtually every earning level we find people who are troubled by their inability to manage their finances. At every level there are some people who are hopelessly in debt and cannot manage from one payday until the next. At the same time we find others who are able to maintain financial security and peace of mind regardless of their income level.

In almost any community you can find families whose income levels and family size are comparable, who live in similar houses in the

Good management
makes the difference.

same subdivision, and yet are in entirely different financial situations. Family A will be involved in one financial crisis after another, while Family B seems to have no money problems. What makes the difference? Obviously it is not how much they earn. It is the way they manage their money. Knowing how to plan their finances, the members of Family B are able to make their earnings do more for them.

There is no question about it! Knowing how to manage money helps a person get the most satisfaction from the dollars spent. The individual or family needs to make decisions about what is important —what to buy now and what to postpone to a later time when more funds are available. It is also important to be an informed consumer: to know how to compare different prices and terms and select the best buy; to know how to make spending decisions that bring the greatest satisfaction.

Read the following incidents. Have any of these things happened to you? Do you know someone in whose life these or similar incidents have occurred?

It's three days before payday and you don't have enough cash around the house to buy lunch or put gas in the car. You have to borrow money from a friend to tide you over.

You drive up to a service station and start to say, "Fill it up," but as you look into your billfold you find you have to say, "Put in a dollar's worth."

You arrive at the supermarket check-out counter and you find that you've selected more goods than you have money to pay for. You don't dare draw a check because your account is almost overdrawn now. So you remove some of the items to reduce your total.

Your personal check is sent back to your favorite department store by your bank, marked "insufficient funds." You had hoped that your latest deposit would clear the bank before the store deposited your check.

You selected some goods on one of your shopping trips that you "just had to have" even though you knew that buying them would prevent you from making your regular charge-account payments, which were already "past due."

> You walk out of the store in which you've just made a purchase and you ask yourself, "Did I get the best value? Did I overpay? Could I have done better elsewhere?"

All of these incidents demonstrate a person's inability to manage his or her money—the inability to plan wisely, the inability to get maximum satisfaction for money spent.

Lifestyle

When you consider these incidents, you will recognize that people spend money for goods and services so that they can establish a satisfying lifestyle. Your lifestyle can be identified by where you've chosen to live, the clothing you wear, the mode of transportation you use, the food you eat, how it is prepared, and how it is served. The way you use all of the resources available to you defines your lifestyle, which is part of what makes you unique. Putting this idea in different terms, we can say that your lifestyle is determined by your personal values, your goals, your needs and wants, and the resources you have at your disposal.

Values

A person develops his value system from several sources. Family beliefs and the culture in which we live are perhaps the greatest influences on the development of our values. Other factors are interaction with friends and the customs and practices of the people in our community. Experiences with institutions such as schools, churches, and social organizations also mold our values. Values, to put it simply, are the beliefs, feelings, and ideas we have about things. They have a great influence on the decisions we make and the way in which those decisions are carried out. They are our perceptions about the things around us, about ourselves, and about qualities we identify in other people. Our values are related to all aspects of our lives—social, political, religious, economic, and aesthetic. In learning to manage our personal finances we are concerned primarily with economic values; but values cannot be compartmentalized easily. We cannot limit our concerns to money and how to use it. For instance, when we earn money through mental or physical work we demonstrate a particular set of values; if we rob a bank or steal from someone to get money we show a different set of values. How we behave is directly affected by our value system.

Some people have not clearly identified their values. Perhaps they have not had to make decisions that forced them to. How would you answer the following questions, and to what values would they be related?

> Why save for a rainy day?
> Why shop for a loan with the lowest interest rate?
> Why give to charity?
> Why file a complaint when someone has taken advantage of you?
> Why should the wage earner buy the maximum amount of insurance when there are young children in the family?

Knowing what you want and why you want it gives direction to your life and determines how you use your money and other resources.

As we take part in our regular activities we are apt to have value conflicts. For example, we value clean, unpolluted air at the same time that we value the convenience of the automobile, one of the major contributors to air pollution. Which value should we respond to? Our values cannot be limited to our personal preferences, without consideration of the environment and the effect our choices will have on other people. If we are to act as responsible citizens we are forced to think twice before we cast our dollar votes by buying products that may be hazardous to others. We need to make choices between one value and another.

Goals

Goals, which are the targets toward which we direct our efforts, are also important in shaping our lifestyle. They enter into the choices we are forced to make in the marketplace. Goals have been described as the "what" of a decision: What are you seeking to attain? What are your dreams? What do you want to accomplish?

Clarifying your values and establishing goals are interrelated processes that set guidelines for your decisions as a consumer. Each person needs to have goals toward which to work even though they are not always achieved. Unless we identify our goals and know where we are headed we cannot map the way. And unless we know where we're going how do we know when we've arrived?

Goals can be short-term, intermediate, or long-term. Some things we work for can be accomplished quickly. Other goals may take months or even years to reach. Success in achieving goals acts as a reward and stimulates a desire to seek new goals. Some people, because of their cultural background or personality type, are unable to wait to achieve long-term goals. They need more immediate gratification. People who have this difficulty in working to achieve long-term goals should identify goals of accomplishment along the way. A succession of short-term goals can have the same effect as a single long-term goal.

Values and goals are not static; they don't stay the same. Rather, they are forever changing throughout the various stages in the life cycle. People of different ages have different interests, desires, and perceptions. The basic needs of an individual may remain constant, but the way in which the needs are satisfied may vary.

Needs and Wants

What we need and what we want are sometimes determined by our goals and at other times help us to define our goals. In order to get the most satisfaction from our spending we should be able to distinguish between our needs and our wants. Needs are those items that are essential. The most obvious needs are the basics that permit us to survive. Such things as food, shelter, and clothing are common needs for all persons. Wants, on the other hand, are those things that are "nice to have." They are the things we think will give us additional pleasure and satisfaction, though without them we could still manage to survive. Often our needs are clouded by what we have established as wants: Meat loaf will satisfy the need for protein in our diet, but will not satisfy our want for steak and the pleasure that steak gives us. There is nothing wrong with wanting steak; but if we start to think of steak as a *need* it may be difficult to live within a limited income.

Besides the basic needs, there are others that must be satisfied. Among these are love, economic security, protection from physical danger, achievement or self-fulfillment, health care, and some form of recreation. Not all of these are related to finances but most of them are. And here, too, the way we fill the needs is affected by the wants we have associated with them.

Resources

Whatever the need or want, the way we attempt to meet it is affected by the resources we have available. The greater our resources, the greater our ability to fill our needs and wants. But success in achieving a rewarding and satisfying lifestyle depends not only upon the amount of resources available to us but also upon the ways in which these resources are used. One type of resource is the money we use to buy those goods and services we think are necessary for maintaining our lifestyle. Other personal resources include time, energy, skills, and so on.

In addition to personal resources, we use, and are required to make crucial decisions about, natural or environmental resources such as water, air, parks, beaches, oceans, and forests. All of us are dependent on our natural resources for survival, for our comforts, and for the quality of life. When technological developments call for increases in the use of resources, how we allocate what we have becomes crucial. We must weigh the consequences of our choices; we need to become knowledgeable about the economic and environmental factors that affect our lives. How will our natural resources be used? Are these uses compatible with our lifestyles? Are our values in keeping with overall social needs? We can no longer "do our own thing" without giving consideration to other members of society and to future generations.

Nature is your
resource, too!

Decision Making

If you want to learn to manage your money you need to be able to make decisions intelligently. You must become a *decision maker*. The ability to make decisions is a skill you need to be successful in making consumer choices throughout your life. Each of us continually has to make decisions as new products become available, as resources change, and as our goals, values, needs, and wants change at different stages of life.

Dr. Robert Hilliard, educational broadcasting specialist for the Federal Communications Commission, is quoted in Alvin Toffler's *Future Shock* as saying, "At the rate at which knowledge is growing, by the time a child born today graduates from college, the amount of knowledge in the world will be four times as great. By the time that same child is fifty years old, it will be thirty-two times as great, and 97 percent of everything known in the world will have been learned since the time he was born." If only a portion of this prediction proves to be true, rational decision making in selecting the things for which we spend money will have to become a vital part of our lives. We won't be able to get by with a little knowledge, some intuition, and luck.

Each of us must decide how and for what to allocate his resources. Money is a limited resource and rational decisions must be made about its use. How you spend your money and what you spend it for must be decided on the basis of your values, your goals, and the amount you have. If you read the incidents at the beginning of this chapter, you saw that it is when people fail to plan or give deliberate consideration to the use of their money that they get into trouble.

Being competent in decision making can be an invaluable asset throughout your life. Each of us is confronted with problems or puzzling questions daily. Some are minor and can be solved in a short time. Others are more involved, use more of our resources, and may have a longer-lasting effect on our lives. It is these long-lasting decisions with which we are concerned in this book.

Steps in Decision Making

The first step in making a rational decision is to identify clearly the problem to be solved. It is at this stage you ask the questions "what?" "when?" and "why?" For example, you might identify a need for transportation. The simplest and most unthoughtful solution would be to go to an auto dealer and select a car. A more rational approach to this problem would be to look for answers to such questions as "what types of transportation are available?" A car may be only one of many. There may be public transportation, car pools, or other transportation services. If a car is the right answer for you, other questions present themselves. How much can I afford for transportation? What can I buy or lease for my limited resources? Which car will best meet my needs? How is it to be financed? If I borrow money or take a loan, when do I pay it off? What will the loan cost? As you can see, this is the probing stage. The first step in the decision-making process is to collect and sort information in order to identify a problem clearly.

The next step in decision making is to weigh the forces for and against the decision under consideration. What are the advantages and what are the disadvantages of the proposed action? Sometimes you will find a conflict of values which requires that you examine your principles and establish priorities. The next time you are called upon to make a decision, take time to list all of the reasons you can think of why you should choose a certain action. Make another list of all the reasons why you should not choose it. Examine your list to see if there are any value conflicts.

Once you take the time to analyze a situation you may find that it has a high priority or a low priority in relation to the other things you value and consider important. Your analysis will help you to place the question or issue in its appropriate place according to your own scale of values.

In making your decision you must: (1) consider all the possible alternatives, in terms of your personal values and the available information; (2) predict the consequences of each alternative on the basis of your information; and (3) select priorities based on your values, needs, and resources, keeping in mind the results or consequences of the decision.

No problem is solved until the chosen decision is put into action. Once the decision is made you should act to carry it out. Later, an evaluation should be made to determine the success or failure of your decision. Has your decision brought about the state of affairs you wanted? If not, what changes should be made? How can this experience help you make decisions of a similar nature in the future?

Throughout this book you will be called on to make decisions. You will be learning the process rather than searching for particular right answers. Right answers are those that are right for you. Becoming competent in the decision-making process will help you find right answers for yourself when you are confronted with new and different choices throughout your life.

The schematic model in Figure 1.1 shows how the decisions we make determine our lifestyle. The model indicates the sources from which our values and goals are derived. It shows that values and goals influence the way we satisfy our needs and wants and use our re-

FIGURE 1.1
Schematic model
of financial
decision making.

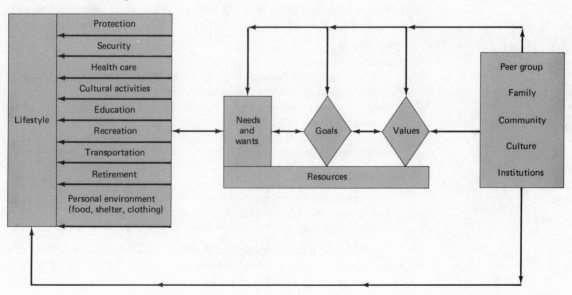

sources. The products and services for which people spend and that contribute to their unique lifestyle are identified as protection, security, health care, cultural activity, education, recreation, transportation, retirement, and personal environment (food, shelter, clothing). It can be seen that peers, family, community, culture, and institutions also influence a person's lifestyle.

Consumer Education

Can a person learn to be a good money manager, make sound financial decisions, and plan spending wisely? The answer is yes! The skills of personal financial management can be learned. Just as a person can learn a trade or occupational skill, learn to play tennis or a musical instrument, so too can he or she learn to manage money effectively. That's what consumer education is all about.

Consumer education can be defined as learning how to gain satisfaction by using your personal and environmental resources to achieve the lifestyle you prefer. From studying reliable consumer information you can gain knowledge of the principles and competence in the consumer skills required for everyday living. The benefits of consumer education can be measured not only in your own life but also in terms of the well-being of future generations.

Objectives of This Book

Anyone can learn to be a better financial decision maker, regardless of the amount of money in his or her pocket. It takes effort, but it is worth it. This book is designed to help you increase your competence as a consumer. You will learn:

> How to plan your spending.
> How to use credit to your advantage.
> How to manage your money so as to get the most value when buying food, clothing, housing, appliances, and transportation.
> How to protect yourself and your family through savings, insurance, pensions, and social security.
> How to maximize the benefits from your health and recreation dollars.
> How to avoid fakes and frauds that cheat you out of your money.

You'll also learn:

> Your responsibility as a consuming citizen.
> The role of taxes in supporting governmental services.
> Where you can go for help at the federal, state, and local levels.

Learning to manage money will put you on the road to getting one hundred cents' worth of satisfaction for every dollar you spend. Learning to manage money will free you from money worries.

GLOSSARY OF NEW TERMS

Consumer education   The process by which a person learns how to gain satisfaction by using his personal and environmental resources to achieve the lifestyle he prefers.

Decision making   Considering the available alternatives and determining the best choice.

Goals   The targets toward which individuals and families work—the objectives toward which we direct our activities.

Lifestyle   The manner in which a person lives. It is based to a large extent on decisions about buying goods and services.

Needs   Those things that are essential to our well-being.

Resources   Things we have on hand or at our disposal to help us meet our daily needs and achieve our goals. Money, time, health, energy, knowledge, skills, and material possessions are examples of resources. So are parts of the environment like water and air.

Values   Those ideas, beliefs, and feelings that are important to us and influence what we do.

Wants   Those things we believe would be "nice to have."

QUESTIONS FOR DISCUSSION

1. Does lack of money influence a person's attitude toward life? How?
2. It has been said that "increased income may not serve as a 'cure-all' for financial problems." Explain why not.
3. What types of financial problems and financial decisions may families face?
4. Explain what is meant by "lifestyle" and list some identifying characteristics of lifestyles.
5. Discuss values and identify factors that contribute to their development.
6. Define "goals" and explain their importance in making consumer decisions. Give examples of long-term, short-term, and intermediate goals.
7. Distinguish between financial resources and environmental resources. Give examples of each.
8. Explain the difference between needs and wants and tell how you would establish priorities for consumer choices.
9. Illustrate how a consumer decision can have adverse effects upon other people.
10. Identify steps in the decision-making process and list ways in which the use of this process can be beneficial throughout life.

SUGGESTED STUDENT ACTIVITIES

1. Identify a purchase you made recently. Explain why you made the purchase and list your satisfaction or dissatisfaction with the item. After studying Chapter I, assume that you were confronted with the same problem that led you to make the above purchase. List what things you would do differently and explain why.

2. Go to a local store and spend some time observing five individuals as they make their purchases. Follow each one through the store. Note whether the shopper's practices were "impulse" or "planned" buying. Describe store practices that encourage impulse buying.

3. Make a list of from five to ten issues that are currently being considered by your town, county, or state. State your position on the issues and explain your reasons. How is your position related to values? Example: The county should raise taxes to provide tennis courts, a swimming pool, and play-ground area for young people.

4. From your observations describe three different lifestyles in your area. Give reasons why you think the families chose different lifestyles. Do you think the lifestyles in all three cases were by choice? If not, explain why not.

5. Using the decision-making process, identify one long-range goal and one intermediate goal. Develop a plan for attaining each goal and put that plan into action. Also develop procedures for evaluating your progress and the success of the completed project.

6. Make out a list of your wants and needs. Analyze your list, checking off those that are unattainable. Arrange your needs in order of priority. List wants according to priority when resources are available.

FOR ADDITIONAL INFORMATION

Gordon, Leland J., and Stewart M. Lee. *Economics for Consumers*. New York: Van Nostrand Reinhold, 1972, pp. 63–189.
This book discusses the role of the consumer in the marketplace and the forces influencing consumer demands and choices. A clear, concise explanation of the American economic system is presented. The authors provide much information to help the consumer analyze his decision-making process and make proper choices. Review questions and suggested projects are included at the end of each chapter.

J. C. Penney Company. "Value Clarification." *Forum*, Spring/Summer 1972, p. 25.
Excellent information on value clarification and suggested procedures for teaching value clarification.

Miller, Roger Leroy. *Economic Issues for Consumers*. New York: West, 1975, pp. 11–29.
Includes a comprehensive chapter on "making up your mind" which examines value clarification, goal setting, planned and impulse buying, decision making, and alternative lifestyles, among other topics. Contains discussion questions, suggested activities, glossary, and bibliography.

Niss, James F. *Consumer Economics*. Englewood Cliffs, N.J.: Prentice-Hall, 1974, pp. 1–11.
This book is an attempt to help readers acquire some knowledge of economics while learning to make rational decisions regarding the use of income. Consideration is given to the ways in which decisions about the use of economic resources affect the environment and the quality of life. Easy to read.

Thal, Helen M., and Melinda Holcombe. *Your Family and Its Money*. Boston: Houghton Mifflin, 1973, pp. 10–48.
Emphasis is given to the management of family resources for the achieve-

ment of family goals. The book discusses the family life cycle as well as values and attitudes in relation to consumer decisions. It is easy to read. Though the focus is on youth, it contains valuable information for all ages.

U.S. Department of Agriculture. *Handbook for the Home: The 1973 Yearbook of Agriculture*. Washington, D.C.: Government Printing Office, 1973. Presents information on family financial management, how to set goals, how to develop a spending plan, and a wide variety of other topics.

2

The Money Plan

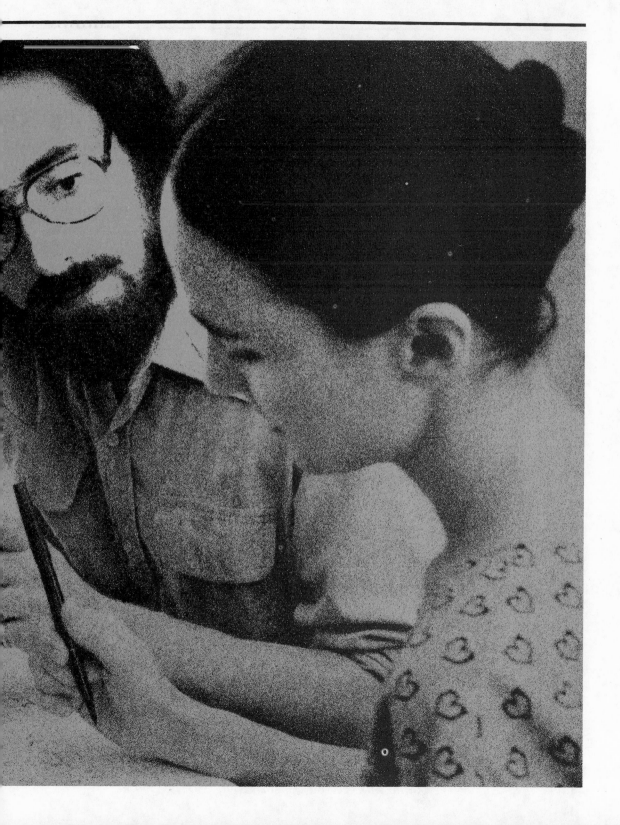

2

No one in his right mind would try to build a house without a plan. The result would be a clumsy thing with its proportions and angles all wrong. However, we often try to arrange our lives and those of our families without a plan.

Similarly, when you are traveling in strange places it helps to have a map to tell you where you are and how to get where you plan to go. Without one, you might exhaust yourself and still not be there.

A money plan is as necessary as a road map or a house plan. It lets you know what you're doing with your money and how to get the most value for the money you spend. In this chapter you will learn how

A house built
without a plan.

to make your own money plan, one that's tailored to your own specific needs. You will learn how to estimate your income, how to calculate your expenses, how to establish your goals, and how to make choices in the use of your money.

Why Should You Plan?

Planning for spending is essential at all stages in life. Young people on fixed allowances need to learn how to plan their spending so that the money they receive satisfies the purposes for which their allowances were given. If an allowance was given to cover the cost of food, clothing, books, and recreation, the person must see to it that expenses for clothing do not use up the money needed for food. Spending all of a week's allowance for recreation and borrowing against next week's allowance in order to be able to eat is evidence of poor planning.

As people mature and begin to earn their own way, proper planning for spending becomes even more important. Single persons with steady incomes begin to look for those things in life that satisfy their needs and wants. In addition to food, shelter, and security, young people want to be able to buy recreation, wardrobes, automobiles, and a multitude of other items according to their own values and desires. How to provide for all of the necessities while satisfying their wants becomes a perplexing problem. Which expenses should come first, which later? Proper planning for spending can help young wage-earners sort out their priorities.

When young people marry and establish their own homes, another set of perplexing questions confronts them. How much can they afford to spend for living quarters? How much should they spend? How much furniture and how many household goods can they afford to buy? Now that they are married, decisions about spending and saving for the future become a joint effort. Plans for spending must be made to satisfy the wants and needs of both partners. Values and desires may need to be modified so that each person is happy with the allocation of the total income.

Proper planning for spending, based on agreed-upon goals, enables young couples to move toward their ultimate objectives and also eliminates one of the major sources of friction in new marriages. One of the most frequent causes of marital disharmony is conflict over money management. Studies have shown that happily married people have learned how to face their financial problems. They are able to arrive at solutions with which they can live. Money problems and the marital problems they cause can be avoided if proper planning habits are established.

Young people who have learned how to plan their spending early in their lives find it easy to carry on their planning when and if they marry. But regardless of your age, now is a good time to learn to plan.

Only through proper planning can a person become a successful money manager.

In the next section is the story of the Armstrongs. They're a typical young couple who are having typical money problems. The items for which they spend their money may be different than those for which you spend yours, but the problem they face is basic.

THE ARMSTRONGS

The Armstrongs had been married for three years. During this time Peggy and Walter had both worked steadily and had furnished their apartment with most of the things that young folks enjoy: a stereo, a television set, good serviceable appliances, and comfortable furniture. They also had a two-year-old Mustang. Up until now they had managed to keep ahead of their debts, and had accumulated about $500 in savings. Peggy was presently in her third month of pregnancy.

The young couple realized that the anticipated change in their family would bring new money problems and reduce their combined income, since Peggy did not expect to return to work after the baby was born. They had a great deal of respect for the common sense of Walter's older brother, Joe, and so they sought his advice.

"We're just staying even now," explained Walter. "How will we be able to manage when Peggy stops working to stay at home with the baby?"

"Well," said Joe, "you've been doing the same thing that a lot of young people do all the time. You've been using your credit and your current income to buy the things that you both thought you had to have or couldn't get along without."

"But using our credit helped us get what we needed to set up a comfortable home when we got married," interjected Peggy. "And besides, we were able to make our payments as we had agreed, and we never let them get out of hand."

"I'm not trying to pass judgment on what the two of you established as your own values. I wouldn't want you to sit in judgment of mine. What's important now is that you've mortgaged Peggy's future income for the things you thought were important to you, and now you're about to lose that income. What you'll need to do is to develop a plan so that you both can live on one income—at least until Peggy is able to go back to work."

"But we've both decided that Peggy should stay home with the baby at least until he or she starts going to school. We both believe that during these early years a mother should stay with her baby," said Walter.

"You both need to sit down and make your own plan so that you'll know where your money is coming from and where it will go," Joe advised. "Call it a budget if you want to. I prefer to call it a spending plan. Make an itemized list of all of your expected income, your current debts, and your current expenses. Be sure to include everything. If you don't have receipts for all of your expenses, make a reasonable estimate. Then we will work together to come up with a spending plan, based on this information, that you can live with."

"That's a lot of work," said Walter.

"Sure it is," answered Joe, "but it will save you a lot of grief and aggravation to do the work now instead of later when you're up to your Adam's apple in debt."

TABLE 2.1
Peggy and Walter's Statement

Income (per month)	Gross pay	Take-home pay
Walter's salary	$800.00	$ 632.00
Peggy's salary	575.00	474.00
		$1106.00

Expenses (per month)	
Rent	$200.00
Food	
At home (includes paper goods and household cleaning supplies)	160.00
Away from home—lunch (Walter)	30.00
(Peggy)	20.00
Clothing (Walter)	20.00
(Peggy)	30.00
Transportation	
Car pool (Peggy)	20.00
Car insurance	15.00
Gas and oil	65.00
Life insurance (Walter)	25.00
Medical and dental care (including drugs)	30.00
Household	
Utilities (all electric)	50.00
Telephone	19.00
Dry cleaning	8.00
Savings (credit union)	20.00
Miscellaneous	
Recreation	40.00
Newspapers	6.00
Magazine subscriptions	16.00
Personal care (haircuts, etc.)	30.00
Alcoholic beverages	20.00
Contributions (Church)	10.00
TOTAL	$834.00

Outstanding Debts	Balance Due	Monthly Payments
Two-year-old Mustang	$1,960.00	$112.00
Furniture store	397.00	40.00
Jewelry store	126.00	15.00
Bank loan	230.00	40.00
Appliance store	322.00	35.00
		$242.00

$30.00 of income not accounted for

"But will we be able to afford some new furniture for the baby's room when we make our spending plan?" asked Peggy.

"I don't know," Joe replied. "However, we'll try to work out a plan that will meet both your short-term and long-term goals."

Next week Walter and Peggy brought to Joe the information shown in Table 2.1.

The Elements of a Money Plan

Could you help Peggy and Walter establish a money plan? Before you try, let us list what they need to know in order to make their plan. As Joe pointed out, they need to know:

1. How much income they have each month.
2. What expenses they have each month.
3. What goals they have set for the future.

These are the three items that everyone must calculate in order to make a money plan. Let's look at each of them a little more closely.

Income

Income is the money that you have coming in regularly. It may be from salary, commissions, pensions, social security, or whatever. As long as it comes in regularly it is considered income.

Worksheet 2.1 lists the money that Peggy and Walter will have coming in during the next month. We label this "regular monthly income." So that you have a better understanding of what the Armstrongs had to go through, itemize your income in a similar table.

The list in the worksheet does not include money that was with-

WORKSHEET 2.1
Money Coming In—
Regular Monthly
Income

		Walter and Peggy's	Your Own
Salary			
	(WALTER)	$ 632.00	$_____
	(PEGGY)	474.00	_____
Commissions		_____	_____
Pensions		_____	_____
Other		_____	_____
Total		$ 1106.00	$_____

	Walter and Peggy's	Your Own
Rent	$200.00	$_____
Car pool	20.00	_____
Car insurance	15.00	_____
Life insurance (WALTER)	25.00	_____
Utilities	50.00	_____
Telephone	19.00	_____
Other		
_____	—	_____
_____	—	_____
_____	—	_____
Regular Charge Payments		
Car	112.00	_____
Furniture	40.00	_____
Jewelry	15.00	_____
Bank	40.00	_____
Appliances	35.00	_____
Others		
_____	—	_____
_____	—	_____
_____	—	_____
Total	$571.00	$_____

held from the Armstrongs' regular pay, for income taxes, social security, hospitalization insurance, and so on. The list shows only the exact amount the Armstrongs received—the take-home pay.

Expenses

Individuals and families, as you know, spend their income on a wide variety of goods and services. These expenses can be divided into those that are fixed and those that are flexible.

Fixed expenses are the monies we spend that do not change from month to month. Examples are rent payments, utility costs, charge payments, and insurance premiums.

Flexible expenses are the monies we spend that *can* change from month to month. In this category we would put our spending for food, recreation, and clothing. Though these things satisfy our desires and needs, the amount of money can be changed according to our ability to pay.

In estimating expenses for the money plan, you need to decide how much you must spend for fixed items and how much you want to

WORKSHEET 2.3
Money Going Out—
Flexible Expenses
per Month

		Walter and Peggy's	Your Own
Food			
At home		$160.00	$_____
Away from home			
	(WALTER'S LUNCH)	30.00	_____
	(PEGGY'S LUNCH)	20.00	_____
Clothing			
Dress	(WALTER)	20.00	_____
	(PEGGY)	30.00	_____
Work		—	_____
Transportation			
Gas and oil		65.00	_____
Other		—	_____
Medical and dental care **(including drugs)**		30.00	_____
Household			
Repairs		—	_____
Supplies			
(INCLUDED WITH FOOD)		—	_____
Laundry		—	_____
Dry cleaning		8.00	_____
Other		—	_____

spend for flexible items. To appreciate how the Armstrongs arrived at their list of expenses, look first at Worksheet 2.2, which covers their fixed expenses. Once the fixed expenses were itemized Peggy and Walter needed to determine their flexible expenses. This was done in Worksheet 2.3, which includes all of the things for which they spent money that were not itemized in their fixed expenses.

Itemizing flexible expenses is the more difficult part because you need to remember more things than you generally care to remember. Compare your expenses with those of Peggy and Walter. No doubt there are others not listed in the table. If you can't remember the exact amount, make an estimate. But be honest with yourself.

Have you accounted for all of your spending? Does your list include that late snack you had, the blouse or the jacket you just couldn't pass up? Cigarettes? That six-pack? Now add your fixed expenses and flexible expenses to arrive at the total expenses, as in Worksheet 2.4.

WORKSHEET 2.3
Money Going Out—
Flexible Expenses
per Month (cont.)

	Walter and Peggy's	Your Own
Savings (CREDIT UNION)	20.00	_____
Miscellaneous		
Recreation (includes paid admissions, records, travel, hobbies, and musical instruments	40.00	_____
Newspapers	6.00	_____
Magazine subscriptions	16.00	_____
Personal care	30.00	_____
Alcoholic beverages	20.00	_____
Contributions (CHURCH)	10.00	_____
Other	—	_____
_____	—	_____
_____	—	_____
_____	—	_____
Income not spent	30.00	_____
TOTAL	$535.00	$_____

THE MONEY PLAN

	Walter and Peggy's	Your Own
Total fixed expenses (FROM WORKSHEET 2.2)	$571.00	$_____
Total flexible expenses (FROM WORKSHEET 2.3)	535.00	$_____
TOTAL	$1106.00	$_____

At this point we have prepared two of the three items we need in order to make a money plan. We have estimated income and expenses. Before going on with the Armstrongs' problem we need to examine the third item of the money plan: goals. Goals, however, are affected by the relationship between money coming in and money going out. Let's see why this is so.

From the estimates that were made previously we can draw up Worksheet 2.5, which compares income and expenses.

If expenses are less than income, there is money left to add to savings—money that can eventually be used to achieve goals. The difference between what is coming in and what is going out gives you the basis for establishing your goals. But if expenses are the same as or more than income there are no funds with which to achieve goals. This is the situation in which the Armstrongs found themselves, even before they learned that Peggy would have to quit her job. What do you do in such a case? You examine your flexible expenses to find where they can be reduced to provide funds for goals. You cannot plan to spend money you don't have.

That's one of the advantages of a money plan. It helps you to see if your expenses and income are out of balance. It also shows you what you need to do to put them into balance. The money plan enables you to match your income and expenses.

	Walter and Peggy's	Your Own
Total monthly income	$1106.00	$_____
Total monthly expenses	1106.00	_____
Difference (+ or −)	$ 0	$_____

Income and expenses
—do they balance?

Goals

Setting goals is the most difficult and complex part in the entire money-management process. Your goals are set by the choices you make to satisfy your own individual preferences—and nobody but you can or should make them.

Data available from the U.S. Bureau of Labor and from regional research organizations show how much the "average" family spends for various goods and services. Table 2.2 is a compilation of such data. People who attempt to make their spending plans according to charts like this one often wind up frustrated and disappointed because they do not "fit" the recommended figures. Nobody is "average." You should establish your own amounts for what you want to and need to buy according to your own values and your own desires. What do you think is most important? What do you think is least important? The decisions you make need to be based on what will give you or your family the most satisfaction—*within your income*.

Obviously, in a family everyone concerned should take part in setting goals; then each person has a stake in seeing that the plan is carried out. The plan helps to establish priorities. Who gets what? Who comes first? When does he or she get it? When decisions are made jointly everyone can pull together.

Now that we have established that the three parts of the money plan are income, expenses (fixed or flexible), and goals, how can Joe advise the Armstrongs?

Drawing up the Plan: Questions to Ask

Income

The family's total income will be reduced because Peggy will stop working. So they must ask themselves what measures they can undertake to increase income. Is a job change feasible for Walter? Can he earn extra money through moonlighting until Peggy is able to assist again? Is there part-time work that Peggy can undertake after the baby is born that will supplement the family income? Of course decisions about increasing family income depend on the goals and objectives of all members of the family.

Expenses

Let's consider the fixed expenses first. The Armstrongs need to examine how fixed and inflexible these expenses really are. Can rent be reduced? Would a different housing arrangement cost less? Would it pay to incur

TABLE 2.2
Annual Budgets at Different Income Levels for a Four-Person Family* in the Urban United States (Autumn 1974)

	Lower Budget		Intermediate Budget		Higher Budget	
Total income	$9,198	100.0%	$14,333	100.0%	$20,777	100.0%
Personal income tax	910	9.9	2,010	14.0	3,899	18.8
Social security and						
disability payments	553	6.0	780	5.4	787	3.8
Total consumption	7,318	100.0	10,880	100.0	14,976	100.0
Food at home	2,403	32.8	3,007	27.6	3,576	23.9
Food away from home	359	4.9	540	5.0	874	5.8
Shelter (renter)	1,322	18.1	1,713	15.7	2,648	18.0
Shelter (owner)	—	—	2,753	25.3	3,460	23.1
House furnishing and						
operations	435	5.9	742	6.8	1,405	9.4
Total transportation	643	8.8	1,171	10.8	1,521	10.2
Total transportation						
(automobile owner)	861	11.8	1,233	11.3	1,521	10.2
Clothing	759	10.4	1.085	10.0	1,589	10.6
Personal needs	231	3.2	310	2.8	439	2.9
Medical care	738	10.1	742	6.8	774	5.2
Reading, recreation,						
tobacco, alcohol,						
education, etc.	423	5.8	786	7.2	1,297	8.7
Gifts and contri-						
butions, life insurance,						
occupational expenses	415	5.7	662	6.1	1,113	7.4

*The family consists of an employed husband, age thirty-eight, a wife not employed outside the home, an eight-year-old girl, and a twelve-year-old boy.

Source: U.S. Bureau of Labor statistics.

the moving expenses? Can the regular charge payments be rearranged? For instance, can the car payments be reduced by spreading them out over a longer period of time or by trading in their present car for a less expensive one? Do they want to do this? Are the savings enough to justify the step?

Consideration also needs to be given to the other regular charge payments. Can these payments be reduced by negotiation with the creditors? Should the debts be paid off from the Armstrongs' savings? Should a loan be taken out to pay off all of the debts and thereby reduce the monthly payments? All of these approaches should be considered in an attempt to rearrange the fixed expenses.

It is in the area of flexible expenses, however, that people are often best able to reduce expenditures. By examining each of the items in the list of flexible expenses, the Armstrongs can decide where they need to make reductions in order to live within their reduced income. Can you see some items in Worksheet 2.2 that could be reduced? Is the money spent for food reasonable? What about the expenses for clothing? Again, the final decisions can be made only in the light of the Armstrongs own values and goals.

In adjusting flexible expenses to meet the money plan, care should be taken that reductions are not too drastic. For instance, the budget for food should always allow for adequate nutrition. The plan should also leave some room for the "good things in life." If too stringent a reduction makes the plan unpleasant, the family or individual may become dissatisfied and eventually abandon it. What the "good things" are depends on personal taste. To one person they might include a good jazz record or a new sweater; to another they might be represented by a six-pack of beer or a good movie.

Goals

How the Armstrongs rearrange their income and expenses to meet the coming change in their lives depends on what they have set as their future goals, just as any money plan you prepare needs to be built upon your own objectives. We do not have any information about the Armstrongs' goals, but when they sit down with Walter's brother they will discuss these and set up a money plan accordingly.

It should be obvious by this time that there are several ways in which finances can be adjusted so that people can live within their income and reach their goals. Preparing a plan lets them see where they might be able to make adjustments. It may also suggest to them that they need to change their goals. For example, if "extra" money is limited, people may decide on less expensive vacations. Or, they may decide to postpone refurnishing a home or to put off purchasing a summer home. On the other hand, if funds are available, people might buy a home sooner or decide to go back to school for advanced degrees.

Now that you have examined the three parts of a money plan—income, expenses, and goals—you should be able to advise the Armstrongs about their problem. If you were Joe, what ideas would you suggest to Walter and Peggy? Could you help them make a money plan?

Why not now make a money plan for yourself? Use a set of worksheets similar to the ones in the pages that follow. The plan may not be perfect the first time. Just start. You can modify it later on the basis of your experience.

Money Plan Worksheet

How much money will be coming in? To answer this question, prepare a chart similar to Worksheet 2.6 to itemize all of the money you expect to receive during the next month. Be honest with yourself, and use amounts you'll actually receive (do not include monies withheld from your salary). Consider that every month has only four weekly pay periods. This arrangement will provide for four extra paychecks per year that will serve as a "cushion" for minor adjustments and unexpected expenses.

Add the items across and down so that you will have totals coming in for each week and for each item of income.

You are on the way to better use of your money! Now you can begin to calculate how much money will be going out. Using a table like Worksheet 2.7, itemize all of the fixed expenses you will have. Do not include items already deducted from your paychecks.

WORKSHEET 2.6
Money Coming In

Source	1st Week	2nd Week	3rd Week	4th Week	Monthly Total
Net salary					
Pension					
Other					
TOTAL					

Item	1st Week	2nd Week	3rd Week	4th Week	Monthly Total
Rent					
Gas					
Electricity					
Telephone					
Insurance					
Charge accounts					
Other					
TOTAL					

Now, with a table like Worksheet 2.8, you can determine how much will be left for you to spend on flexible items; these are the items about which you have a choice.

WORKSHEET 2.8
Money Left for
Flexible Expenses

	1st Week	2nd Week	3rd Week	4th Week	Monthly Total
Total income (from Worksheet 2.6)					
Total fixed expenses (from Worksheet 2.7)					
Amount available for flexible expenses (first line minus second line)					

In order to plan your flexible expenses you will need to have some idea of how much you are presently spending for these items. So keep a record in a notebook of your daily expenditures. Start the day with a record of how much you have in your pocket. At the end of the day subtract what you have left in order to figure out your spending. Have you accounted for all of your spending? At the end of the week enter the expenditures in a table modeled on Worksheet 2.9. Do not duplicate the fixed expenses.

WORKSHEET 2.9
Money Going Out—
Flexible Expenses

Item	1st Week	2nd Week	3rd Week	4th Week	Monthly Total
Food					
Clothing					
House furnishings					
House operations					
Savings					
Transportation					
Education					
Medical care					
Occupational expenses					
Recreation					
Personal needs					
Gifts					
Contributions					
Tobacco					
Other					
TOTAL					

PERSONAL FINANCE FOR CONSUMERS

WORKSHEET 2.10
Money Planning

Item	Planned Spending	Actual Spending	Necessary Adjustment for Next Month
Food			
Clothing			
Transportation			
Other			
TOTAL			

Compare these totals with the totals in your version of Worksheet 2.3. Have you anything left to meet planned wants or goals? By comparing the totals actually spent with what you had available for flexible expenses you can determine where you need to make adjustments.

Now that you see how your spending compares with your income it's time to make your plan for future spending. Plan your weekly spending for next month using your experience of the past month as a guide. Keep a record of your daily spending. Use a chart like Worksheet 2.10 to check each week's spending and your total for the month against the plan. If necessary, make adjustments in the plan to fit the way you live.

How much have you set aside for reaching your goals. A sound plan needs to have some money saved or set aside for future wants and needs. A table like Worksheet 2.11 can help you specify what your goals are and how much you will need to reach them.

Continue to make a plan for each month. Adjust your plans as income and expenses change. You're on the way to a richer and fuller life.

WORKSHEET 2.11
Goals

Things I Need and Want in the Next Three Months	Cost	Things I Want after Three Months	Cost
	_____		_____
TOTAL	$	TOTAL	$

GLOSSARY OF NEW TERMS

Fixed expenses Expenses that occur on a regular basis and that cannot easily be altered, such as mortgage or rent payments and car payments.

Flexible expenses Expenses that can be changed or adjusted upward or downward. For example, you can spend a lot of money on expensive cuts of meat, or you can choose less expensive cuts and spend less money.

Income All monies received, whether from salary, interest, dividends, rent, commission, or another source.

Money plan A clearly developed outline showing how you expect to spend your income. It can help you get the most value from your dollars.

QUESTIONS FOR DISCUSSION

1. What can be considered as income in making a money plan?
2. Identify items included in flexible expenses.
3. Why should family members cooperate in planning the use of the family income? What are some questions they should consider?
4. Describe problems that may arise when families do not have a money plan.
5. Explain the relationship of goals and values to the money plan.
6. What are the advantages of making a money plan?
7. What steps are involved in making a realistic money plan?
8. Suggest ways of increasing your income assuming that you need and want to increase your flexible spending.
9. Suggest ways in which a person in debt might reduce fixed expenses such as rent, insurance, charge payments.
10. How can a family reduce their flexible expenses to balance their spending plan?

SUGGESTED STUDENT ACTIVITIES

1. Interview two or more employers and find out: (a) the average salary for a specific type of job; (b) the deductions taken out monthly (taxes, social security, insurance, and so on); and (c) the net take-home pay.
2. Interview five people of different ages and socioeconomic conditions to find out the three things they want most. Ask them to list their wants in order of importance. Prepare a report on how wants vary according to age and socioeconomic status.
3. List two items you would like to have. One you will need within the next month, the other within a year. Develop a money plan to show how these two items could be obtained and paid for.
4. Observe ten commercials. Make a list of the techniques used to influence wants, values, goals, and lifestyle.
5. Pick out some "emotionally charged" situations (funerals, weddings, birthdays, Valentine's Day, and so on) and investigate the impact they have on the use of financial resources.
6. Among your friends or members of your family, identify a person who is having money problems, whom you would like to help, and who would accept your advice. Use the suggestions for making a money plan in this chapter to assist your friend or relative in developing a realistic plan. Work with the person long enough to know that he or she understands the procedures and to help evaluate his or her progress. Prepare a written report of your project and explain how it reinforced your own learning.

FOR ADDITIONAL INFORMATION

Family Decisions: A Simulated Choice/Chance Game. Pullman, Wash.: Cooperative Extension Service, Washington State University.
Participants are made aware of various alternatives in decision making and of the probabilities of positive and negative outcomes. Shows the influence of values on decisions.

Fletcher, Adele Whitely. *How to Stretch Your Dollar.* New York: Benjamin Co., 1970, pp. 7–15.
A pocket edition of a book that covers a wide variety of topics concerning the use of the family dollar. Emphasizes planning before you buy.

Hendricks, Gary, and Kenwood C. Youmans. *Consumer Durables and Installments Debt: A Study of American Households.* Ann Arbor, Mich.: Institute for Social Research, University of Michigan, 1973.
Reports findings from a study of spending and saving patterns in 1,400 U.S. households, including the amount a consumer will spend for durable goods and how much debt families will incur for such purchases.

J. C. Penny Company. *Dynamic Consumer Decision-Making.* New York, 1972.
A learning kit that presents three case problems. It includes cassette, slides, transparencies, flip chart, worksheets, and a simulation game. These materials help the learner to make decisions on the basis of what is important, to recognize the reward for deliberate, informed decision making, and to realize that the quality of life and of the environment is affected by consumer decisions.

"Make a New Budget for Times Like These." *Changing Times*, pp. 6–11.

Points out the way inflation has made spending plans obsolete. Gives charts showing changes in the cost of some items in one year. Emphasizes the importance of planning and of making the plan flexible.

Niss, James F. *Consumer Economics*. Englewood Cliffs, N.J.: Prentice-Hall, 1974, pp. 12–18.

The steps in making a financial plan are explained and illustrated with charts. Includes some good "think-it-over" statements which should stimulate an examination of values.

Raines, Margaret. *Consumers' Management*. Peoria, Ill.: Charles A. Bennett, 1973, pp. 26–61.

This book is directed to the teen-ager primarily; however, adults will find easy-to-read information and good coverage of a variety of topics, such as planned spending, credit, food, clothing, and housing.

U.S. Department of Agriculture. *A Guide to Budgeting for the Family*. Home and Garden Bulletin No. 108. Washington, D.C.: Government Printing Office, 1965.

A helpful guide for family use. Explains what to include in the budget and ways to set up a spending plan.

3

**Managing
Credit**

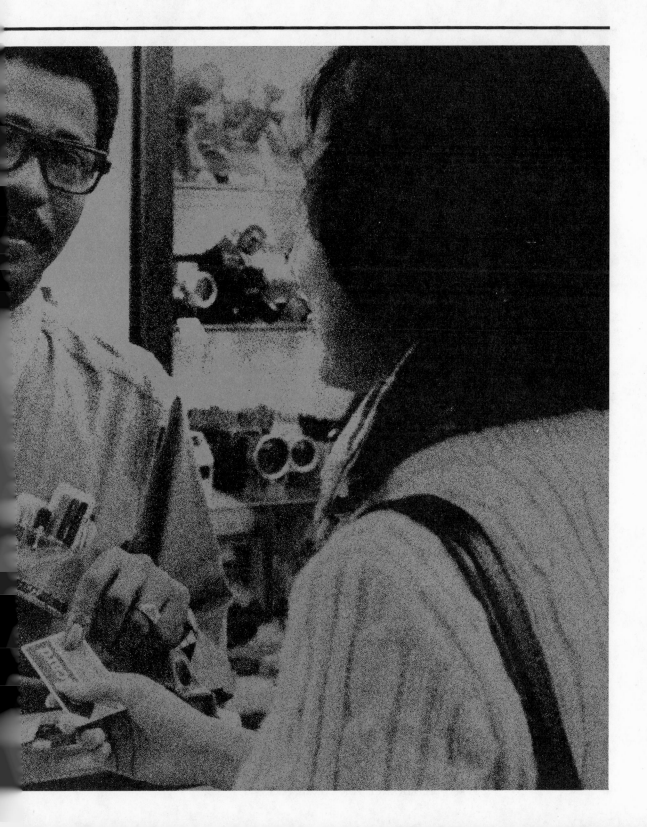

3

You will recall that in the story about Peggy and Walter in Chapter 2 they reported the following "outstanding debts."

	Balance Due	Monthly Payments
Two-year-old Mustang	$1,960.00	$112.00
Furniture store	397.00	40.00
Jewelry store	126.00	15.00
Bank loan	230.00	40.00
Appliance store	322.00	35.00

These debts were what the Armstrongs owed for items that they had purchased from merchants and for money that they had borrowed from the bank. The monthly amounts are payments that they had promised to make in order to pay off their debts. *Credit* had been extended to them.

In this chapter you will learn about credit. You will find out what it is and how much it costs. You will also learn how to manage credit for yourself, how to avoid getting into financial difficulties because of credit, and what to do if you do get into "credit trouble."

What Is Credit?

When we discuss credit in this chapter we are referring to consumer credit, which is often called installment credit, short-term credit, or even consumer loans. All of these terms mean money or purchasing power granted to consumers. Merchants and retailers allow customers like you to have the goods or services you want solely on the basis of your promise to pay for these goods or services at some later date. You have use of the goods immediately but can defer payment until later. Similarly, banks and other lending agencies will lend you money which you can use to buy the goods and services you want. You have use of the purchased item immediately and repay the bank later.

Through the use of credit, thousands of consumers have been able to enjoy goods and services before accumulating the money to pay for them. In this way sellers of goods have been able to get more of their goods into the hands of their customers. It is argued that credit so used has enabled manufacturers and retailers to expand their businesses and create more jobs for more people, who in turn have been able to buy more of the manufactured goods. This oversimplification is used to illustrate how credit has served to expand the American economy.

The explanation does not show, however, the dangers that arise for individual customers when they have used more credit than they can afford. Many consumers have overextended their buying and have

Credit is like fire. Will it be master or servant?

sunk hopelessly into debt because of their excessive use of credit. Advocates of strict credit controls point to the ever-increasing debt load that consumers have assumed; this, they argue, stimulates demand and contributes to inflation. The rise in the total amount of consumer credit outstanding foretells a "day of reckoning," according to the critics. As can be seen from Table 3.1, there was a steady increase in the total

TABLE 3.1
Total Consumer Credit Outstanding, 1965–1974, in Millions of Dollars

Year*	Installment	Noninstallment
1965	70.9	18.9
1966	76.2	19.9
1967	79.4	21.4
1968	87.7	23.0
1969	97.1	24.0
1970	103.1	27.1
1971	111.3	27.1
1972	127.3	30.2
1973	147.3	33.0
1974	156.1	34.0

*The computations were made at the end of each year.
Source: *Federal Reserve Bulletin*, Washington, D.C.: by Federal Reserve Board, Federal Reserve System Board of Governors, published monthly.

amount of consumer credit from 1965 through 1974. Each year more and more people have owed more for the goods and services they use.

Under the circumstances it is reasonable to ask, "Is credit bad?" Credit is good or bad depending on how you use it. Using credit is like using fire. If you use it wisely it can bring you comfort and satisfaction and add to your well-being. Use credit poorly and it can bring disaster.

In order to be able to decide whether you should use credit you should know something about the different kinds of credit and how much they cost. Ordinarily as a consumer you will use either or both of these kinds of credit:

1. Sales or purchase credit;
2. Cash loans or borrowing credit.

Sales or Purchase Credit
There are three important types of sales or purchase accounts available. These are:

1. Installment accounts;
2. Revolving charge accounts;
3. Open charge accounts.

Installment Accounts
Installment accounts are the form of credit generally used to purchase durable or semidurable goods such as automobiles or refrigerators. The installment sale involves a written contract, according to which the seller actually owns the item until it has been paid for in full. The contract of sale specifies that the seller has the right to the goods if the buyer does not pay as agreed. Payments under this type of plan are usually made in equal monthly, bimonthly, or weekly installments over a period of one, two, or three years.

Charges for installment sales vary. In most instances charges are made for the unpaid balance as in revolving accounts, described in the next section. However, under provisions of the Truth-in-Lending Law (Consumer Credit Protection Act of 1968), the installment contract must state:

1. The annual percentage rate;
2. The total of all finance charges, including all add-on charges such as loan fees, investigation fees, and required insurance;
3. The purchase price;
4. Any down payment or trade-in allowance;
5. The net amount being financed with credit;
6. The size of weekly or monthly payments;
7. The due dates of payments;
8. The total number of installments before the debt is entirely paid.

All of this information must be given to the buyer, in writing, before credit is extended and before the buyer signs the contract. With this information available you can compare the total cost of installment credit with the cost of any other type of credit available to you.

Revolving Charge Accounts

A revolving account permits you to buy up to a stated amount, which depends on your credit rating, your income, and other facts about your ability to repay that the merchant thinks important. Your payments will be either a certain portion of the total amount due or a fixed amount, depending on the plan. You are permitted to buy goods at any time so long as you don't owe the seller an amount greater than the credit limit of the plan.

Charges are usually based on the unpaid balance. All revolving contracts and monthly bills must state the "nominal annual percentage rate." The "nominal" rate on this type of credit equals 12 times the monthly rate. The usual charge of most retail stores, 1.5 percent a month, is shown as a nominal rate of 18 percent a year.

However, stores that charge the same nominal rate may actually levy different charges for their revolving credit depending on how they arrive at your monthly balance. Some stores apply a credit charge to your bill *before* deducting any payments or credits for returned merchandise. Other stores deduct all payments and credits before applying the credit charge. Still others use an average daily balance to arrive at the charge. Table 3.2 illustrates the cost to the buyer using the different methods of calculating charges. Obviously, store A makes more money, since the buyer who purchases in store A is paying more for his credit than the customer who buys in store B or C.

You may be using a revolving credit plan when you use a department store charge plate or a bank credit card. If the purchase you make on a credit card is paid for within the normal billing period, then there is no charge for the credit. If, however, you choose to pay only a portion of the total amount due, the balance is maintained as a revolving charge. You are generally billed for 1.5 percent of the unpaid balance each

	Store A	Store B	Store C
Opening balance	$200	$200	$200
Payments and credits	$100˙	$100	$100
Closing balance	$100	$100	$100
Monthly rate	1.5%	1.5%	1.5%
Actual finance charge	0.015 × $200 = $3.00	0.015 × $100 = $1.50	0.015 × $150 = $2.25
Actual annual rate	36%	18%	27%

TABLE 3.2
Three Methods of Calculating Finance Charges*

*Store A calculates the charge *before* deducting payments; store B applies its charge *after* deducting payments; and store C figures on the basis of the average daily balance. In the calculation for store C, we assume that the $100 payment was made in the middle of the month.

MANAGING CREDIT

month. This "service" charge is what the credit is costing you. You should refer to your credit card for specific details of the credit charges, how they are computed, and the limit of the credit to which you are entitled.

Most department stores and large specialty stores have their own credit plans. Some stores extend credit to their customers indirectly through a sponsoring bank, credit card agency, or other financial agency. In this case the credit agency reimburses the merchant for your credit purchases and then collects from you. The merchant pays the credit agency for this convenience, but the system allows the merchant to use the money you owe him before it is collected from you.

Open Charge Accounts

With an open charge account you agree to pay in full for all of your purchases within a certain time after being billed, usually 10 or 30 days. There is no direct service charge or interest for this type of account. The merchant is absorbing the cost of the credit. In some stores this may be reflected in higher prices charged for goods. Stores with open charge accounts watch payment records carefully and transfer slow-paying customers to revolving accounts, in which there is a charge for credit.

It is important that you compare the prices you pay in a store that offers open accounts with those in other stores that do not offer this service. You may be paying for the convenience in higher prices, even though you are not being charged any interest.

Cash Loans or Borrowing Credit

Cash loans are the amounts you borrow from a bank or other lending agency, such as a finance company, loan office, credit union, or loan agent. The cash enables you to make your purchases from stores without asking them to extend credit. Such loans generally cost less than other types of credit.

In loan credit, single-payment and demand loans are similar to open charge accounts; installment loans are similar to installment accounts; and ready-check loans are similar to revolving charge accounts.

Single-payment loans, offered by banks and lending institutions, may run for 30, 60, or 90 days. A loan of this sort requires a signed note with a specified date of repayment. Interest and principal become due on the date specified, and you make your repayment all at once. *Demand loans* are single-payment loans with no specific due date; they are subject to "call" or "demand" by the lender—that is, you must pay the loan back whenever the lender asks you to. Demand loans are not generally considered to be consumer loans; they are most often used for commercial purposes.

Installment loans—ones that are repaid in regular installments—may be made on the signature of the purchaser alone, but when collateral or some other security is required, this condition is specified in the note. *Collateral* is a form of security that serves as a pledge assuring the performance of a contract or the discharge of an obligation. Usually title to the collateral is technically transferred to the lender by way of a separate document, which is returned to the borrower when the loan is repaid.

Ready-check loan credit is a system of revolving credit that is used by banks. The borrower is given a book of special checks, which he can use to draw on the bank for more than he has in his checking account—up to a certain limit. Each month he receives a statement itemizing all the checks he has written that have cleared the bank. The borrower may elect to make a deposit to cover all the checks drawn; in this case the bank will add to his bill a nominal bookkeeping charge. Or the borrower may pay a percentage of the amount he owes; then the bank will make a service charge of about 1 percent per month.

Credit cards issued by banks offer a form of credit like that of charge accounts at retail establishments. Purchases that you make from "participating" merchants are recorded on sales slips, which you sign before leaving the store. These sales slips are immediately sent to the bank by the seller, and he is credited with cash for the amount of the sale. At the end of the billing period the bank sends you a statement of all the purchases you have made during that period. You may pay the entire balance due, in which case there is no service charge, just as with an open charge account. Or you may elect to pay just a portion of the balance due, in which case you are charged for the credit, usually 1.5 percent per month on the unpaid balance; this is similar to the charge on a revolving account.

Cash loans are more difficult to get than credit cards. Different cash-lending agencies charge different annual percentage rates for their services. Some lenders require security to guarantee that the loan will be repaid. A general rule is that the easier it is to get the loan, the more it will cost you.

The Truth-in-Lending Law requires that the lender state in writing not only the total finance charge and the annual percentage rate, but also the following:

1. When finance charges begin;
2. The number of payments, their due dates and amounts;
3. The total of all payments;
4. Penalties for default or late payments, or for paying ahead of schedule;
5. The nature of any security (collateral) held by the creditor.

A copy of the statement must be given to you.

Figuring the Cost of Installment Credit

There are many devices available that can help you figure out how much installment credit will cost you. Charts and tables are available from banks and office supply stores. Even though the seller is required by law to tell you how much the credit is going to cost, it is possible and often helpful to figure it out yourself.

For instance, if a dealer offers a new car for $2,072.00 with a down payment of $272.00 and monthly payments of $59.75 for 36 months, how much would the car really cost you? We can calculate the total amount by the following steps.

1. How much is to be financed?

Cash price	$2,072.00
Minus Down payment	− 272.00
Amount to be financed	$1,800.00

2. How much are you repaying?

Monthly payments	$ 59.75
Times Number of payments	× 36
Total amount repaid	$2,151.00

3. What is the cost of the credit?

Total amount repaid	$2,151.00
Minus Amount financed	−1,800.00
Cost of credit	$ 351.00

4. What is the total cost of the car?

Total amount repaid	$2,151.00
Plus Down payment	+ 272.00
Total cost of car to you	$2,423.00

WORKSHEET 3.1
Calculating the Cost of Installment Credit

1. The amount to be financed
   - Cash price $_____
   - *Minus* Down payment (if any) −_____
   - Amount to be financed $_____
2. The amount that will be repaid
   - Monthly payments $_____
   - *Times* Number of payments ×_____
   - Total amount repaid $_____
3. The cost of the credit
   - Total amount repaid $_____
   - *Minus* Amount financed −_____
   - Cost of credit $_____
4. The total cost of the TV
   - Total amount repaid $_____
   - *Plus* Down payment (if any) +_____
   - Total cost of TV $_____

For some practice in this technique, determine how much it would cost you to buy the television in the following advertisement.

19" COLOR TV!

ONLY $399.⁴⁴

NO DOWN PAYMENT

100% FINANCING
$25. A MONTH
(24 MOS TO PAY)

Follow the same steps, setting them up in the same way, as shown in Worksheet 3.1.

Figuring the Cost of Revolving Credit

How much will credit cost when you buy with a revolving account?

Suppose you want to buy a TV set that is marked $400.00. The store requires that you make payments of $25.00 per month and charges 1.5 percent on the unpaid balance. How much, in total, is the TV set going to cost you? Assume that the store calculates the credit charge *before* deducting each payment.

When you make your first payment to the store, the accounting department will add 1.5 percent of $400.00 (which is $6.00) to your account and subtract your $25.00 payment. This will leave a balance of $381.00. The next month, the store will add 1.5 percent of $381.00 (which is $5.72) to your account and subtract your second payment of $25.00, leaving a balance of $361.72. By the time you have completed all of your payments your account will look like Table 3.3. As the table shows, the cost of the credit is $60.95 and the total cost of the TV $460.95.

Now, as an exercise, calculate the cost of buying $100.00 worth of merchandise on revolving credit when you are required to pay $10.00 per month and the store charges 1.5 percent on the unpaid balance. Use a table like Worksheet 3.2.

Figuring the Cost of Cash Loans

How much would it cost to finance the car discussed in the section "Figuring the Cost of Installment Credit" if you were to obtain a cash loan from a bank or other lending agency? The amount to be financed, you'll remember, was $1,800.00. Typically, with a loan from a bank at 8 percent interest, you would pay $162.00 a month for 12 months. Multiplying $162.00 times 12, we see that the total payment is $1,944.00.

TABLE 3.3
The Cost of Credit in a Revolving Account

Payment Number	Balance at Beginning of Month	Finance Charge	Balance Plus Charge	Amount of Payment	New Balance
1	$400.00	$ 6.00	$406.00	$ 25.00	$381.00
2	381.00	5.72	386.72	25.00	361.72
3	361.72	5.43	367.15	25.00	342.15
4	342.15	5.13	347.28	25.00	322.28
5	322.28	4.83	327.11	25.00	302.11
6	302.11	4.53	306.64	25.00	281.64
7	281.64	4.22	285.86	25.00	260.86
8	260.86	3.91	264.77	25.00	239.77
9	239.77	3.59	243.36	25.00	218.36
10	218.36	3.28	221.64	25.00	196.64
11	196.64	2.95	199.59	25.00	174.59
12	174.59	2.62	177.21	25.00	152.21
13	152.21	2.28	154.49	25.00	129.49
14	129.49	1.94	131.43	25.00	106.43
15	106.43	1.60	108.03	25.00	83.03
16	83.03	1.25	84.28	25.00	59.28
17	59.28	0.89	60.17	25.00	35.17
18	35.17	0.52	35.69	25.00	10.69
19	10.69	0.16	10.85	10.85	-0-
		$60.85		$460.85	

Then the cost of credit in this case would be $144.00, as compared with $351.00 for the dealer's installment credit.

But the payments of $162.00 per month for 12 months are not as easy to make as those of $59.75 per month for 36 months under the dealer's plan. It stands to reason that with the lower interest plan you must pay back the money faster, in larger installments. On the other hand, if you want the convenience of using the money for a longer time, you must pay more for it. Since the terms can differ so widely, you should shop around for the terms that best suit you.

More About the Cost of Credit

Credit is a service and you must, of course, expect to pay for it. Whether the cost is called interest, finance charge, carrying charge, service

WORKSHEET 3.2
The Cost of $100.00 of Revolving Credit

Payment Number	Balance at Beginning of Month	Finance Charge	Balance Plus Charge	Amount of Payment	New Balance
1	$100.00	$1.50	$101.50	$10.00	$91.50
TOTAL		$_____		$_____	

charge, or insurance, you need to decide if the credit is worth it. Is it worth paying more for what you buy to have the advantage of using it while you are paying for it? Are you willing to pay the cost for the extra satisfaction you get?

There are a number of factors that enter into the charge that the store or bank levies for the use of credit. Obtaining information about you as a borrower costs the lender time and money. The lender must also maintain records each time an account is opened and a payment or purchase is made. Since the lender's money is tied up for the length of time you owe him, he is entitled to a fair "rental" for the use of his money. There may also be a need to insure against damage to the product, or to insure the life of the borrower and his ability to repay. This credit insurance, which repays your loan in the event that you die or are disabled, is available to you as the borrower and is added to the cost of your credit. Before you agree to accept this insurance you should realize that it is relatively high in cost for the protection it gives you. Often the protection you get is limited. Furthermore the insurance is sold at a flat rate regardless of the age of the borrower. The lender of the loan receives a commission on the insurance if you buy it and is very likely to encourage you to do so. Consider whether you need this type of insurance before you agree to buy. Compare the price you will have to pay for this insurance with similar insurance from other sources.

All of these costs go into the total cost of credit in dollars and cents. Lenders have a variety of ways of expressing the charge. Some terms you'll see are *percent, per annum, percent per month, annual rate, nominal rate,* and *annual percentage rate.* Some of these we've mentioned already, but the sheer variety of them can be confusing. Fortunately the Consumer Credit Protection Act requires that every seller advise the buyer of the annual percentage rate, as well as of the total cost in dollars and cents of all finance charges. Be sure you receive *in writing* all the credit information to which you are entitled under this act. Some sellers make oral statements that they can later deny to circumvent the provisions of the act. The cost of credit is no longer a mystery known only to a select few. Since everyone can know what the credit is costing, everyone ought to be able to make reasonable decisions about credit.

Deciding About Credit

With so many different kinds of credit available, how can you decide which is best for you? You decide in the same way that you decide if any purchase is right for you. Does it meet your needs? How does it compare with other alternatives?

First, you need to determine if the cost of the item fits into your money plan. Is the item the one you have planned for? Can the payments you are going to undertake fit into your planned expenses? Will

Shopping for credit.

there be enough money left after fixed and flexible expenses to meet these new payments?

There are always many tempting things to buy. You may be encouraged to buy because there is "only a small down payment" or because of the promise of "easy payments." But ask yourself: Small for whom? Easy for whom? You need to recognize the limits placed on your capacity to pay by the size of your income and your current expenses. To put it simply, you can use as much credit as you can afford to pay for.

Once you have decided that you can afford the payments and that credit does fit into your money plan, you are ready to consider the other things that help you make a decision about the kind of credit to use. Just as you would examine a coat for cost, fit, and material, examine the kind of credit. Is this credit the best buy for you? Is there someone else who can provide similar credit at a lower cost?

Also ask yourself if the terms of credit fit your needs. Is there a

Does the credit fit
your needs?

penalty if payments are late? What happens if you are not able to make payments on time? Do you lose the goods? Do you lose all you have paid up to that time? Can you buy back the item if you pay the amount that is past due?

Do not let yourself be carried away by the enthusiasm or the promises of the person who is giving you the credit. He wants to make a sale. Take your time. Do not let yourself be rushed. Read the agreement *before* you sign. If you do not understand it, do not sign it.

Reliable lenders or merchants will be glad to explain what the agreement says. They should also be willing to have you take it to someone who can explain it to you and whom you trust. It shows the lender that you are a responsible individual when you are concerned about the obligations that you are about to undertake.

If the lender objects, take your business elsewhere.

Difficulties with Credit

A lender will extend credit only if he believes that the borrower will repay as promised. The promise to pay is the foundation on which the entire credit industry rests. It has been said that credit worthiness is measured by the three c's: *character, capacity,* and *capital.* "Character" means the willingness of the person to pay as agreed, the trustworthiness of the individual. "Capacity" refers to the ability to meet the obligation when it is due, and this in turn depends on the difference between income and expenses. The best character in the world is meaningless without the ability to pay. "Capital" means the net worth of the individual, determined by the difference between what he owes and what he owns. Our possessions provide the margin of safety for the lender, because if our capacity or income proves inadequate to repay the debt, we can draw on capital to do so. Capital is also evidence of past behavior, indicating a person's sense of value and frugality.

Before merchants or lenders extend credit to you, they will want to know something about who you are and your past experiences with credit. They get this information from a credit reporting agency or

Stop! No credit for you.
Credit is a privilege.

bureau. The report the agency gives them tells them how you have handled your credit obligations in the past and if there have been any problems. If there is something in your past record that leads the lender to believe you are a poor risk, you may be refused credit.

The credit reporting agencies do not approve or disapprove your request for credit. They only report what others have told them about you, and sum up the information with a document known as a *credit report*. The merchant makes the decision as to whether or not he will give you credit. He makes this decision on the basis of the information given him.

If you believe there are things that have happened in your past which might lead the merchant to believe you are a poor credit risk, tell him about them. Be honest with the lender when asking for credit. He will find out if you are not being honest with him, so tell him before he makes the credit check.

Sickness or unemployment may have prevented you from paying your bills on time in the past. There may have been other legitimate reasons that interfered with your ability to pay but that no longer apply. Tell the lender or merchant about them. Your explanation about your past record may influence the merchant in making his decision.

If you are denied credit because of a credit report, you have the right to know what is in your credit file. Thanks to a law called the Fair Credit Reporting Act, effective April 25, 1971, the user of the credit report must let you know in writing:

1. That your request for credit was denied;
2. The name and address of the credit agency that made the credit report.

You may then go to the credit bureau and ask to see your file. There is no charge if you do this within 30 days. If you think there is an error in your file, you say so. The credit bureau will investigate the item and let you know the outcome. If you disagree with the outcome you can file a written statement giving your version and why you disagree with the findings. When such a statement is filed it must go along with any subsequent credit report containing the disputed information. If any item is found to be incorrect and is deleted—or if any item is disputed—the credit bureau must, at your request, inform all persons who have used your file in the last six months.

Upon written request, you may also see your credit file even if you have not been refused credit, but the credit bureau may charge you a nominal fee for the information.

Whenever you are denied credit, demand to know if a credit report or credit information was involved. Then follow it up at the credit reporting agency. Do not let any credit grantor deny you credit without telling you why you were denied. If you do not like the answer, challenge it. Ask for proof in writing.

You cannot hide from
your creditors.

When you use credit you have received goods or services on the promise that you will pay in the future. The lender depends on your word that you will pay as agreed. If you cannot make your payments, go to the lender. Tell him your problem. Most times he would rather arrange for a slower period of repayment than face the possibility of losing all of his loan or of having to repossess the property. If he believes you, he may rearrange your payments to meet your situation. Protect your credit reputation. Do not try to avoid the lender if you cannot pay.

The lender will work hard to find you if you try to avoid him. He is willing to pay collectors to help him find you, and they are experts at doing so. The lender does this to protect himself from losing the money he lent you; you would do the same if you were in his position.

If you cannot negotiate with the lender and you cannot pay him as you agreed, try to get someone to talk to him for you. Your employer, your foreman, your clergyman, or your union representative may be able to suggest someone who can speak for you. Ask these people. Your local branch of the Legal Aid Society or your community credit counseling service might also be available to help. Ask about it.

The Role of Credit in Your Life

Credit can help you get the things you want or need before you have cash to pay for them. Millions of people do it this way, and credit has helped them to live a better life. It has given them the opportunity to enjoy things while they were paying for them.

However, credit has also caused many people grief and hardship. Credit has encouraged people to get into debt beyond their ability to pay. Now you know how much credit costs, how to decide if you should use credit, and how to determine if you can afford it. You know what to do if you get into credit difficulties. So use your credit wisely!

Play the Shopping Game

Pick an item. Something you want very much (TV, car, freezer, complete stereo system, boat). Shop the stores for the one you want and determine the cash price.

Now figure out the total cost if:

1. You pay cash;
2. You borrow the money from a bank;
3. You borrow from a loan office;
4. You borrow from a credit union;
5. You buy on installment.

To do this, go to a bank, a loan office, and a credit union and find out what the payments will be. Check the installment terms at the store that sells the item. Then use a chart like Worksheet 3.3 to figure your total cost.

What have you learned? How would you buy this item? With cash? With credit? Which credit plan?

GLOSSARY OF NEW TERMS

Annual percentage rate   This is the effective rate a person pays for credit; it includes basic finance charges as well as any additional fees, such as credit investigation fee, service charge, or mandatory insurance premiums.

WORKSHEET 3.3
The Cost of Credit from Four Different Sources

	Monthly Payments		Number of Payments		Total Cost
Retailer	$_____	×	_____	=	$_____
Bank	_____	×	_____	=	_____
Credit union	_____	×	_____	=	_____
Loan office	_____	×	_____	=	_____

Cash loan   A loan made directly by a bank or lending agency upon your signature. Often it is based on the cash value of your life insurance policy, your savings account, or other collateral. You obtain cash to use for a specified time for a negotiated rate of interest. With a single-payment loan, both the principal and interest charges are paid in one lump sum. An installment cash loan is repaid in scheduled payments over a period of time. With a ready-check cash loan you borrow money simply by writing a check; if you don't repay it all when you receive the first statement a service charge is added.

Collateral   A form of security that serves as a pledge to assure the performance of a contract or discharge of an obligation. It may be a bill of sale, a stock certificate, or some other tangible property.

Consumer credit   Purchasing power granted consumers to buy goods and services on a promise to pay at a later date.

Credit report   A document used by credit bureaus to advise creditors of a person's past credit history.

Fair Credit Reporting Act   This law, which went into effect in 1971, attempts to regulate the action of credit bureaus and prevent them from dispensing erroneous information about private citizens. If an individual has been denied credit, employment, or insurance because of an unfavorable report, the company must tell him the name and address of the agency which issued the report. The individual has the right to know everything in his file at the credit agency (if he so requests) except medical information. He may have disputed information reinvestigated and false or unverifiable data deleted.

Installment account   A means by which an item of durable goods can be bought and paid for through scheduled payments over a specified period of time. A finance charge is added to the cash price. The buyer does not own the goods until all payments have been made.

Open charge account   A credit system under which the customer pays for the purchase within a certain period, such as 30 days. There is no service charge if the payment is made on time.

Revolving charge account   A credit system under which the maximum amount that may be owed to the store at any time is determined when the account is opened. The customer pays for purchases over a period of time. Interest is charged on the unpaid balance.

Truth-in-Lending Law   This law, properly called the Consumer Credit Protection Act of 1968, requires the lender or merchant to state the total finance charges and the annual percentage rate plus other information about the credit transaction.

QUESTIONS FOR DISCUSSION

1. Discuss the statement that credit is a privilege, not a right.
2. Explain what is meant by "credit rating," and what you can do to establish a good credit rating.
3. Identify some kinds of information recorded by credit bureaus, and name some potential sources of this information.
4. Identify factors that contribute to the cost of credit.

5. What information must the lender furnish the borrower, according to the federal Truth-in-Lending Law?
6. What are the different types of credit? Explain the unique features of each type.
7. What type of credit is usually the cheapest? Explain why it is generally cheaper than other kinds.
8. What can happen if you are not able to make your credit or loan payments on time? Suggest action the consumer should take when unable to meet his financial obligations.
9. Would you expect a family's credit to vary from stage to stage in the life cycle? How might it vary?
10. What would you do if you were refused credit? Identify the provisions of the Fair Credit Reporting Act which afford protection to the consumer.

SUGGESTED STUDENT ACTIVITIES

1. Collect and compare credit applications from a department store, furniture store, car dealer, bank, and loan company. Be sure to read the fine print. List the various points you agree to when you sign a credit contract.
2. Assume you want to borrow $500. Choose one of the following and interview the credit manager: a credit union, finance company, loan association, life insurance company. Report the cheapest source of credit. (You may wish to do this with a friend.)
3. Make a survey to find out the number and types of credit cards possessed by your class or by any ten people. Prepare a chart showing the credit policies of three lending institutions whose cards turned up in the survey.
4. Compare the costs of the same items in stores that offer credit and those that do not. Explain your findings.
5. List two items you would like to buy. Identify the cost of each item if you paid cash. Then figure the cost if the items were purchased on credit. Identify the source and type of credit.
6. Collect advertisements of consumer credit and classify them according to type and source. Which kinds of credit are most heavily advertised? Can you think of any reasons? Prepare a written report of your findings.
7. Compile a list of places to call to report dishonest credit practices to ask, advice about credit, and to check a creditor's reputation before signing a contract.
8. Prepare a list of "come-on" or persuasive techniques used to encourage buying ("no down payment required," "take as long as you like to pay," etc.).
9. Visit a pawn shop and ask the manager to explain the operation of his business.
10. Make a list of guidelines that would be useful to a person shopping for credit.
11. Prepare a list of advantages and disadvantages of (a) paying cash, and (b) using credit.

FOR ADDITIONAL INFORMATION

"Are You Using Your Truth-in-Lending Rights?" *Changing Times*, November 1973, pp. 17–18.
A refresher on the Truth-in-Lending Law and what it means to credit users.

"Credit Reform: Which Way to Go?" *Consumer Reports*, May 1974, pp. 382–384.
A discussion of opposition to the proposed Uniform Consumer Credit Code (UCCC) and an alternative. The article also points out some serious omissions in the code.

Finkelstein, Milton, and Arthur Nitzburg. *Living in a Consumer's World*. New York: Globe, 1974, pp. 61–74.
The chapter on borrowing to buy a car explains the language of credit, how to shop for a loan, contracts, and interest cost. Easy reading.

"How to Shop for Credit." *Consumers Report*, March 1975, pp. 171–178.
Explains different types of credit and how to shop for the best interest rate, and offers recommendations about using credit.

"Is Borrowing to Pay Bills Smart?" *Changing Times*, April 1975, pp. 23–24.
Discusses debt consolidation and offers a word of caution. Suggests what to look for, where to shop, and how to plan for paying the debt off.

Mandell, Lewis. *Credit Card Use in the United States*. Ann Arbor, Mich.: Institute for Social Research, University of Michigan, 1972.
A comprehensive study that examines the use of credit cards, attitudes toward credit cards, and economic implications.

Money Management Institute. *It's Your Credit—Manage It Wisely*. Chicago: Household Finance Corporation, 1970.
Well written and easy to understand; presents information on the wise use of credit.

Schoenfeld, David, and Arthur A. Natella. *The Consumer and His Dollars*. Dobbs Ferry, N.Y.: Oceana, 1970, pp. 169–191.
Discusses the historical development of credit, the kinds of credit, and credit cost.

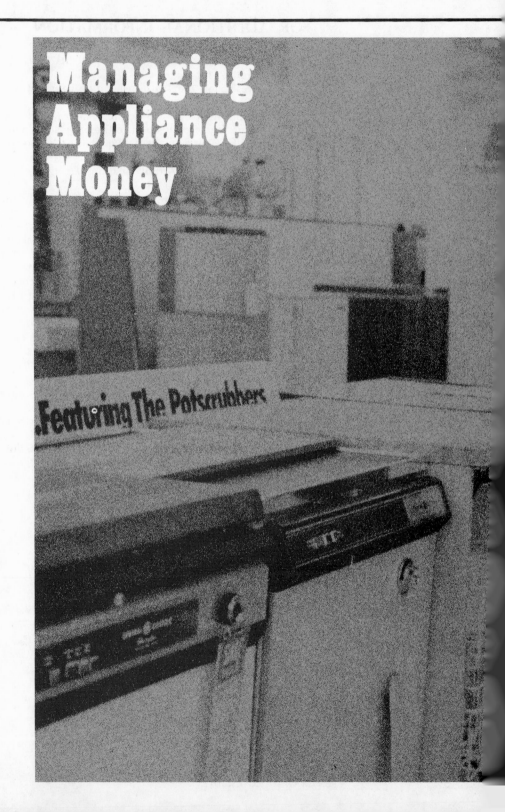

4

Managing Appliance Money

...Featuring The Potscrubbers

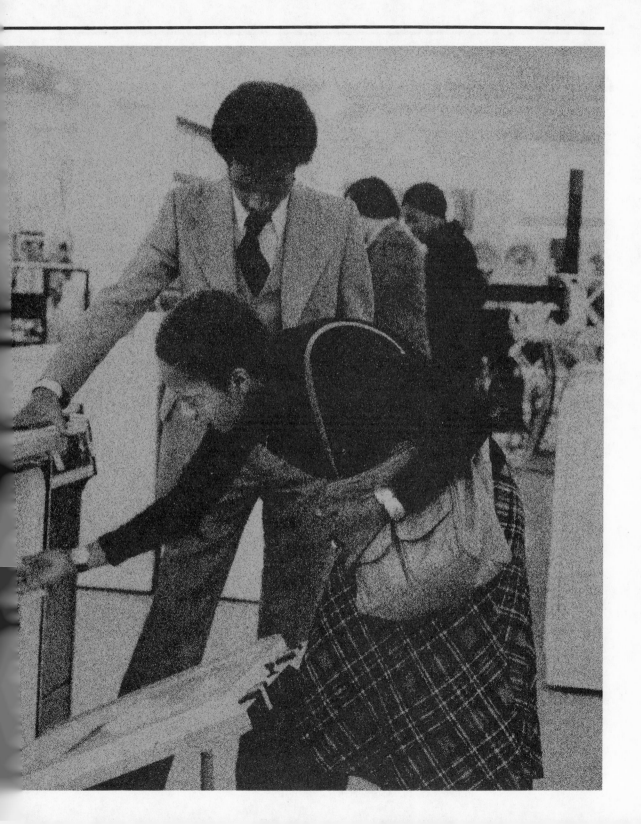

4

Most people want to have the best in time-saving and energy-saving equipment to make their lives fuller and easier. Since each piece of equipment that you buy for yourself or for your family represents an investment—and often a sizeable one—you want to get the most for the money you spend. *Before* the purchase is completed, careful consideration should be given not only to the advantages of the item, but also to the disadvantages.

In this chapter you will learn what you need to know to make your decision about buying an appliance. You will learn how to compare important features and how to evaluate costs and benefits.

Read the story of the Keenes, who bought "A Refrigerator like Mary's." As you read what happened to them, try to put yourself in their place and decide what to do. But read the remainder of the chapter before making a final decision.

A REFRIGER-ATOR LIKE MARY'S

"Look, Jack, here's a refrigerator just like Mary's and it's $50 less than they paid for theirs," Fran Keene said to her husband. He examined the advertisement that Fran was looking at, and sure enough the refrigerator bore exactly the same make and model number that Joe and Mary Stout had in their home.

The Stouts were long-time friends of Fran and Jack and lived in their own home close to the apartment where the newly married Keenes had set up housekeeping several months ago.

"We sure need to get rid of this old refrigerator that your mother loaned us," said Jack, "and Joe and Mary say that their box not only supplies plenty of ice cubes for drinks, but holds enough food for themselves and the four kids for a week. Imagine, we'll be able to do all our food shopping at one time with a big box like this to store it in."

"Yeah, and we won't have to fight with those crazy ice trays any more either."

"Can we afford the payments of $21 a month?" asked Fran.

"Of course," said Jack, "that's less than $5 a week. Let's go down to look at it this afternoon. Do you know where Max's is?"

"That must be that little store that just opened on the side street. I don't know anyone who's bought there, but we'll find it."

That afternoon they went to the store and the refrigerator was indeed the same as Mary's. There was a big tag on it which said "$50 off." They arranged for delivery the next day. The salesman was very nice. He told them that they wouldn't need to make a down payment and had Jack sign a paper agreeing to payments of $21 per month, as advertised. He assured them that they were getting a terrific value, which Max's was able to offer only because the store owner was new in the city and was willing to sell goods at low prices as a way to introduce himself to customers.

When the box arrived, Fran plugged it in and went shopping to stock up on her groceries for the week. That night, when Jack got home, she proudly showed him the new refrigerator with her groceries neatly stored within.

"Sure looks empty in there," he said; "not like Mary's."

"Of course, stupid, Mary has four kids. Wait until we have four children and our box will be stuffed like theirs," retorted Fran.

"That's a long time away, isn't it? Well, let's have a cold drink now."

They discovered that in order to use the ice cube dispenser they would need to have a water line directly into the refrigerator. The janitor, whom they called in to advise them on how to install the ice cube maker, told them they would have to bring in a line from the basement. The plumber told them that the installation of a water line to the new refrigerator would cost between $100 and $150, depending on how long it took to run the pipe. He could not give them a firm price until he found out what he had to go through to get the line in.

Jack called the store, Max's, to seek advice, and was told that everybody knew you had to have a water line to be able to use an automatic ice cube maker.

Because of the expense of installing the water line and the fact that the box was more than they needed at this time, Jack asked the salesman whether he could exchange the box for a smaller one that didn't make ice cubes automatically.

"Of course not," replied the salesman. "We don't do business that way. You bought it—now it's yours."

"Then I'll stop making payments on it if you won't exchange it," argued Jack.

"You do that and you'll not only lose the refrigerator but have a law suit on your hands for the full amount of $756. According to the sales contract you signed with us, and which we have sold to the Gypum Loan Company, if you fail to make your payment on time each tenth of the month they have the right to repossess the appliance and sue you for the balance due on the contract."

"Seven hundred and fity six?" Why, that box was supposed to be $50 off. Twenty-four payments at $21 a month would be only $504."

"It sure would," said the man, "but your note was for 36 months and that amounts to $756, and I'd advise you to see that your payments are made on time 'cause the loan company doesn't like to wait for their payments too long before they repossess."

What did Jack and Fran do wrong?

Should the refrigerator be defective before the end of the warranty, who would be responsible for repairs? Would Fran and Jack be obligated to continue making payments to the Gypum Loan Company if the motor burned out at the end of one year? Does your state have laws that protect consumers in Fran and Jack's situation? In what way could you profit by Fran and Jack's mistake?

In case you are called on to make a decision about buying a refrigerator, it would be wise to keep the following points in mind.

1. The primary function of a refrigerator is to keep food fresh and safe, and to provide for storage.
2. The size needed depends on family size and frequency of shopping.
3. Storage space in the refrigerator should be related to use.
   a. Large space is needed for items such as watermelons, tall bottles, and turkeys.
   b. Smaller storage spaces are needed for small containers; you may also want a covered space for butter and a special space for eggs.
4. Adjustable shelves, pull-out shelves, and door storage make for convenience and extend space.
5. Crispers for fresh fruits and vegetables should have tight-fitting covers to prevent drying out of the contents.
6. "Frost-free" refrigerators, which do not require defrosting, are more expensive to operate than those that must be manually defrosted, because they use more electricity.
7. The cabinet should be easy to clean, have a durable finish, and have adequate insulation.
8. A refrigerator-freezer with separate doors provides more freezing space than one with a single door, and the temperature in the freezing compartment can be maintained at zero degrees.
9. Side-by-side refrigerator-freezers are convenient but expensive. It might be cheaper to purchase a separate refrigerator and freezer if space is available for both units.
10. Automatic ice makers eliminate filling ice trays but require the installation of a waterline.

Types of Appliances

Let's consider other appliances so as to avoid the pitfall Jack and Fran encountered in buying a refrigerator. Home appliances may be classified into *major appliances* and *small appliances*.

The group of major appliances includes the larger, more expensive items, such as ranges, washing machines, dryers, refrigerator-freezers, waste compacters, microwave ovens, dishwashers, and food waste disposals.

Some small appliances are designed to make you beautiful—for instance, hair dryers and nail-care sets. Others, such as vacuum cleaners, fans, or floor polishers, keep your living space clean and comfortable. Others permit you to have food cooked and served most any place in the house or on the patio. Many of these appliances are portable and relatively inexpensive, and a wide variety is available from which to choose.

Meeting Your Needs and Wants

Appliances and household equipment should be purchased on the basis of your present and future needs and wants. You should bear in mind that there are individual differences among people and among families. What might be ideal for one can be disaster for another. For example, large families with growing children need many items that are very different from those required by a single person or a couple with no children. This seems to be a simple truth, but it is often forgotten when household goods are purchased.

You should be sure, of course, that the appliance will fit your money plan—that you can afford it. If you decide that you can, it may seem wise to buy the appliance on "sale" rather than at the regular price. Initial price, however, is not the only consideration. The following list of questions should be helpful in evaluating whether an appliance will suit you.

Is the appliance you are considering really needed? Will you use it?

Will it make the housekeeping jobs easier or faster?

Is it easy to use, clean, and adjust?

Will it make the home safer, more liveable, more enjoyable?

Will it make more space available by replacing items that are taking up too much space now?

Or will it take up space that shouldn't be given up?

Do you like the way it looks?

Will it cause excessive heat or noise in the home?

Could you find a better use for the money you are going to spend for equipment?

Will it complicate your way of life—or your family's?

Is the appliance too small or too large for the task to be performed? If it is too small it will be ineffective. If it is too large it will waste energy, besides costing more to purchase.

Does the appliance have the special features you need? Remember that the more elaborate the gadgets, dials, and buttons the greater the cost and the higher the odds that something will go wrong. And when it does, fewer repairmen will know how to make the needed repairs.

Before you decide on the appliance you want, shop the stores. Make notes as you visit different dealers. Compare the advantages and disadvantages before you make your final decision. Only if the

Is the appliance right
for *you*?

positive factors outweigh the negative ones should you decide to make the purchase.

Other Guidelines for Buying Appliances

Before you settle on a piece of equipment, even if you think it will meet your basic needs and wants, you should take some other factors into account.

First, the equipment should be economical to operate. Rising costs of energy make it important that you compare the appliances you are considering in terms of energy utilization. How much energy or fuel will your choice require? How does its operating costs compare with the costs of other models? Examine the amount of energy that each model will use in a given period of time.

If you have the choice of gas or electricity as the energy source for your appliance, check to determine which form is more economical in your community. Your local gas and electric company can give you the information. Of course you should consult your personal preferences as well; perhaps you like gas better than electricity, or vice versa.

You should also check out the "hidden" costs. Don't wait until you get the appliance home, as Fran and Jack did, to find that you need a special water line. And what about gas and electricity—do you have the right lines or circuits? If not, how much will they cost?

The manufacturer of the equipment should be well established and reliable, one who stands behind the product and provides you with detailed information about how the product is constructed, about the finish, about the special features, and about how to use them to best advantage. Instructions for the general care and use of the appliance should also be provided by the manufacturer.

The retailer from whom you buy your equipment should be reliable too. He or she should be willing to demonstrate the appliance, to give you an estimate of the installation cost, and to provide information about servicing. The retailer should be able to install the equipment efficiently and properly. In addition, you'll want to find a merchant who has a reputation for being fair in servicing appliances and replacing parts.

A *warranty* is a legal guarantee by a seller or manufacturer of the performance and quality of the item offered for sale. In examining a warranty, you should ask yourself these questions: Does the warranty tell you what the manufacturer's responsibility is in case the product fails to perform properly at any time within the stated period? Is it written in easily understood terms? Does the warranty state what is provided free and what must be paid for (parts, labor, service)? How long is the warranty in force? Must you purchase the item from an authorized dealer to receive the stated benefits—and is the merchant you are buying from an authorized dealer?

Often seals and tags are attached to the appliance to identify it as guaranteed, certified, approved, or tested. Know who makes the promises that are printed on these seals and tags, who made the tests, what the certification includes, and what are the terms and length of

Find the hidden costs.

the guarantee. The *American Gas Association (AGA) seal* certifies that gas appliances have been tested for safety, performance, and durability. The *Underwriters' Laboratories, Inc. (UL) seal* certifies that electrical appliances have been submitted by the manufacturer for testing; those bearing the UL seal have met certain safety standards for fire, electric shock, and other hazards.

Good Housekeeping and *Parents' Magazine* offer "seals of approval" to items that are advertised in their magazines. While *Good Housekeeping* states that it "guarantees replacement or refund to customer" for improper performance, the publishers do not guarantee the safety or wholesomeness of the product. The guarantee by *Parents' Magazine* is granted only to products advertised in the magazine that the publishers believe are "suitable for families with children." There is no responsibility on the part of the magazine as to how good a product is, and the criteria used in evaluating it are not stated. Under these circumstances the validity of these "seals of approval" is open to question. You should be guided by your own good sense in making decisions about "sealed" products and not rely upon the magazines' recommendations.

The guidelines we have been discussing are general buying guides for all appliances or types of equipment. For information about specific things to look for in particular kinds of equipment you should check sources such as *Consumers' Research Magazine* (formerly *Consumer Bulletin*) published monthly by Consumers' Research, Inc., and *Consumer Reports,* by Consumers Union. You can find these publications in the library or at a local newsstand. If the current issues don't have an article about the appliance you are interested in, check the back issues at the library. The publishers of *Consumer Reports* also put out a *Buying Guide* once a year.

Friends who have similar appliances are also a good source of information. Ask them what is good about the item and what is bad. Find out if they would buy the same kind of appliance again. Their answers will give you a better understanding of how the appliance will suit your needs. But remember it is your needs that count, not theirs.

Take advantage of special offers that dealers make from time to time. Sometimes a year-end model or one from a "close-out" sale will do the job you need to have done at less cost. But be certain that you are getting what you think you are during these "special events." Evaluate your purchase on the basis of what you know about the item, not on the basis of the salesman's promises.

The Method of Payment
Household appliances may be purchased for cash or on installment credit. Sometimes you may be able to get an "extra reduction" if you offer the merchant cash.

If you use credit in purchasing your appliance, you will pay for this service. Know how much the credit will cost you. Just as you have checked with different dealers for quality and style to suit your needs, shop different dealers to compare credit costs before you obligate yourself. Compare the cost of each deal, being sure to include all charges. Be certain you read and understand the agreement before you sign it. Don't let a fast-talking salesman or saleswoman tell you that the fine print is not important and rush you to sign the contract.

Service for Your Appliance

Service costs are an essential but often overlooked item of expense in managing your equipment dollar. Provide some funds in your money plan for unexpected repairs. The following suggestions will help you minimize the cost of servicing your equipment.

Read the instruction booklet before you use your equipment. Follow the manufacturer's instructions about the care and use of the item.

Check the equipment to see that it is properly installed before you begin to operate it. Ask your utility company to check for you if you are in doubt.

Do not tamper with equipment that is out of order, unless you know what you're doing. You might cause greater damage and increase your service costs.

Keep the warranty slips, the sales slip, the serviceman's address and phone number, and receipts for service in a handy place so that you can refer to them quickly when needed.

Before you call the serviceman, check the instruction manual. Check electricity, water, and gas for proper connection. Check the fuse box.

When you call the repairman, know the details about your appliance: the name of the manufacturer, the model number, the date of installation. Write these on the instruction booklet so you can find them easily.

Describe the problem as best you can. Ask for an estimate or learn the serviceman's rate for home calls. Be prepared to pay for the service call even if the repairman finds your appliance in perfect order.

When the serviceman arrives, be home or have someone responsible there to find out what has to be done and the cost. Ask for an itemized bill for service and parts. Let the serviceman work uninterrupted. Time spent in talking to you may be charged to you. Be prepared to pay cash for repairs unless arrangements have been made previously for credit.

For service problems that you and your local dealer or repairman cannot resolve, write or call the Major Appliance Consumer Action Panel (MACAP), 20 North Wacker Drive, Chicago, Illinois 60606. The phone number is (312) 236–3165. This agency is established on an industry-wide basis to handle consumer complaints about the products of the major appliance manufacturers. If your complaint is legitimate, they authorize the dealer to make restitution.

Appliances and the Energy Crisis

The United States has only 6 percent of the world's population and yet we use 32 percent of the world's energy. We are doubling our energy demands every fifteen to twenty years. The demand for electricity is doubling every eight to ten years. It is becoming apparent that conservation of energy is a must and will be for years to come.

The home is a big energy user. Almost one-fourth of the nation's energy is used in the home. Heating and cooling rank highest among home uses, followed by hot-water heating, cooking, refrigeration, lighting, and the running of small portable appliances.

Most people take for granted the appliances in the home. When we first see or read about a new appliance we may consider it a luxury or an extravagant use of funds. But once we acquire it either as a gift or as a purchase we generally become convinced that it is essential to our lifestyle.

Therefore, in selecting and purchasing appliances, serious thought should be given to conserving energy. Ask yourself: Will the appliance under consideration contribute to the energy drain, or will it be more efficient than an older appliance? Can I do without it altogether?

Appliances That Help Conserve Energy

Electric Broilers Some appliances perform the same functions as others but use less energy in the process. The small electric broiler, for example, uses less electricity than a range broiler, according to tests made by Consumers Union. This table-top appliance, sometimes called a toaster-oven, does a variety of cooking jobs. The heat for baking and roasting comes from the bottom. For broiling and top-browning the heat comes from the top.

Some toaster-ovens have only one heating unit, and the entire appliance can be flipped over so that the heating unit is on the top for broiling and toasting and reversed for baking and roasting. There are several models, and there are variations in the services they will perform. So if you're interested in purchasing a toaster-oven be sure to make comparisons. Ask yourself the following questions.

Does it perform the jobs you expect?
Is it the right size for the space you have and the amount you want to cook?
Does it automatically turn off and ring a bell to tell you?
Is it easy to clean?
Does it cook evenly, according to test reports?
Are the instructions complete and easy to understand?
Will you use it enough to warrant making the purchase?
Are there other, more appropriate ways to conserve energy?

Microwave Ovens Microwave ovens are gaining in popularity as a time-saving and energy-saving way to cook food. Sales are predicted to increase tremendously in the years ahead. Microwave energy, much like the radiant energy of a television, is produced by a magnetron. When food in the microwave oven absorbs the energy, the molecules become agitated, and this process produces the heat that cooks the food. Most foods can be cooked in one-fourth the normal cooking time with microwave energy. Although many foods, such as roasts, will not brown in the microwave oven unless they have a relatively long cooking period (fifteen to twenty minutes) some models are available with browning units that operate like the broiler in a conventional range.

Utensils made of glass, china, ceramic pottery, and paper are used to hold the food while it is cooking. Metals should not be used, since they reflect microwaves, nor should china with metallic designs or bands. Browning utensils are available from some manufacturers.

Microwave ovens are as safe as other household heating appliances. They must meet strict government regulations, which state the maximum microwave energy emission that is allowed during the useful life of the oven. The standards also stipulate that every microwave oven have at least two operating safety interlocks that automatically shut off radiation whenever the door is opened. There are no recorded injuries from the use of microwave ovens.

The microwave oven requires less energy than other ovens when used in preparing meals for a family of four or fewer, and it does not heat the kitchen as conventional ranges do. This cuts down on the need for cooling in the kitchen, a need that is costly in terms of energy.

The microwave oven is a versatile appliance. It can be used for thawing frozen food, reheating food quickly, and heating a bowl of soup or cup of coffee, as well as for roasting and baking. It enables persons employed outside the home to enjoy a home-cooked meal in a short time. The portable units which are available can be moved to the patio, den, or another area. Anyone who purchases a microwave oven should spend some time learning to make the best use of it.

Dishwashers Once considered a luxury appliance, the dishwasher is presently considered essential by many people. One in four families owns a dishwasher, and it is estimated that 40 percent of the homes in the United States will be equipped with dishwashers in a few more years.

Some recent studies have shown that when properly loaded and used a dishwasher uses less hot water than is used in washing dishes by hand. This is especially true when the water is left running in the washing-by-hand process. Approximately three to five gallons less water needs to be heated when a dishwasher is used. Thus while the dishwasher uses energy to operate, there is still a saving of energy.

Dishwashers are popular because they save the time and energy of the homemaker. The kitchen can also be kept more orderly, because used dishes can go right into the dishwasher. Dishes come out cleaner and more sanitary than if hand washed and dried. However, the proper water temperature (140°–160°F) must be maintained.

As with other appliances, you should study the instruction booklet in order to get maximum use out of a dishwasher. If you do not understand the instructions, ask for a demonstration from your dealer.

Some Ways to Conserve Energy in Using Appliances

In the summer, schedule heat-generating activities such as cooking, vacuuming, and ironing for the cooler evening or morning hours. That way, if you have an air conditioner, it will not have to run so much of the time. Even if you don't have an air conditioner you'll appreciate the difference.

Set the thermostat on the air conditioner higher, so the air will be cooled rather than chilled. When an air conditioner is installed, make sure it is the correct size and the most efficient unit for the space to be cooled.

Check the hot-water heater to see if the temperature setting could be lowered a few degrees.

Conserve energy but don't be *too* enthusiastic.

PERSONAL FINANCE FOR CONSUMERS

Reduce the use of hot water by washing laundry in cooler water and adjusting the amount of water to the size of the load. If the water level cannot be regulated, wait until you have a full load to wash.

Run the dishwasher only when it's full.

Select the most efficient appliance for the task. A microwave oven uses less energy than a regular one for some cooking tasks. Portable ovens or similar appliances use less energy than the range oven for small baking jobs. And new smooth-top ranges offer greater efficiency for top-of-the-stove cooking.

Avoid using the range oven for long periods with only one or two items in it. It's better to plan a complete oven meal than to bake two potatoes. Start without preheating the oven.

Use proper-size pans with flat bottoms to avoid wasted heat.

Be sure to lower the temperature when food being cooked reaches the boiling point.

Buy the correct-size refrigerator for your use or your family's, and remember that the frost-free model uses more electricity.

In using a refrigerator and freezer, avoid (1) overloading, (2) opening the door too often, and (3) allowing thick frost to build up. Check to see if you refrigerate items that do not require refrigeration.

Reduce the intensity of lights where you can and turn them off when they are not being used.

Product Safety

A two-year study by a national commission on product safety revealed that twenty million Americans are injured each year as a result of incidents connected with household consumer products; 30,000 are killed; and 110,000 are crippled or disabled. The annual cost of the injuries is more than $5.5 billion. As a result of these startling facts Congress passed a Consumer Product Act, which went into effect on December 26, 1972. A new federal regulatory commission, known as the Consumer Product Safety Commission (CPSC), was created and given wide authority. Among other things, the commission can:

Require companies to perform certain tests to certify that their products meet safety rules.

Force manufacturers of new products, before distribution, to provide the commission with information showing that the products have met required standards.

Refuse admission to the United States to imports that fail to meet regulations.

Ban a product if no feasible standard for it has been developed and the hazard of injury, death, or illness exists.

Issue warnings about specific products or appliances. Order the recall of unsafe products.

A study of the authority vested in the CPSC indicates that the commission can have a profound impact upon manufacturers. The law also provides for action by consumers, consumer organizations, and public interest groups.

There are stiff penalties for violations: $2,000 for each violation, up to a maximum of $50,000; criminal penalties up to $50,000 and one year in prison. Consumers may sue for enforcement or petition for implementation of the product safety standards.

The commission may also conduct research on products and collect data on injuries caused by unsafe products. It may initiate studies for improving product safety and train researchers in product safety investigations.

SUMMARY

Ask yourself:

> Is the appliance needed?
> Will it make work easier or more efficient?
> Will it make my home safer, more liveable, more enjoyable?
> Will it make more space available than present equipment?

Also consider the disadvantages:

> Will it cause excessive heat and noise?
> Can I use the money to better advantage?
> Will it take up space I cannot spare?
> Will it increase the amount of energy used?
> Will it complicate my or my family's way of life?

Then weigh the positives and negatives before deciding.
Before buying the appliance, look for these things:

About the model
> Does it meet my needs (size, style, special features)?
> Is it easy to operate, clean, and service?
> Is it well constructed?

About the manufacturer and dealer
> Are they well established and reputable?
> Are they willing to give information about service and installation?

About the warranty
> What does it provide?
> How long is it in effect?
> Who pays for what?

About the price
> Can I afford it?
> Is if the *best* price for me?
> What's included in the price?
> What does the credit cost me?
> What will the operating costs be?
> What can I expect the service costs to be?

GLOSSARY OF NEW TERMS

American Gas Association (AGA) Seal Certifies that gas appliances have been tested for safety, performance, and durability.

Consumer Product Safety Commission (CPSC) A federal agency with authority to see that a wide variety of products and appliances meet required standards and safety regulations.

Major Appliance Consumer Action Panel (MACAP) A group of independent consumer experts set up by major appliance manufacturers to resolve consumers complaints about major appliances such as refrigerators, ranges, air conditioners, dishwashers, etc.

Underwriters' Laboratories, Inc. (UL) Seal Certifies that products have been checked for safety from fire, electric shock, and other hazards.

Warranty A legal agreement whereby a seller or manufacturer guarantees the performance and quality of items offered for sale.

QUESTIONS FOR DISCUSSION

1. What factors should be considered when selecting an appliance?
2. What is a warranty? Explain important points that should be included in a warranty.
3. Name two tags or seals which are often attached to appliances and explain what they mean.
4. Name some reliable sources of information about appliances. Identify the consumer services provided by MACAP.
5. What costs need to be considered in addition to the basic price of the appliance?
6. Explain how choosing an appliance is related to each person's or family's needs and preferences.
7. If an appliance were purchased on a retail installment plan, how might the rate of interest compare with the rates for other types of credit available to consumers? (See Chapter 3.)
8. If you were dissatisfied with a refrigerator you bought last month, what would you do?
9. Name the major users of energy in the home. Rank these appliances according to the relative amounts of energy used.
10. Identify the measures you would take if your washing machine suddenly stopped functioning.

SUGGESTED STUDENT ACTIVITIES

1. Identify three appliances that do essentially the same job but vary in price. Read the warranties, seals, and other information and choose the one that would best fit your needs. Explain the reasons for your choice.
2. Select a home appliance which you are interested in purchasing in the future. Obtain as much essential information as needed to make an intelligent choice of a particular brand and model. Report to the class your choice and your reasons for making it.

3. Estimate the costs per month of operating a gas range and an electric range with similar features. Which one is more economical in your area? Investigate the additional cost for electricity or gas for a self-cleaning oven. State whether this feature would be worth the additional cost, and if so, why.

4. Compare the cost of buying a major appliance at a discount store with the cost at a department store. Check for extra charges for installation and delivery. Which store offers the better deal?

5. Make a list of some major kinds of equipment used in the home. Survey five families who own appliances on your list. Find out how long each appliance has been owned, its service record, and its present condition. Then prepare a chart that shows the usual service needs and life expectancy of each type of appliance.

6. Make a list of basic household appliances that would be needed by a newly married couple. Arrange them according to the priorities that should be followed in purchasing. Take the top three on your priority list, and draw up specifications of the features and sizes that would be required. Recommend models that measure up to the specifications.

7. Make a list of persons or places you could contact for information about:
   a. Air conditioners,
   b. Refrigerators,
   c. Ranges,
   d. Televisions and stereo equipment.

8. Prepare a list of suggestions for cutting energy costs through selection and use of appliances.

FOR ADDITIONAL INFORMATION

"At Last They're Doing Something About Dangerous Products." *Changing Times*, February 1975, pp. 35–37.
> Gives a sampling of instances in which the CPSC has ordered recalls or banned dangerous products.

Fletcher, Adele Whitely. *How to Stretch Your Dollar*. New York: Benjamin Co., 1970, pp 52–59.
> Discusses selection and purchasing of some major appliances.

General Services Administration. *Washers and Dryers*. Bulletin No. 2200–0079. Government Prtinting Office, n.d.
> The federal government has prepared a series of consumer publications designed to make available information the GSA has assembled in purchasing items for government installations. This bulletin is one in the series. Write the Superintendent of Documents for a complete, up-to-date list.

"How Much Your Electric Appliances Cost to Run." *Changing Times*, February 1975, p. 6.
> Presents a chart showing the operating costs of approximately fifty appliances, based on information from the Electric Energy Association.

Morton, Ruth, Hilda Geuthier, and Virginia Guthrie. *The Home, Its Furnishings and Equipment*. New York: McGraw-Hill, 1970.
> Considers the home budget for furnishings and equipment. Presents shopping techniques for obtaining quality.

Seaduto, Anthony. *Getting the Most for Your Money*. New York: David McKay, 1970, pp. 86–97.

Considers when, where, what, and how to buy. Discusses appliances and home furnishings along with other matters.

U.S. Department of Agriculture. *Handbook for the Home; The 1973 Yearbook of Agriculture*. Washington, D.C.: Government Printing Office, 1973.

Provides helpful suggestions on large and small appliances for the kitchen and laundry, for personal care, and for recreation. Energy conservation is also considered.

5

Managing Housing Money

5

Housing usually represents the largest expense item in an individual's or family's money plan. Costs for housing include not only rent or mortgage payments, but related expenses such as utilities, insurance, decorating, maintenance, and repairs. Special assessments such as school taxes, trash pickup fees, and water and sewer taxes may also be added to your housing costs.

In this chapter you will learn how to make the most of your housing expenditures, so that they give you or your family the greatest satisfaction. You will learn how to decide the kind of housing you need, how much you can afford to spend, and how to use insurance to protect your home and the things you have in it.

Read the following account of the Shorts. They are involved in a typical family argument about housing. Once you have read about their problem, we can examine what you need to do to manage your housing money well.

TO BUY OR RENT

Bill and Mary Short had lived in their present home for a rental of $235.00 per month for the past several years. Bill would have liked them to own their own home. Since getting out of the service they had lived in three different cities, and he felt that owning a home would enable them to establish roots in the community. To him, renting was a transient way of living. He argued, "Owning is cheaper than renting. All we have to show for the time we've lived here is rent receipts. If we owned this house our payments would be going toward buying it. We would be building equity in the house and after time we would own it outright."

Mary didn't agree. She believed that owning a home tied a person down too much. "What if you were offered a promotion that required that we move to another town?" she asked. "Wouldn't you want to take it? And maybe, when the kids get older I'll want to live closer to downtown so that I can go back to work. Besides, if we owned our house I know that I would be the one to take care of it instead of the landlord, who does it now. I know that I won't be able to depend on you to do the minor repairs."

"Just making the mortgage payments isn't all there is to owning a home, she argued. "It'll cost us more, and we can't afford it now when the children are growing up and have many needs."

"But look at the Long's next door," said Bill. "They're paying only $235 on their house and in time they'll own it. Anyway, if we have to move to take a better job sometime, we can sell the house."

In order to settle the argument, they went to see the Longs to find out the details of how Ray and Doris had purchased their home. They learned that the Longs had paid $34,400 for their house, which

was similar to the Shorts. The down payment when they had purchased the house was $4,400, leaving a $30,000 mortgage that they
obtained from a local institution at 8 3/4 percent for 30 years. The
mortgage payments were $236.10 per month. But taxes and insurance

were not included in the monthly payments. Also, Ray pointed out, they had had to put in a new hot water heater just recently when the old one broke down. In time they would need to make other repairs, including a new roof and maybe even a heating system.

"Well," said Bill, "I certainly hadn't thought this through enough to make a decision. I guess Mary and I will have to talk about the business of buying a little more thoroughly before we decide."

Do you think Bill's arguments were valid?
Were Mary's arguments valid?
Do you think the Shorts should buy or rent? Why?

What Kind of Housing Do You Need?

People differ widely in their needs and wants when housing is concerned. Some people prefer small, compact accommodations; others want a large amount of living space. Some want to do gardening and yard work; others want indoor space for their leisure-time activities. Most important, as family size varies, housing requirements vary.

The life stage of the person or family plays a part in housing. Single, newly married, or childless people obviously have different needs than those with children. And when the children are small the needs are different than when they are nearly grown.

You need to decide whether you want to live in a house or an apartment; in the city, the suburbs, or the country; in a new area or an older neighborhood. Your own needs will dictate how many rooms you should get for yourself or your family. Will each child have his own room, or will boys share one room and girls another? Is a separate dining room or study needed? Must there be an attic or a basement? Is a carport or garage required?

To help you in thinking about the kind of housing you want and need, let's consider the major types one by one. Volumes have been written about each type, but the capsule presentation here will help you narrow your focus.

Apartments

Young adults, either single or married, often prefer an apartment to any other type of housing. Some become accustomed to apartment living while they are students, and they recognize that it provides a certain amount of freedom and less responsibility than a house. There is no yard to care for, and the apartment owner assumes the responsibility for repairs and upkeep.

Many apartment buildings provide a swimming pool, tennis courts, a recreation center, and laundry rooms. Apartments are frequently located near public transportation, a shopping center, and the bright lights of a town or city. However, an increasing number are being built in suburban areas.

Apartments can be rented furnished, in which case all you need to move in are linens, personal belongings, and perhaps a TV or stereo. But as you begin to acquire more furniture and personal belongings and feel a desire to have your living space show a greater reflection of your own personality, you might consider an unfurnished apart-

Does the housing fit your needs?

ment. This is often the second step on the housing ladder. It permits you or your family to acquire furnishings to suit your own desires; if you chose wisely, the things you buy may be suitable for a house you'll acquire later. The family attic, furniture auctions, and antique shops can provide items to refinish or restore. Paint, attractive fabric, time and effort, plus a little creativity and a small amount of money, can turn an unfurnished apartment into attractive living space.

Duplexes

A duplex is usually designed and built for two families to live side by side under the same roof. Each unit is separate; it has its own heating system, and generally includes a laundry unit, range, refrigerator, and other kitchen appliances. A duplex has many of the advantages of an unfurnished apartment. It may also have a yard or patio you can use.

As you become more affluent you may wish to purchase the duplex—live in one side and rent the other. Duplexes can be a good financial investment.

Duplex living is of course enhanced when the two families sharing the unit get along with each other. This is also a factor in selecting an apartment, but in the duplex it is probably more important.

Townhouses

Another type of living space is a townhouse. Townhouses are self-contained dwellings, generally built in a row with no space between units. Some recent designs feature clusters of units. Each unit has its own front and back entrance. Individuality is achieved through variation in construction and in the finish of the roof and exterior walls. Some townhouses have their own patios and garages. All have their own utilities, such as heat, laundry facilities, and appliances. Most townhouses are either two or three stories high. This would be a disadvantage for a physically handicapped person.

Townhouses are usually individually owned and can be transferred from one owner to another. Often they can be rented. One advantage is that they are frequently the cheapest way of owning a home, especially in areas where land cost is enormous.

Condominiums

Condominiums, another form of housing, are apartment complexes in which a person buys his own apartment and pays a fee for the management of the complex. The central administration takes care of the grounds and various other features, such as security and the renting of condominiums whose owners are not year-round residents.

Owners of a townhouse or condominium are eligible for the tax benefits of a homeowner. This includes the deduction from taxable income of property taxes and interest paid on the money borrowed for the mortgage.

Mobile Homes

Mobile homes may offer advantages for some individuals or families. Their most obvious characteristic is that they can be moved to other locations should their owners be transferred. A mobile home is usually bought completely furnished, and the average cost is less than the cost of an unfurnished house. Mobile homes are used by many people who cannot afford to own another type of housing.

There are certain restrictions as to where mobile homes can be anchored. However, many attractive mobile home parks have been established in convenient locations. For a low rental fee these parks provide a cement pad and water and electrical connections. In warmer climates, screened porches or decks are often added to provide additional space and relieve occupants of the cramped feeling of mobile home living. Some parks have space for pets and flowers and also a central coin laundry.

In areas struck by tornadoes, some mobile home parks have been completely destroyed. The mobile homes seem to offer little protection because of their light weight and tight construction.

Some couples live in a mobile home until they are able to afford a house, and then move the mobile home to a lakeside lot to use as a retreat or second home.

Single-Unit Houses

To own a house is the dream of many families. It may be a new house in a recently developed subdivision, an older house in a well-developed area, a house on a small plot of land in the country, or any other kind. It will be your responsibility to learn how to judge quality and how to choose the necessary space for family activities. You can have greater privacy in your own home, and each family member can have space to enjoy his or her own hobby. Family preference and nearness to work, school, shopping areas, and other services, along with the cost, are important factors to consider in making a decision.

Selecting a New House   A new house can afford certain advantages as well as some disadvantages. Let's consider some of the advantages. It will be clean and will probably have certain built-in appliances, such as a range and a dishwasher. It may have a disposal unit, washer-dryer combination, and a refrigerator. In some new houses the floors are carpeted. If you make a decision on a specific house before construction is completed, you can often choose the colors for carpeting and wallpaper and the kind and color of the appliances. The newly built home will probably cost less for repairs than an older one, since the roof, furnace, plumbing, painting, and wall finishes are all new.

Along with the advantages there are usually some disadvantages. The lawn and shrubbery probably will not be well established. A lot of effort is required to develop a good lawn and to have shrubbery growing well and where you want it. Cracks may develop in the wall plaster as the house settles. Leaks may occur in the basement because of drainage problems. Sometimes appliances don't work properly. You ought to be sure to get a warranty on all appliances and the furnace. The house may not be as well insulated as it should be, and in this case it will cost more to heat and cool. With recent increases in fuel cost, inefficient heating and cooling could be a major expense. Since there are no prior records to use in judging the cost, a thorough examination should be made of the insulation. If you are not competent to make a judgment, you'd better get a professional!

Selecting an Old House An old house usually is cheaper than a new one and is located in a well-established neighborhood. The taxes may be lower, since the street, sewerage, and water mains have already been paid for. The lawn and shrubbery are well established. The present owner's bills can give you an idea of the cost of utilities.

A well-constructed old house may be a good investment. If you are handy with tools and a skillful painter, renovating an old house to meet your family's needs can be fun. However, it is usually best to live in an old house for several months or even a year before making changes. In this length of time you can tell whether the present arrangement is an added charm or an inconvenience.

Renovating an old house can be a family affair. Each person can tackle part of the job. A little can be done whenever time permits and cash is available. A great deal of satisfaction can be gained from seeing an old house take on a new face and from knowing that you did it yourself.

In selecting an old house, you should make a thorough check of the construction, the soundness of the foundation, the heating and cooling systems, the plumbing and wiring, and the roof. Look for evidence of termites. If you do not know how to make these checks, get help from someone who does.

Where Do You Want to Live?

For many, location is as important as the housing itself. Choice of a location is dictated in many instances by the family's customary way of living as well as by the final cost. Within your price range, there are many possibilities.

You may be concerned about the schools that are available. Convenience in transportation, as well as in other facilities and services, must also be considered. Find out about the professional services, stores, churches, fire and police stations, and recreational facilities nearby.

What about the neighbors? Would you and they be compatible? Would you enjoy living near them? Do you think that you would find common interests? Would you feel safe staying alone in the house or apartment? Has the neighborhood been plagued with burglaries? The police department may be able to advise you.

The costs of living in the location you choose are another factor to be considered. What transportation costs will you incur in this location? Will public transportation be available, or will you need an extra car? What is the cost of insurance? How do the utilities compare in cost with other neighborhoods? What is the tax rate? Are the community services in your price range? Will living in the neighborhood put pressure on you to "keep up with the Joneses"?

How Much Can You Spend for Housing and Related Services?

People differ in the amounts they are willing and able to spend for housing. Many figures have been published about how much a person should spend, but what you spend depends on what you want in living facilities and how this relates to the other goals in your or your family's plan for living.

To decide how much to spend, evaluate how important housing is to you. Is it more important to spend for housing than for education, travel, hobbies, or recreation? How much are you willing to give up in other things in order to buy, rent, or maintain the housing you want? Take into account the things that are important to you about housing, such as schools and play space for smaller children. The special needs of physically handicapped or aged members of the family may also have to be considered.

Your current earnings, the total family income, and your non-housing expenses must enter into the decision about the amount you can spend for housing. If you have large expenses for medical services, school tuition, past debts, or loans, they will need to be considered before you commit your money to housing. Can you meet the monthly housing costs out of your current monthly income and have enough left over to take care of the other ongoing needs, plus a fund for emergencies? Do you expect any change in your or your family's earning capacity, either upward, or downward? How will such a change affect your ability to meet your housing costs?

Buy or Rent?

Once you have decided how much you can afford to spend on housing each month, where and in what kind of housing you or your family would like to live, you can turn your attention to the buy-or-rent decision, the one that so preoccupied Bill and Mary Short.

Many people who rent wait patiently for the day when they will start to buy their own homes. Others who own are moving to apartments. Renting and owning each have advantages and disadvantages. To decide between them, you need to look at your family, its size, its stage in growth. Consider your occupation, your financial situation, the housing market in your area, and your personal preferences, as well as the income tax advantages for mortgage interest and real estate taxes. Table 5.1 lists a few simple questions to put to yourself.

Getting Advice

If you have decided to rent and have found the place that meets your needs in terms of location, costs, services, space, and so on, then it is most important that the responsibilities of you and your landlord be spelled out carefully. If a lease is to be signed, be sure that you understand what is included in the document. For how long a term are you leasing? How can you terminate the lease? Exactly what does the landlord provide, and what are your obligations? If you do not understand the lease, take it to someone who can explain it to you. Do not hesitate to ask someone to help you interpret it. There is no reason to feel ashamed of having to do so. It takes special training to understand most legal documents. You show that you have good sense when you ask for help about something you are not equipped to handle yourself. You go to a plumber when a pipe breaks, or to a carpenter to build a house. You may need a lawyer or another trained person to help you understand a lease.

If you have decided to buy, there are even more factors that need to be taken into consideration. The services of a reputable realtor or real estate agent can be a great help to you in making decisions about the kind of house you want to buy and where it should be located. He or she can tell you what you need to know; the final decision, of course, must be yours.

When you are building or buying a house you will surely need a lawyer to look after your interest. Your lawyer will review all papers and agreements to make sure that they include all the necessary provisions. If you do not have a lawyer, find one by asking friends, relatives, your employer, your bank, or another financial institution. You may also be directed to a competent lawyer by your local branch of the Legal Aid Society or by the local bar association.

TABLE 5.1 Your Buy-or-Rent Decision Chart	The Question	If Yes	If No
	Can you estimate your future needs for housing?	Buy	Rent
	Do you know which neighborhood you prefer?	Buy	Rent
	Do you expect to be in the same location for many years?	Buy	Rent
	Can you make an adequate down payment, arrange suitable mortgage terms, and pay closing costs?	Buy	Rent
	Can you make up your mind to assume responsibilities, and do you welcome them?	Buy	Rent
	Do you have a dependable source of income?	Buy	Rent

A lawyer will protect your interests when you buy or rent.

Financing a Housing Purchase

In arranging financing of a home you will want to shop for a loan much as you would shop for other items. There are many sources of home financing. Home loans may be secured from commerical banks, life insurance companies, mortgage companies, mutual savings banks, private lenders, and savings and loan associations.

When you use a loan to finance a house, you are said to have *mortgaged* the house—that is, the property is pledged to the lender as security. The word "mortgage" is also used loosely to refer to the loan itself. Mortgages are generally based on one of three types of loans: *conventional loans, Federal Housing Administration (FHA) insured loans,* and *Veterans' Administration (VA) guaranteed loans.*

In obtaining a conventional loan, the borrower deals only with the lender. The loan is made on the basis of the borrower's credit rating, and the security is just the value of the house. The down payment required is usually larger and the repayment period shorter than for a VA or FHA loan. The amount that can be borrowed for a conventional loan varies from 75 percent to 90 percent of the property value, depending on the lender's policy. The repayment period is usually 20 years but may be as long as 30 years. Interest rates fluctuate according to the general mortgage market. When money is plentiful, rates are lower, and when it becomes scarce in relation to demand, rates go up.

Once you have a partially paid-up conventional loan you can usually borrow additional funds in case you wish to remodel or make improvements on your house.

With an FHA insured loan, the Federal Housing Administration assures a private lender that he will be paid should the borrower default. This makes it easier for low-income and high-risk families to obtain loans. The amount that can be borrowed varies. You may borrow as much as 97 percent of the FHA appraisal value of the property up to a total of $15,000. As the size of the loan increases, the percentage that can be borrowed is lowered, according to a certain formula. For instance, a $35,000 loan can represent no more than 95 percent of the value of the property. The absolute maximum that can be borrowed on a home loan is $45,000. For a loan of this magnitude the percentage borrowed cannot be greater than 90; in other words, the borrower must have made a 10 percent down payment.

FHA loans can be extended up to 30 years. At the discretion of the Federal Housing Administration, the length of the repayment period can be changed. The rate of interest, also regulated by the FHA, varies in relation to the current cost of money. If the FHA guaranteed loan rates are too low in relation to money market rates, lenders can ask for "points" to make up the difference. A point is a charge of 1 percent of the amount loaned and is paid by the *seller*. You should check with local lenders about the current cost of an FHA loan and about any change of policy regarding the amount of the loan, down payment, and repayment period.

A VA loan (often referred to as a GI loan) is guaranteed by the Veterans' Administration, which insures the local lender against loss of the property or default in payment. A VA guaranteed loan is available only to qualified veterans. You can borrow a larger portion of the appraised value of the house with a VA loan, if you are a veteran, than with an FHA or conventional loan. The time for repaying the loan can be extended to 30 years. The rate of interest is regulated by the Veterans' Administration. Lenders may also charge points for a VA loan.

The FHA and the VA generally serve urban areas. The Farmers' Home Administration and the Federal Land Bank Association serve the rural areas. When shopping for a loan, you would be wise to contact the appropriate federal agencies to check on their guaranteed housing loans. They will be listed under U.S. Government in your local telephone directory. The FHA and the VA will refer you to local lending agencies that will assist you in making application for a loan; the Farmers' Home Administration and Federal Land Bank Association will aid you directly.

In securing any type of housing loan you should remember that:

> Lenders are generally willing to make loans if they are satisfied with your ability to repay and if the value of the property is equal to the loan.

The higher the down payment, the lower the monthly payment; often you can even negotiate a lower interest rate. This is so because the more money you put down, the less risk there is for the lender.

The lending institution will have a qualified appraiser determine the current market value of the house. The cost of the appraisal is usually paid by you. When there is no other limitation, the appraised value is the maximum amount you can borrow.

For several years the larger part of your monthly payments goes to pay interest on the loan. What is left is used to reduce the mortgage.

Monthly payments frequently include real estate taxes and insurance premiums. These funds are held in a special account called a trust account and are used by the lender to pay tax and insurance bills as they come due.

It pays to shop for the lowest possible interest rate. Even one-half of one percent can mean several thousand dollars on a $30,000 loan over a period of 30 years.

It is wise to investigate the lender's policy regarding prepaying the loan. Would you be penalized if by chance you received a sizeable sum of money and wanted to pay off your loan early?

An FHA or VA loan takes longer to process than a conventional loan and may delay completion of a purchase. Sometimes four to six weeks are required for approval of the loan.

The buyer pays the *closing costs*, which include legal fees, fees for a title search and a survey of the property, fees for recording the mortgage, and possibly others.

Property Insurance

If you buy a house you will want to protect it and its contents through property insurance. And if you are renting you will want to insure your belongings.

When you buy a home the agency that provides you with a mortgage will *insist* that you maintain insurance on it in order to protect the agency's investment. You as the owner need to consider protection against fire, windstorm, and other damages against claims arising out of personal liability, and against loss from theft. In many instances, as we noted in the last section, payments for property insurance are included with the monthly payments you make to the lending agency.

Fire Insurance

Fire insurance reimburses the policyholder for any damage caused by fire. This insurance is the most basic protection you can have. It is generally written for one-, three-, or five-year terms. The amount of coverage should be based on the replacement cost of the property, not on the original cost. The cost of the land on which the property stands should not be included in establishing the value, since land is not destroyed by fire. Thus a house that has a current market value of $45,000 and is standing on a lot valued at $5,000 would carry fire insurance with a face value of $40,000. This house may have cost the owner only $20,000 when he bought it a number of years ago, but the policy must cover the full replacement cost, as reflected in the present market value. You should review your fire insurance periodically to be certain that your home has adequate coverage. If you do not maintain insurance to cover 80 percent of the replacement value, you become a coinsurer and the insurance company will pay any loss claim on the basis of the ratio of the insurance you carry to the amount that represents 80 percent. Thus if you carry $30,000 of insurance on a $50,000 home, you would receive only three-fourths of any claim for fire damages $\left(\dfrac{\$30,000}{80\% \times \$50,000}\right)$.

Extended Coverage

Extended coverage is insurance protection for damages to your home from windstorm, hail, explosion, or a similar force of destruction. Extended coverage can be added to the basic insurance for a very reasonable cost; it should be considered when property insurance is written.

Personal Property Coverage

Personal property coverage is protection from loss by fire or theft of household items such as furniture and appliances as well as personal belongings like clothing. The amount of personal property coverage generally depends on the amount of basic insurance on the dwelling. A $30,000 basic fire insurance policy might allow 10 percent, or $3,000, for personal property coverage. "Floaters" can sometimes be added to cover loss of personal property from other causes, or for larger amounts. If you wish to maintain this type of coverage, you should know exactly how much protection you are receiving and what is included. If the coverage is not adequate to meet your needs, you should arrange for whatever additional protection you require and can afford to pay for. The cost of course depends on how much protection you want to buy.

Personal Liability Coverage

Personal liability insurance protects you from damage suits that may arise from accidents in your house or on your property. It also protects you from claims resulting from the actions of members of your family or your pets. It does not cover automobile accidents. Some policies with personal liability coverage may also provide some medical payments for those injured in your home or on your property.

Insurance Protection for Renters

If you rent a home or an apartment you will not need to carry basic property insurance or extended coverage. However, you should insure your household goods and personal property against fire and theft. It is also recommended that you carry personal liability coverage in case someone is injured in your home by your family or by your pets.

Liability claims against you can cause serious consequences, and insurance that protects you against such claims is a prudent investment.

Packaged Policies

All of the various types of property insurance may be purchased in one package, in what is often referred to as a homeowner's policy. Combining these various protections into one policy costs less than purchasing a separate policy for each risk. Perhaps you will not want *all* of the coverages in the package, but you may find that the complete package or a modified package with a little less coverage costs no more than just the basic items you prefer.

The longer the term for which a policy is written, the less it will cost per year. A three-year policy costs less per year than a one-year policy, and one for five years costs less per year than either.

Deductibles

When you purchase property insurance you will be able to save a substantial amount on the premium if you agree to a deductible clause of $50 or more. With this clause you assume the risk of paying the first $50 of a claim. The insurance company makes a substantial reduction in the premium for including a deductible clause. Deductibles enable the insurer to save the expense of handling many small claims, and these savings are passed on to the policyholder in lower premiums. The larger the deductible amount, the greater the premium reduction. The main purpose of insurance is to protect you against big losses that would be catastrophic to you and your family. You should be able to cope with small losses from your own resources.

SUMMARY

Answer for yourself the following questions:

1. What are your housing needs? They depend on your marital status, family size, stage of life, personal preferences, social activities, hobbies, and the number and sex of your children.
2. Where do you want to live? This depends on your preference, your school and shopping needs, the other services and conveniences you require, the character of the communities under consideration, and the costs of living in them.
3. How much can you spend? This depends, first, on your feelings about a home. Which is more important: a home, or other things like recreation, travel, and education? Also, what special housing needs do you have? What major nonhousing expenditures *must* you make? How much of your income is available for housing?
4. Should you buy or rent? This decision depends on your ability to estimate future housing needs; the firmness of your neighborhood preference; whether you have enough money for down payment, closing costs, and

other buying expenses; the stability of your income; how long you expect to remain in the same location; and your willingness to take on responsibilities.

5. Whom do you ask for advice? About a lease: a lawyer. About buying: a real estate agent, lawyer, or bank officer.

6. Where can you get the best loan? This depends on your credit rating, the amount of down payment you can afford, the types of loans for which you qualify, the policies of the lending institutions in your area, and the length of time you need to pay off the mortgage.

Remember: Shop for your best housing buy just as you would for any other service or product.

GLOSSARY OF NEW TERMS

Closing costs   Legal fees and fees for such things as survey of the property, title search, and recording of the mortgage, generally paid by the buyer of property.

Conventional loan   A housing loan obtained from a bank, savings and loan association, life insurance company, another financial institution, or a private lender, and secured by the value of the property and the integrity of the borrower.

Federal Housing Administration (FHA) loan   A housing loan, obtained through a bank or savings and loan association, that is insured by the Federal Housing Administration. The FHA guarantees to reimburse the lender, up to the approved amount, if the borrower defaults.

Lease   A legal contract between the tenant and the landlord. It states the responsibility of the tenant and the obligations of the landlord.

Mortgage   The placing in pledge of property as security that a loan will be repaid as agreed. If not paid as agreed the property reconveys to the grantor.

Realtor   An agent, licensed by the state, who assists in bringing together the buyer and seller of real estate.

Veterans' Administration (VA) loan   A housing loan, obtained through a bank or savings and loan association, that is guaranteed by the Veterans' Administration. The VA assures the lending institution that the mortgage will be repaid, up to the amount approved by the VA, should the borrower default in payments. Only veterans can qualify for VA mortgages.

QUESTIONS FOR DISCUSSION

1. Explain how housing needs vary for individuals and families at different stages of the life cycle.

2. List the things you consider essential in your housing.

3. Identify the different types of housing available for persons in your community. To what extent are housing needs met? Make recommendations for improving the housing to provide adequately for everyone in your community.

4. What factors might influence the type and location of living space for a single person, a growing family, and "empty nesters"?
5. Explain the advantages and disadvantages of renting and buying. Should cost be the deciding factor? Explain why or why not.
6. List what you think should be the rights and responsibilities of the tenant and the landlord.
7. List the different types of institutions that lend money for the purchase of a house. Describe the various kinds of loans and the features of each.
8. Can you think of some energy-saving features to look for in selecting housing?
9. Discuss the types of insurance coverage needed by most homeowners. How about renters?
10. Suggest some ways in which insurance costs can be cut.

SUGGESTED STUDENT ACTIVITIES

1. Collect pictures of different types of housing in your community: for example, a low-priced home, a moderately priced home, and an expensive one; a mobile home, an apartment, a townhouse, a condominium, and a room in a boarding house. List the cost of each in terms of down payment and/or monthly payments (including taxes and insurance). List factors other than cost that must be considered in deciding which living facility should be selected. Describe your own situation and identify the type of housing that fits your needs. Explain the reasons for your choice.
2. Check the want ads and talk to friends and real estate brokers to discover the costs of renting apartments and houses in your community. Use a table like Worksheet 5.1 to report your findings.

WORKSHEET 5.1
Rental Costs

Number of Rooms	Cost			
	Unfurnished Apartment	*Furnished Apartment*	*Unfurnished House*	*Furnished House*
1				
2				
3				
4				
5				
6				

3. Carol and Bill want to buy their own house. The house they want costs $30,000. They have only $3,000 in savings. Find out the answers to the following questions.
   a. Would they be able to get a loan in your community? They have a combined income of $16,000 a year and a good credit rating.
   b. What type of loan could they qualify for?
   c. What rate of interest would they have to pay?
   d. With a home of their own, what added expenses would they have?
   e. What would their monthly payments be?
   Taking all these things into account, what advice would you give them?
4. Secure a copy of a lease that a person is required to sign when renting. Identify the commitments you would make if you signed it. Find out whether you would be penalized if you were suddenly transferred to another city.
5. Make a list of items to inspect before renting or buying a house. You might include features of the yard, the basement, the outside of the house, the inside, and the neighborhood. After finalizing the list, examine a new home for sale and one for rent using your checklist.
6. Choose one of the following situations and prepare to serve on a panel discussing whether it would be more advantageous for the people to own or to rent housing.
   a. A young couple recently married are moving to a new city where both will be employed. Their salary will be $12,000.
   b. A single young man who has recently graduated from college is working in a city approximately 100 miles from his parents' home. He is earning $15,000 a year.
   c. An older couple, whose children are married and living away from home, are nearing retirement. Their retirement benefits will be approximately $575 per month.
   d. A married couple who are both employed have two school-age children. Their combined yearly salary is $18,000.
7. Consider your expected income when you finish school and your other resources. Interview two or three local realtors, and keeping in mind your likes and needs, find out what type of housing is available in your price range. List other expenses you will probably have in addition to the cost of housing. Describe your satisfaction or dissatisfaction with your findings.

FOR ADDITIONAL INFORMATION

"Are You Sure You've Got Enough Home Insurance?" *Changing Times*, February 1975, pp. 7–11.
   Explains how to figure out how much coverage you need to cover increases in replacement cost caused by inflation.
Garrett, Pauline G. *Consumer Housing*. Peoria, Ill.: Charles A. Bennett, 1972.
   Contains valuable, in-depth chapters on planning for housing, selecting housing, renting, buying, selling and moving, financing a home, and housing for senior citizens and the physically handicapped.
"The Legal Side of Owning a House." *Changing Times*, July 1973, pp. 7–10.
   This article presents some legal trouble spots to watch out for in buying and selling a house.

Margolius, Sidney. *How to Finance Your Home*. Public Affairs Pamphlet No. 360A. New York: Public Affairs Committee, April 1971.

This twenty-page pamphlet offers valuable and concise information on selecting and buying housing. It discusses buying versus renting, selecting a house according to income, factors to consider in house selection, signing a binder and contract, and mortgages.

"Mobile Homes Take Hold." *Ebony*, January 1972, pp. 43–46, 48.

Discusses the advantages of mobile home living, people who have bought mobile homes, and their reasons for the choice. Cost and financing are considered.

Money Management Institute. *Your Housing Dollar*. Chicago: Household Finance Corporation, 1973.

This booklet contains valuable, easy-to-understand information on housing needs; how much to spend on housing, whether to rent, buy, or build; selecting housing; financing, buying, or building a house; home insurance; and planning a move.

U.S. Department of Agriculture. *Selecting and Financing a Home*. Home and Garden Bulletin No. 182. Washington, D.C.: Government Printing Office, 1970.

Contains information on analyzing housing needs, renting versus buying, how much to spend for housing, selecting housing, shopping for a mortgage, and insuring a home.

"Zap! You're a Condominium." *Apartment Life*, Vol. 6, No. 5 (September 1974), pp. 4–6.

This article discusses what a tenant can do if the apartment he is living in is converted into a condominium. It includes information about buying a condominium and lists characteristics of buildings most likely to convert.

6

Managing Transportation Money

6

The automobile has become the most common means of transportation in the United States. Other modes of transportation, such as buses, trolleys, and trains, play a lesser role in getting people from one place to another. In addition to its convenience, the automobile identifies a person's position in society. A car, along with our other material possessions, seems to tell our friends and neighbors who we are. We need to be able to decide how much we can afford to spend for all that a car gives us. But often it is hard to realize the costs that are involved in owning and operating a car.

In this chapter you will find some guidelines to help you decide how to spend your money for your transportation needs. You will see how to determine the total cost of purchasing a car, and you will learn about the different types of insurance that you are most often required to have when you own a car. We'll begin with the account of Richard and Sandra Young, who found themselves disagreeing about the value of a car.

LET'S BUY A CAR

"Meet me at my office when you finish lunch," Richard said to Sandra over the telephone. "I want to show you a set of wheels I can get."

The Youngs had been married for two years and both worked downtown. Their combined income was $1250 per month. Almost

PERSONAL FINANCE FOR CONSUMERS

their entire income was needed to meet their living expenses and to make the payments for the household furniture and appliances they had purchased when they got married. They were beginning to regret that they had purchased such expensive items, but they had wanted the best.

Nevertheless, they had managed to save about $500 and were proud that they were beginning to get some money ahead, even though they wouldn't be clear of payments for at least another year.

On that day when Sandra met him after lunch, Richard took her to a used car lot where there was a convertible that looked just perfect. It was the kind of car they had many times talked about owning when they were making their plans for the future.

"Ain't it a beaut?" asked Richard.

"It sure is," said Sandra. "How much does it cost? Can we afford it?"

"It's only one year old and costs over $5000 new. One of the fellows in my office told me about it. I can get it for only $3,500. With a down payment of $500 the payments will be only $119.18 a month for 30 months. You know our TV and stereo payments of $80 a month will end next month, so all we'll be adding is $39.18, and we can afford that! Of course, we won't be able to put any more in the bank for a while, but look at what we'll save on trips if we have our own car."

"But what will we run it on," asked Sandra, "if we're planning to use all of our extra money to make these payments?"

"The fellows tell me it's very easy on gas and we'll be able to cut down on something else. Say yes, Sandy. You know this is the kind of car we always wanted and it's a bargain at this price."

"Let's talk about it when we get home," she said, still a little in doubt. "We'll have some time to consider it. And besides, if I don't get back to work soon, I might not have a job."

What do you think the Youngs should do about purchasing this car? How would you help them make a decision? What do they need to take into consideration? Before attempting to answer these questions, read the rest of this chapter.

Do You Need a Car?

Owning a car is sometimes a necessity. Our public transportation facilities have not kept up with our rapidly expanding cities. Before you decide to buy a car, however, consider whether it is the best means of transportation for you.

Which will it be?

If there is no other way of getting to and from work, then of course a car becomes a necessity. You may, however, find that there are public facilities available. A car then becomes a convenience. As a convenience or a source of pleasure it needs to be evaluated along with other sources of pleasure or convenience. Which convenience do you prefer? Which pleasure do you prefer? If a car is not a necessity, you should also consider that your convenience and pleasure are contributing to the environmental pollution that is plaguing all of us. Is your pleasure worth this added cost?

Assuming that you want a car for convenience or pleasure more than anything else, then you have to decide whether you can afford it, whether it will fit into your money plan. Unless you can provide the money to buy yourself a pleasure or convenience, it is futile to think of buying.

Buying a Car

The price you pay for a car will depend upon its age, make, model, equipment, condition, and so on. Before you decide on the car you want, you will need to make these decisions: How much can you afford to spend? How big a car do you need? What body style? With what options? Reading such material as "Annual Auto Roundup" in *Consumer Reports* or *Performance Data for New Passenger Cars and Motorcycles*, issued by the Superintendent of Documents, Government Printing Office, Washington, D.C., will help you make up your mind.

What Size Car?

Subcompacts are the very little cars. While some American manufacturers are beginning to introduce these into the market, most are of foreign origin. Subcompacts usually cost less to operate than larger cars but are not suitable for families or for long trips. Availability of service must also be considered when choosing a subcompact, for parts must be imported from overseas and few mechanics have the skill or equipment to work on them.

Compacts are up to three feet shorter than intermediates and can accommodate four adults in reasonable comfort. The imported models are generally more expensive than domestic compacts. While not as comfortable as intermediates, compacts are good extra cars for small families that presently have only one car.

Intermediates are about one foot shorter and one to two inches narrower than full-sized cars. The four-door models are comfortable for six passengers, and with six-cylinder engines intermediates get only about two miles less for every gallon of gas than similarly equipped compacts of the same make.

Full-sized cars will seat six adults and provide comfort on long trips. They are bulky to handle in heavy traffic and tend to consume greater quantities of gasoline—an economical and environmental handicap. If you need to carry many people often and for long distances, a station wagon may be more advisable.

Body Styles and Options

Most foreign and American cars come in two-door or four-door styles. While many people prefer two-door styles for their sporty looks and because they cost less, four-door models are easier to get into and afford more leg room for back-seat passengers. Some cars are available as three-door coupes or "hatchbacks." These coupes, however, are less desirable than a small station wagon for carrying cargo.

A number of options are available on most cars. You should decide before you go shopping for a car exactly which options you want and plan your purchase so that you can wait one or two months for delivery instead of being obliged to take the car the dealer has on hand that is "loaded" with options. Heavily equipped cars not only cost more, but also consume extra gasoline. The options you can select include engine size, transmission type, disc brakes, air conditioning, tires, tinted glass, vinyl roof covering, upholstery, power seats, exterior trim strips, automatic speed control, rear window defogger, heavy duty suspension, limited-slip differentials, remote-control outside mirror, and undercoating. Each contributes to the overall cost of the car, and careful consideration must be given in deciding which is essential, which is "puffing," and which you can afford to buy and continue to live with.

Shopping for a Car

When shopping for a new car look at the bottom sticker price, then subtract shipping and any other charges that are not for optional equipment. This gives you the car's base price. To determine the dealer's cost for this car, use the following factors: 0.77 for a full-sized car, 0.81 for an intermediate, and 0.85 for a compact or subcompact. Multiply the sum you obtained by subtracting shipping charges by the appropriate factor. This will give you the dealer's cost. For example, if you see an intermediate with a sticker price of $4,355 and subtract shipping and other charges of $210, you get $4,145 as the base price. Multiplying by 0.81, the factor for intermediates, gives you $3,357.45 as the dealer's cost. There may be other discounts that the dealer earns, but this gives you a close approximation. Add back the freight and other charges. If the dealer quotes you a price with about 10 percent added to his cost, then you have a fair deal. How much you pay above or below the fair price depends upon such things as demand, the dealer's financial position, and your bargaining ability, to name but a few.

Your Old Car

Complicating the purchase of a car may be the fact that you want to trade your old car. A U.S. Department of Transportation study shows that the most economical way to own a car is to run it until you have to junk it, in spite of the fact that repair bills will increase with the age of the car. These repair bills over the long run will not equal the depreciation cost you incur when you buy a new car. Appearance, comfort, and the reliability of a new car often induce people to trade cars periodically. In addition, many owners of large cars are converting to small, more economical cars. Before trading your old car for a new one, calculate how much your old car is worth before talking to the new car dealer. In normal times, you can obtain the approximate value of used cars through the *National Automobile Dealers Official Used Car Guide*. (Your bank's loan officer will have a copy you can see.) This guide shows the average price paid for all types of used cars at wholesale auctions. When the used car market is changing rapidly the official guidebook does not reflect the marketplace. In such instances it is well to read the newspaper ads, especially those placed by dealers. These ads reflect the market trends almost on a daily basis and give you an accurate picture of what is taking place in the market. Using the tables found in the front of the dealers' guide, make price adjustments for special features of your used car to obtain its full value. Subtract this price from the price you expect to pay for the new car. This is the cash difference, which is the amount you must actually pay. When bargaining with a dealer, look for one whose price is reasonably close to this cash difference price. Even though the price for the new car and the trade-in offer are important, the final cash difference is the price that most concerns you.

Warranties and Sales Contracts

While it is wise to get the best price you can from a dealer, you also want to deal with one who has a reputation for service. Often the dealer who shaves his original price makes it up in his service department. And unless you can repair a car yourself you will have to depend on your dealer to take care of the problems that will most certainly arise in your new car. If you know nothing about the dealer's reputation for service try dropping into his service department in the morning when people are bringing in their cars. Striking up a conversation with these customers will give you a clear insight into the dealer's service policies.

The manufacturer issues the warranty, but the dealer does the work. While he is supposed to make these warranty repairs without any loss, most often he winds up losing money on them. This is a powerful incentive for him to skimp on, or even neglect to take care of, these repairs.

Be sure to have copies of your contract, warranty agreement, and any other papers signed by the dealer. Sales contracts vary widely, and if you do not like some of the contract conditions or want to add some of your own (such as a firm delivery date), ask the dealer to amend the contract *before you sign*. Standard warranties for most cars are for 12 month or 12,000 miles, whichever comes first. American Motors has an all-inclusive warranty that can be doubled to 24 months or 24,000 miles for a premium of $95. If you cannot get satisfactory warranty repairs, go to the service manager. If necessary move up higher to the general manager or the owner and, if you must, to the zone service manager. If you still are not able to get satisfaction check your local library for a copy of *What To Do With Your Bad Car*, by Ralph Nader, Lowell Dodge, and Ralf Hotchkiss (published by Grossman), and follow their advice on writing complaint letters to the factory. If all else fails, consult a lawyer to determine if legal action is indicated and worthwhile.

Buying A Used Car

For the average one-car family, the best used car buy is a recent model of a subcompact, a compact, or an intermediate. The advantage of a recent model is that the greatest drop in the price of a car occurs in the first year of the car's life. You must be careful that such a recent model car does not have excessive mileage or serious defects. Generally, buy the smallest car that fills your needs and buy a new car rather than a luxurious used car at the same price. Over time a luxury car is likely to cost more in tires, fuel, and parts.

The most likely source of a used car is the used car lot of an established dealer. He has a larger investment in his establishment and thus is most apt to have a better service department to put a used car into shape. He usually keeps only those used cars he thinks will give the best service. He sells the less desirable ones to used car dealers and to used car auctioneers. Used car dealers are therefore not a very good place to look for serviceable cars. Nor should you resort to private newspaper ads. Often these are "fronts" for disreputable dealers and at best the private seller cannot guarantee or repair the car. No matter where you want to buy a used car, the following should be kept in mind:

> Examine the car's surface for repairs to the body that indicate more extensive damage. Check for rust; operate the windows, doors, and seat adjustments. Check the interior for excessive wear spots.
> Take the car for a road test. Check for looseness in steering, worn shock absorbers, poor brakes, engine roughness, smoke from the exhaust pipe.
> Have an impartial, reliable mechanic check the car thoroughly for defects. Some localities have diagnostic clinics where mechanics specialize in making elaborate tests to determine the condition of a car. The cost of $20 to $25 is well worth it.

Paying for a Car

Some cars are bought with cash. However, if you do not have cash or cannot arrange for a cash loan that would be advantageous to you, then you will probably arrange for financing with installment credit. This enables you to use the car while you are paying for it. Generally the dealer will require that you make some down payment and that you pay the balance due over a stated period of time with equal monthly installments.

It is not necessary that you obtain credit from the dealer who sells you the car. Generally dealer-offered credit arrangements are the most expensive. There are many institutions that provide credit for auto purchases. Shop to find the credit arrangement that is best suited to your needs. You may be asked to carry life or disability insurance to cover the amount of the credit. As you learned earlier, in the chapter on credit, this insurance cost may be excessive. Find out how much it costs and decide if you want to buy it from the lender or from some other less expansive source.

The Consumer Credit Protection Act requires the lender to state the cash price of the car, the trade-in allowance or down payment, and the total finance charges; all other charges must also be itemized. Be sure to examine the figures closely and make comparisons so that you will know the total charges at various lending agencies. Check the following:

To whom will you make payments?

What rebate, if any, will you get for paying off the debt faster than agreed?

What penalties are charged for late payments?

What repossession rights does the finance company have?

Will you have the right to "fair notice" before the car is taken from you for nonpayment or for slow payment?

What rights do you have to redeem the car if it has been repossessed?

What about any money left after repossession and resale of the car—who gets it?

Auto Insurance

When you finance the purchase of a car you agree not only to meet the monthly payments, but also to keep insurance in force throughout the life of the loan, in order to protect the lender's investment. Even if you pay cash for the car, it is important that it be covered by insurance, for your own protection. The cost of insurance will depend on such things as the age of the car, the risk category in which you fall, where you live, and from whom you buy the insurance. You will want to shop for insurance just as you did for the car, comparing the kind and amount of coverage as well as the cost. It is not necessary to buy the insurance from the lender who gives you credit.

There are three basic types of insurance that are available to you as the owner of a car:

1. *Liability insurance* protects you, the owner, against damage that the car may cause to someone else's property or personal health. You need to carry an amount of insurance that is sufficient to protect you and your heirs from claims against you for bodily injury or property damage. Most states require a certain minimum coverage under their motor vehicle safety laws. But it is a good investment to carry more coverage than the minimum.

   Some states now require drivers to have *no-fault* liability insurance. With *no-fault* insurance the injured party receives damages, up to a limited amount, regardless of whose fault it was that the accident occurred. Claimants are paid immediately but have the right to sue if claims are above a stated limit. *No-fault* insurance has reduced the number of law suits because of accidents and has brought about a reduction in liability insurance costs. There is a movement to require all states to allow no-fault insurance.

2. *Comprehensive insurance*, sometimes called *fire and theft insurance*, pays you for physical damage to your car or loss of the car from causes other than collision. It may cover damages in addition to those caused by fire and theft, such as those resulting from vandalism, flood, or hail. The insurance cost and the payments for damage are based on the actual cash value of your car, not on what you paid for it originally.

3. *Collision insurance* provides payment if your car is damaged in a collision, regardless of who caused the damage. This type of insurance is generally written with a deductible of $50, $100, or more; you pay for damages up to the deductible amount, and the insurance company pays for any damages above that amount. The higher the deductible amount, the lower the premium. And whatever the deductible, your premium will decrease as the car depreciates in value. Despite this decrease, it is generally not advisable to carry collision insurance for cars that are more than five years old, since the cost then is high in relation to the value of the car.

The Cost of Owning a Car

The cost of owning a car includes many things beyond the initial price. The various costs can be divided into several categories:

1. *The price paid.* This includes all initial costs, including credit charges, sales tax, and so on.
2. *Depreciation cost.* This is the decline in value of the car over the years that you own it. For example, if the car cost a total of $3,500 and you plan to trade it in after 5 years when it will be worth $500, the total depreciation will be $3,000. The average annual depreciation cost will be $3,000 divided by 5, or $600; this is the average decline in value each year that you drive. The depreciation is above average for the first four years and less than average in later years. Remember that the day you drive a new car off the lot, it is a used car worth hundreds of dollars less than you paid for it.
3. *Fixed expenses.* These are the regularly recurring expenses, such as insurance, license fees, ad valorem taxes, and so on.
4. *Flexible expenses.* These are the day-to-day operating expenses, such as those for gas, oil, tires, maintenance, and repairs, and the additional expenses that are incurred when the car is used for vacation trips or to provide outings for the family.

The U.S. Department of Transportation in an estimate of expenses over 100,000 miles of driving (April 1974) determined that it cost an average of 15.9 cents per mile to operate a standard size car, 12.9 cents for a compact, and 11.2 cents for a subcompact. In 1972 the average cost per mile of a 1972 car driven 100,000 miles was 13.6 cents per mile for standard size cars, 10.8 cents per mile for compacts, and 9.4 cents per mile for subcompacts. With the observed rise in gasoline prices during 1975 and the further increases in gas prices contemplated in order to reduce gas consumption, drivers of any size car can expect appreciable increases in the cost per mile of operating their cars over the ensuing years. People are switching to compacts and to subcompacts because of the increases in operating expenses

How much does it
really cost?

and because they understand that the cost of operating their autos is probably the largest item in their spending plan. Economy, rather than luxury and opulence, seems to be the guide in auto selection.

Knowing the total cost of owning a car will help you decide if you want it more than some other pleasure or convenience. Next to a home, a car is generally the most important expenditure of the family. Only by recognizing *all* of the costs involved in car ownership can you decide if the expenses can fit into your money plan.

Saving Money and Fuel

It makes good sense to keep tight rein on the cost of maintaining and operating a car. The high cost of repairs, the increased cost of fuel, and the continued warnings that unless fuel is conserved there is a possibility of a shortage for years to come—all these remind everyone of the importance of maintaining and operating a car efficiently.

Each time you fill the tank with gasoline you "ante up" a substantial sum of money and you dip into the total energy supply. Have you stopped to think what use you could make of the money if you did not spend it for gasoline? Ask yourself these questions: Is this trip really necessary? Should I use gas for this purpose? Could I get to my destination by other means—walking, riding a bike, joining a car pool, using public transportation? Wouldn't it be just as enjoyable to plan more recreational activities at home? If you do not have a game room, music center, patio with facilities for cooking outside, or other provisions for expressing your interests, why not consider using some of the money you now spend for gas to develop them?

If you have decided that a car is essential for your work, transportation, and recreation, then you want to know how to cover the miles with a minimum of expense. Perhaps you already know and are doing many of the things in the list that follows; if so, check them off in your mind and give consideration to those not checked.

1. *Maintaining your car in good running condition.* With each new car sold there is an operator's manual, in which the manufacturer suggests regular checkups and tells you what should be done to keep the car in good condition. Read and become familiar with what should be done, and take the car to the dealer or a reliable service department for preventive maintenance. Keeping a car in top repair can reduce costly "wear and tear," and save gas as well. If you view your car as an investment, think of this as essential for keeping it at its peak value. Remember, a well-tuned engine won't pollute the air as much, and will increase your miles per gallon of gas.
2. *Weight and wind resistance.* A factor in gas mileage is the weight of the car. Once you've bought your car you can't control its basic weight, but you can eliminate excess weight in the trunk or back seat. Check to see if you are carrying unnecessary weight. If you are transporting heavy objects, remove them as soon as you reach their destination. Wind resistance is also important. Do not leave luggage racks, ski racks, or bike racks attached unless in use, since they increase the resistance and therefore reduce the gas mileage.
3. *Tires and wheel alignment.* Underinflated tires can lower gas mileage by as much as a mile per gallon. Find the correct air pressure in your owner's manual. By investing about $1.50 in a tire-pressure gauge you can check your tires and keep them properly inflated. By increasing the air pressure about four pounds above the level recommended in the owner's manual, you can increase mileage for short trips around town. However, you should not inflate the tires above the maximum levels embossed on their side walls. With increased air pressure the ride will likely be a little rougher.

    Examine the way in which the front tires are wearing. An uneven pattern of wear is an indication that the wheels are out of alignment. A $5 wheel alignment job may save you a $50 pair of tires.
4. *Driving habits.* The right driving habits can bring you tremendous savings on gasoline. Driving on the expressway at a steady cruising

speed of 55 miles per hour or below will use less fuel than driving faster or more erratically; you should be aware that most cars get the maximum mileage in the 30 to 40 mile-per-hour range. Starting and pulling away from traffic lights with moderate acceleration is another habit that will save fuel. So is looking far ahead, anticipating stops, and adjusting your acceleration accordingly. You should turn off the ignition if you must wait more than a few minutes. Turn off the air conditioner except when the weather is uncomfortably warm. Plan your driving, if you can, for times when traffic is light, in order to avoid frequent stops. Eliminate unnecessary trips; plan to complete as many errands as you can at one time, while the engine is warmed up. Join a car pool or organize one if this has not been done in your area.

Remember that the biggest saving is usually in the gas tank. So don't be a show-off driver. It may be unexciting not to "scratch off" with squealing tires or to take the curves without leaving your tire tracks, but the extra money it will leave in your billfold will enable you to have fun in other ways. You will also have the satisfaction of knowing that you are helping to conserve energy resources.

5. *Fuel.* Never use premium gas unless your car requires it. Refer to the owner's manual for the type and octane recommended for your car. It is better to refill your tank when it is one-quarter full than when it is empty, since impurities and condensed water settle to the bottom of your tank and, if drawn through the fuel lines, can damage the fuel pump or carburetor. Observe the price of gasoline. Often you will find a difference of at least five cents per gallon between dealers.

SUMMARY

Before buying a car, ask yourself these questions:

> Can I get along without a car?
> Is it a necessity or only a pleasure and convenience?
> Are there other conveniences or pleasures I want more than a car?
> Can I afford it?
> What is the best price, including credit and taxes?
> Which dealers are reputable?
> Which is the best credit plan for me?
> Where should I go for detailed information on models, performance, durability, and so on?
> What kind of insurance will I need?
> How much will the insurance cost?
> What will the other costs be, including depreciation, fixed expenses, and flexible expenses?
> How can I help to conserve energy and reduce pollution?

GLOSSARY OF NEW TERMS

Collision insurance   Insurance that provides payment to you if your car is damaged in a collision, regardless of who caused the damage.

Comprehensive or fire and theft insurance   Insurance that pays for physical damage to your car or loss of the car from causes other than collision.

Depreciation   The decrease in value over the number of years an item will be used.

Liability insurance   Insurance that protects you against damage that your car may cause to someone else's property or personal health.

No-fault insurance   A type of insurance coverage that pays for damages regardless of who is responsible for them. It is presently applied to medical and personal injuries only, for limited amounts, and is required only in some states.

Options   Equipment on automobiles that is not included in the base price, such as special lights, air conditioning, special tires, and so on.

QUESTIONS FOR DISCUSSION

1. List points to consider in deciding on the types of transportation needed for a typical family.
2. List ways in which a person or a family can economize on transportation costs and car operation.
3. How might a person's values influence his or her choice of a car?
4. Why do you suppose some dealers have less "mark-up" on new cars than others?
5. How would you determine dealer's cost on a new car?
6. Discuss the importance of automobile insurance, the types available, and why insurance is required when you take out a loan to purchase a car.
7. Discuss depreciation. When does the car depreciate most rapidly? Explain the relationship of depreciation to insurance cost.
8. What considerations should be given in selecting a used car for yourself?
9. How would you go about establishing the value of your car, assuming you intend to trade it in for a new one?
10. What effect will a gasoline shortage have on the amount of travel by private car? On public transportation? On car sales and the type of cars bought? On family lifestyle?

SUGGESTED STUDENT ACTIVITIES

1. Prepare a list of questions to ask when purchasing a new or used car. Include items such as:
   a. Total cost and what it included;
   b. Sources and cost of financing;

c. Insurance required;

d. Cost of operation.

Use the questions to interview different automobile dealers. Compile your findings and present them to the class.

2. After doing considerable reading and talking to mechanics and dealers, compile a list of guidelines for use in buying a used car. Identify the advantages of a used car as opposed to a new car.

3. If you have made a tentative choice of a used automobile, look up its value in your library. Two annual publications provide this information (1) *Official Used Car Guide of the National Automobile Dealers Association*, and (2) *The Kelly Blue Book*. The *Buying Guide* of the *Consumers Reports* will tell you how to compute the total cost. Consider the following questions before you buy.

   a. Do I really need a car?

   b. What are some alternate modes of transportation if I do not purchase a car?

   c. Considering the total cost (monthly payments, taxes, insurance, upkeep, and so on, can I really afford it?

   d. Is it a good buy?

   e. Would I be paying a reasonable interest rate on the loan?

   f. Would the insurance I have allowed for protect me and those driving or riding in the car adequately?

   g. Does the insurance firm have a reputation of settling claims fairly and on time?

4. Choose a place at least 500 miles from your home where you would like to go for a vacation. Find out the bus, train, and/or airplane fares for the trip, and calculate the cost of going by car. Take into account the amount of time required and the cost of food and lodging. Then make a comparative analysis of these various means of transportation. Explain your conclusions.

5. Obtain warranties from a number of car manufacturers and used car dealers for the purpose of comparison. State your findings.

6. Calculate the total depreciation to date of your car by using the following information.

   The value of a typical car depreciates by approximately 30 percent the first year; 18 percent (of the original price) the second year; 14 percent the third year; 11 percent the fourth year; 9 percent the fifth year; 6 percent the sixth year; and 2 percent the seventh year.

7. Figure out your total transportation costs for the past month, and from these figures determine the approximate costs for a year.

8. Find out how much it costs to operate a standard-size car in your area or community. (Automobile clubs or leasing agencies can provide information.)

9. Make a chart comparing the finance charges on car loans by a local bank or finance company and by a local car dealer.

10. Interview a representative from a reputable insurance company for information on essential auto coverage, deductibles, costs, classifications of drivers and areas, and types of policies.

11. Prepare a list of suggestions for conserving fuel and reducing the cost of operating an automobile. You should be able to think of many tips besides those given in this chapter.

FOR ADDITIONAL INFORMATION

Car Buying Made Easier. Dearborn, Mich.: Ford Motor Company, 1974. 60 pp. (updated annually)

A paperback booklet containing practical tips on what to look for in choosing a car. Although prepared by Ford Motor Company, most of the information can apply to any make.

Consumers Union, *The 1975 Buying Guide Issue of Consumer Reports*. Mount Vernon, N.Y.: Consumers Union, 1975.

This guide, published in December each year for use the following year, generally includes a summary of products tested during the year and reported in the monthly magazine *Consumer Reports*. These summaries are up-dated and additions are made where needed. This very helpful guide can be purchased for $3.00.

"Fix Up the Old Car and You're Dollars Ahead." *Changing Times*, May 1975, pp. 32–34.

Offers practical advice on repairing your old car and demonstrates how much more economical it is to repair an old car than to buy a new one.

Fletcher, Adele Whitely. *How to Stretch Your Dollar*. New York: Benjamin Co., 1970.

Contains brief, to-the-point information on your transportation dollar. Discusses points to consider in buying and operating a car.

Jackson, Charles R. *How to Buy A Used Car*. Radnor, Pa.: Chilton Book Co., 1974. 90 pp.

The author, a pro in managing large used car sales, tells the tricks of the trade. He also discusses financing, guarantees, and advertising.

Mead, William B. "Living with Less Oil." *Money*, March 1975, pp. 34–37.

This article tries to put the oil problem into perspective. It also includes a driver's guide to gasoline economy.

National Automobile Dealers "Official Used Car Guide." National Automobile Used Car Guide Co., Washington, D.C.

The bible of the used car industry. Published monthly.

Saalbach, William E. *Learning To Be A Better Buyer*. River Forest, Ill.: Laidlaw Brothers, 1974, pp. 72–93.

A paperback, in *The Consumer and The American Economy* Series. The author discusses choosing transportation and owning a car and considers various forms of transportation. Easy to read.

Time-Life Book of the Family Car. Chicago: Time-Life, 1973.

Presents excellent information on care of the car, price financing, maintenance, insurance, emergencies, conserving energy, and defensive driving. Includes illustrations of how to do mechanical work on a car. The material has been checked for accuracy by four major automobile manufacturers.

"Ways to Make Every Gallon of Gas Go Further." *Changing Times*, May 1974, pp. 35–37.

Some worthwhile hints on conserving gasoline regardless of the size of your car.

There are also some inexpensive booklets that provide useful information on saving money and energy. A publication called *Citizen Action Guide to Energy Conservation*, available from the Public Documents Distribution Center, 5801 Tabor Avenue, Philadelphia, Pa. 19120, gives excellent counsel on how to save fuel. It costs $1.75; ask for item 1AA. A number of booklets on automobiles have been put out by the Consumer Information Center, a branch of the Public Documents Distribution Center, General Services Administration, Pueblo, Colo. 81009. Of these, *Gasoline: More Miles per Gallon* (booklet 005C, 1974, 35¢) contains tips for saving fuel with the right driving techniques and proper maintenance. *Miles per Gallon Ratings for 1975: Cars and Light Trucks* (booklet 236C, 1975, no charge) provides just what its title suggests; it excludes cars that are certified to meet California pollution standards. *Three Rules for Maximum Tire Life* (booklet 013C, 1975, 25¢) gives tips on how to get the maximum safe mileage from your tires. You can ask to be placed on the Consumer Information Center's mailing list if you want to receive quarterly editions of the index of publications.

7

Managing
Food
Money

7

Eating has as much to do with who we are and how we live as anything else.

Families spend from 25 to 40 percent of their income for food. If their sole criterion in food shopping is to buy what they like to eat, they may be getting satisfaction for the money they spend, but not necessarily good nutrition or the best value. If you are like most people it is very difficult to change your likes and dislikes about food. Good management of your food buying does not mean changing the way you like to eat or the foods you prefer; it means changing the way you buy your food.

In this chapter you will learn the advantages of planning your food buying. You will learn about your own food needs, and you will find tips on getting the most value for your food dollars. You will learn about food labeling regulations and the meaning of "unit pricing" and "open dating."

Read the story that follows. Think of yourself in the same situation. How would you behave? As you read try to think of the suggestions you might make if you were advising Susan.

THE QUICK SUPPER

"Oh my, it's four o'clock. John will be home at five-forty and I haven't begun to get our supper ready. I was so wrapped up with fixing Alice's new party dress for her that I didn't realize it was so late.

"Now let me see. . . . I'll have to fix something quick. I've got frozen meat pie in the fridge, but I don't have time to thaw it. The leftovers from last night would make a good stew, and that's what I wanted to make with them, but it's too late to start that now. Guess I'll have to run over to the Quick-chek at the corner and get something for the four of us.

"Alice, set the table and watch out for Billie. I'll be back in a few minutes."

With these words, Susan flew out of the house on her way to shop for the evening meal. She knew that she could have saved some money by going to the supermarket for her supper needs, but that would take a longer time than she felt she could spare, so she headed for the corner Quick-chek.

Her problem was to find something that she could prepare in a few minutes. She made it a point to have a hot, nutritious meal for her family every evening. She knew how important it was.

Arriving at the corner store, she dashed to the meat counter to look at the variety. There were some lovely roasts, but there wasn't enough time to prepare one. "Guess it'll have to be steaks or chops. They're awfully high today, but I'll only buy two steaks; John can have one and the children and I can divide the other. Even so, I'll be spending more than I should, but it's just this once. I can save on tomorrow's supper by using the leftovers from last night."

On the way to the check-out counter she noticed some pies and decided to have one for dessert. "I could have baked today, and mine are really much better than these bought pies, but, oh well."

There were a few other items she saw on her way out: cereal for tomorrow's breakfast, spaghetti and tuna fish for the children's lunches, and so forth. She picked them up.

"The last time I 'picked up' these things," she recalled, "I bought the kinds they didn't like. I guess I'll not make that mistake again—even if those kinds are on 'special.'"

She still got a twinge when she thought about the time she'd had to give away a whole basket of items that had accumulated in her cabinet. She had purchased them at various times on "special," not noticing that they were varieties her family wouldn't eat. Now she was buying the right kinds, even though they were costing her a few cents more.

Supper that night was a success. Everybody enjoyed it, even though the kids would have liked more meat. John had talked about the vacation schedules being made up at his shop, and both children joined in with suggestions about where they would like to go for their vacation.

"With the money so tight, I wonder if we'll even get to go any-place," thought Susan. "How can we possibly afford to spend on extras when I can hardly make our food allowance last?"

What do you think of Susan's shopping habits? What suggestions would you make if you were advising her? Before you try to answer these questions, read the material that follows.

Nutrition

Wise food management calls for skill in buying, preparing, and serving foods which are both appetizing and nutritious. Let's first consider nutrition. Each person needs to know how to select the foods necessary for developing and maintaining optimum health. Whether you are responsible for buying food for yourself or for a family or for making choices when eating out, you need to know which combinations of foods give you adequate nutrition.

The food we eat supplies us with nutrients our body needs for:

1. Energy,
2. Body-building,
3. Regulation of body processes.

Energy in the food we eat is measured in calories. Some foods provide more calories that others. If we consume less calories than required for the energy we expend, then our bodies lose weight; if we consume more calories than required, we gain weight. The average adult needs between two and three thousand calories a day. Thirty-five hundred calories over and above the body's requirements add one pound of body weight.

Only carbohydrates, protein, and fats supply the calories a body needs. Vitamins and minerals do not supply calories but are essential for growth and maintenance of body tissue and for regulation of body processes.

Each nutrient has its own function to perform, but all of the nutrients work together in body metabolism to maintain health. If one or more nutrients are missing in the diet, the body is unable to function at maximum potential—physically, emotionally, and intellectually. Despite their high standard of living, many Americans are malnourished. Good nutrition develops over time and requires constant attention to the kinds of food you eat.

This is why it is recommended that you eat appropriate quantities of a wide variety of foods. Eating various foods from the four basic groups will provide all of the essential nutrients.

The Basic-Four Food Plan

The basic four food groups, developed by the United States Department of Agriculture in 1956, form a simple daily food guide that can be used for planning nutritious meals and making sound food selections. Different foods are grouped according to the nutrients they supply most abundantly. The basic-four guide is easy to learn and to use. It allows people at any economic level to choose foods that fit their individual preferences.

The basic-four plan states the number of servings from each group that should be included for an adequate daily diet. Using the basic food groups as a guide enables a person to make a wide variety of choices in planning a nutritionally sound menu plan. Alternate plans may be required to provide for the special nutritional needs of people like vegetarians and older persons. But it is well to remember that in any plan the basis of good nutrition is eating a variety of foods from the basic four groups.

Table 7.1 lists the food groups, the recommended daily servings for each group, and examples of the amount counted as a serving in each group.

Nutrition Labels and USRDA

USRDA is a set of initials with which persons concerned with nutrition and good health should become familiar. USRDA stands for "United States Recommended Daily Allowances" and should not be confused

	Basic Food Group	Servings Recommended per Day		What Counts as a Serving*
TABLE 7.1 Basic-Four Food Guide	**Meat Group**	2 or more		2 to 3 ounces of lean cooked meat, poultry, or fish. As alternates: 1 egg, ½ cup cooked dry beans or peas, or 2 tablespoons of peanut butter may replace ½ serving of meat.
	Milk Group	Child, under 9 Child, 9 to 12 Teen-ager Adult Pregnant Woman Nursing Woman	2 to 3 3 or more 4 or more 2 or more 3 or more 4 or more	One 8-ounce cup of fluid milk—whole, skim, buttermilk—or evaporated or dry milk, reconstituted. As alternates: 1-inch cube cheddar-type cheese, or ¾ cup cottage cheese, ice milk, or ice cream may replace ½ cup of fluid milk.
	Vegetable-Fruit Group	4 or more, including: 1 good or 2 fair sources of vitamin C 1 good source of vitamin A—at least every other day		½ cup of vegetable or fruit. Or a portion: for example, 1 medium apple, banana, or potato, half a medium grapefruit or cantaloupe. *Good sources:* Grapefruit or grapefruit juice, orange or orange juice, cantaloupe, guava, mango, papaya, raw strawberries, brussels sprouts, sweet red pepper, green pepper, broccoli. *Fair sources:* Honeydew melon, lemon, tangerine or tangerine juice, watermelon, asparagus, cabbage, cauliflower, collards, garden cress, kale, kohlrabi, mustard greens, potatoes and sweet potatoes cooked in the jacket, rutabagas, spinach, tomatoes or tomato juice, turnip greens. *Good sources:* Dark-green and deep-yellow vegetables and a few fruits, namely: apricots, broccoli, cantaloupe, carrots, chard, collards, cress, kale, mango, persimmon, pumpkin, spinach, yams, turnip greens and other dark-green leaves, winter squash.
	Bread-Cereal Group	4 or more		Count only if whole-grain or enriched: 1 slice of bread or similar serving of baked goods made with whole-grain or enriched flour, 1 ounce ready-to-eat cereal, ½ to ¾ cup cooked cereal, cornmeal, grits, spaghetti, macaroni, noodles, or rice.
	Other Foods	As needed to round out meals and meet energy requirements		Refined unenriched cereals and flours and products made from them; sugars; butter, margarine, other fats. Try to include some vegetable oil among the fats used.

*Amounts actually served may differ—small for young children, extra large (or seconds) for very active adults or teenagers.

Source: U.S. Department of Agriculture, *Your Money's Worth in Food,* Home and Garden Bulletin No. 183, Washington, D.C.: Government Printing Office, 1974.

with RDAs, which are the Recommended Dietary Allowances established by the National Research Council. The USRDAs are the amounts of vitamins, minerals, and other nutrients from food that a person should eat daily to remain healthy. The USRDA system was developed by the U.S. Food and Drug Administration so that people could use nutrition information to plan more nutritious meals for themselves and their families and could get more for their food dollar.

USRDAs were selected from tables of Recommended Dietary Allowances of the Food and Nutrition Board of the National Academy of Sciences–National Research Council. They represent the amounts of nutrients needed every day by healthy people, plus an excess of 30 to 50 percent to allow for individual variations. Thus many adults need only two-thirds or three-fourths of the USRDA for several nutrients, and children about half.

There are three USRDAs. The best known, and the one that will be used for nutritional labeling, is for adults and children over four. The second is for infants and children under four. The third is for pregnant women and women who are nursing their babies.

Perhaps you have noticed a difference in the labels appearing on some food products. The Food and Drug Administration has begun implementation of a new program that will bring about basic and far-reaching changes in the labeling and advertising of food products. This FDA program is designed to inform the consumer of the identities, quantities, and nutritional values, according to USRDAs, of a wide variety of foods available in the marketplace. In other words, what you see on the label is what you will get in the container. Many companies are already putting nutritional information on their labels. When the program is fully developed, all foods for which a nutrition claim is made and all fortified foods will display the nutritional information.

A standard format has been established that processors must follow in nutritional labeling. In addition to the usual information found on products, the label must give:

>serving size
>servings per container
>calorie content
>protein content
>carbohydrate content
>fat content
>percentages of USRDAs of protein, vitamins, and minerals

This information must appear on the label immediately to the right of the main panel. Figure 7.1 shows examples of the way the labels will look.

Some other key points to remember about the new FDA labeling rules are:

1. Although it is not required, the label may specify the types of fat

(polyunsaturated or saturated), the number of grams of each type, and the milligrams of cholesterol and sodium.

2. Regulations have been established by the FDA to distinguish between a food and a drug. This is to discourage the high consumption of unnecessary and harmful quantities of certain vitamins.

3. Nutritional labeling helps shoppers to count calories, get the right nutrients for people on special diets, plan nutritious meals, compare the nutritional qualities of similar foods, and determine the nutritional values of prepared and complex foods such as "TV dinners."

Nutrient labeling will enable you to know what nutrition you are buying in the marketplace. Of course, to be a wise consumer you must have learned what you need in order to keep your body healthy. Unless you know your nutritional needs you cannot read the labels intelligently.

Health Foods and Food Additives

You can be misled by the promotion of so-called health foods. The terms "health foods," "organic foods," and "natural foods" are usually used to describe foods grown without chemical fertilizers or the use of pesticides. There is no hard evidence to prove that these foods are any better or more nutritious than foods grown with chemical fertilizer and pesticides. Promoters of health foods have not been able to support

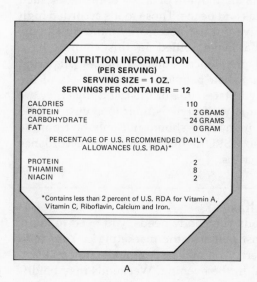

NUTRITION INFORMATION
(PER SERVING)
SERVING SIZE = 1 OZ.
SERVINGS PER CONTAINER = 12

CALORIES	110
PROTEIN	2 GRAMS
CARBOHYDRATE	24 GRAMS
FAT	0 GRAM

PERCENTAGE OF U.S. RECOMMENDED DAILY
ALLOWANCES (U.S. RDA)*

PROTEIN	2
THIAMINE	8
NIACIN	2

*Contains less than 2 percent of U.S. RDA for Vitamin A,
Vitamin C, Riboflavin, Calcium and Iron.

A

NUTRITION INFORMATION
(PER SERVING)
SERVING SIZE = 8 OZ.
SERVINGS PER CONTAINER = 1

CALORIES	560	FAT (PERCENT OF	
PROTEIN	23 G	CALORIES 53%)	33 G
CARBOHYDRATE	43 G	POLYUNSAT-	
		URATED	2 G
		SATURATED	9 G
		CHOLESTEROL*	
		(20 MG/100 G)	40 MG
		SODIUM (365 MG/	
		100 G)	830 MG

PERCENTAGE OF U.S. RECOMMENDED DAILY
ALLOWANCES (U.S. RDA)

PROTEIN	35	RIBOFLAVIN	15
VITAMIN A	35	NIACIN	25
VITAMIN C		CALCIUM	2
(ASCORBIC ACID)	10	IRON	25
THIAMINE (VITAMIN			
B₁)	15		

*Information on fat and cholesterol content is provided
for individuals who, on the advice of a physician, are
modifying their total dietary intake of fat and cholesterol.

B

FIGURE 7.1 Examples of nutritional labels. (A) A label showing the minimum information. (B) A label including optional information on cholesterol and sodium content and on the quantity of each type of fat. [From U.S. Department of Health, Education, and Welfare publication number (FDA) 74-2039.]

claims that such foods help to prevent diseases or extend the number of years a person will live. (However, certain foods—whole-grain breads and cereals, unrefined sweeteners, and lean meats—emphasized by the health food movement *do* belong in every person's daily diet.) Since health foods are often more expensive than ordinary ones, buying them will affect your money plan; they are not a wise choice.

As consumers we should also be aware of the difference of opinion concerning the additives in our food. Proponents say that additives keep food from spoiling and enable mass distribution at lower prices. Opponents argue that they are a hazard and are only used to enable companies to make more money. There is no simple solution. The problem is presently being researched.

Cultural and Sociological Influences on Food Choices

Nutrition is based on the food we eat and how the body uses it. But food means more than just something to eat to meet one's needs for survival. Food has many cultural and sociological implications.

In every society food plays an important role in culture. Food is used for expressing hospitality and for celebrations on holidays and special occasions. It is associated with religious beliefs and is sometimes thought to have magical qualities. Food is used for punishment (bread and water) and for reward (ice cream, cake, or candy).

Certain foods are considered to have high status, such as steaks, caviar, and lobster, while others are thought of as lower in status, such as beef stew and black-eyed peas and beans. Those foods accorded high status are usually more expensive but not necessarily more nutritious.

Different nationalities that have settled in this country have brought with them their food preferences and methods of preparing food. Studies have shown that when people from other parts of the world come to live in the United States, one of the last things they are likely to give up in adopting a new lifestyle is their food customs. So when we select our daily food items they should not only be from the basic four groups and adhere to USRDAs but should be in accordance with our cultural likes and practices.

Planning Your Food Purchases

Now that you know which foods your body needs, you need to know how to plan to obtain the most value in the marketplace. Your food habits probably fall into a pattern. You may have a moderate breakfast, a light lunch, and a main meal in the evening. Weekends may be different because of a difference in the way you spend your time. Any pattern that suits you or your family is a good one if during the entire day you consume a variety and sufficient quantity of foods—meats, milk, fruits and vegetables, and breads and cereals—as suggested by the basic-four food guide.

Using a system or guide in planning meals and snacks is one of the best ways to assure an adequate diet. You can develop your own system, or you can check your daily menus by the basic-four plan. The idea is to have a pattern to follow so that meals can be planned and checked for nutritional adequacy quickly and easily.

Planning meals and snacks in advance enables you to (1) take full advantage of weekly food sales and foods that are in season, (2) reduce the number of trips to the grocery store, (3) make the best use of leftovers and items on hand, and (4) prepare meals in advance and freeze them for special occasions or for when an unannounced visitor arrives.

The Shopping List

Once you have a good idea of the foods you will be eating for the next few days or the next week, you are ready to make a shopping list. List the foods you will need to prepare the meals that you have planned. Check all storage space to determine which items are already on hand. Also check the storage space to see if there is adequate room to store the food you plan to buy. It is poor planning to buy items that need to be kept frozen or refrigerated when you do not have the space. It is a good idea to keep a regular shopping list of staples. When items on the list run low they can be marked for purchase. If you are preparing a new dish, it is wise to check the recipe to make sure you have included on your list all ingredients needed. Those extra trips back to the store take time and add transportation costs.

When preparing your list, be sure to study the food ads in your newspaper. Include advertised food specials on your shopping list when they are reasonable in price and fit into your menu plan or can be substituted for other foods you had planned to serve. Use "cents-off" offers and coupons. Time and energy can be saved by observing the store layout and organizing your shopping list in the order in which items are placed in the store. It is best to select frozen and refrigerated items last.

How Much to Buy

Food purchased in larger quantities is usually cheaper, but not always. It's best to compare the unit prices if you have any doubts. (See the discussion of unit pricing later in this chapter.) However, you should buy no more than you can use or store safely until it can be used. Do not buy large quantities of staple goods, such as sugar and flour, unless you have tightly covered containers for storage. This practice is to prevent contamination by insects and rodents. It is best to purchase new food items for the family in small quantities to test their acceptability.

Where and When to Stop

Where you do your shopping generally makes a difference in how much you pay for food. It is best to check prices and make your own com-

TABLE 7.2
Cost (in cents) of a
three-ounce serving of
cooked lean meat from
selected kinds and cuts
of meat at specified
retail prices per pound

Kind and Cut of Meat	Price per Pound of Retail Cuts (in cents)									
	40	45	50	55	60	65	70	75	80	85
Beef										
Roasts										
BRISKET, BONE IN	21	23	26	29	31	34	36	39	42	44
CHUCK, BONE IN	18	20	22	25	27	29	31	33	36	38
CHUCK, BONE OUT	14	16	17	19	21	23	24	26	28	30
RIBS (7TH), BONE IN	18	20	22	25	27	29	31	33	36	38
ROUND, BONE IN	13	15	17	18	20	22	23	25	27	28
ROUND, BONE OUT	12	14	16	17	19	20	22	23	25	27
RUMP, BONE IN	17	20	22	24	26	28	31	33	35	37
RUMP, BONE OUT	14	15	17	19	20	22	24	26	27	29
Steaks										
CHUCK, BONE IN	18	20	22	25	27	29	31	33	36	38
CHUCK, BONE OUT	14	16	17	19	21	23	24	26	28	30
CLUB, BONE IN	23	26	28	31	34	37	40	43	45	48
PORTERHOUSE, BONE IN	21	23	26	29	31	34	36	39	42	44
ROUND, BONE IN	13	15	17	18	20	22	23	25	27	28
ROUND, BONE OUT	12	14	16	17	19	20	22	23	25	27
SIRLOIN, BONE IN	17	19	21	23	26	28	30	32	34	36
SIRLOIN, BONE OUT	16	18	20	21	23	25	27	29	31	33
T-BONE, BONE IN	22	25	28	30	33	36	39	41	44	47
Ground beef, lean	10	12	13	14	16	17	18	20	21	22
Short ribs	23	26	29	32	35	38	41	44	47	50
Fresh Pork										
Roasts										
LOIN, BONE IN	20	23	25	28	30	33	36	38	41	43
LOIN, BONE OUT	14	16	17	19	21	23	24	26	28	30
PICNIC, BONE IN	21	24	27	29	32	35	37	40	43	45
Chops										
LOIN	18	20	22	25	27	29	31	33	36	38
RIB	20	23	25	28	30	33	36	38	41	43
Cured Pork										
Roasts										
BUTT, BONE IN	14	16	18	20	22	23	25	27	29	31
HAM, BONE IN	14	16	17	19	21	23	24	26	28	30
HAM, BONE OUT	10	12	13	14	16	17	18	20	21	22
PICNIC, BONE IN	18	21	23	25	27	30	32	34	37	39
PICNIC, BONE OUT	14	16	18	19	21	23	25	27	28	30
Ham slices	12	14	16	17	19	20	22	23	25	27
Lamb										
Roasts										
LEG, BONE IN	17	19	21	23	25	27	29	31	33	35
SHOULDER, BONE IN	18	21	23	25	27	30	32	34	37	39
Chops										
LOIN	18	21	23	25	27	30	32	34	37	39
RIB	22	25	28	30	33	36	39	41	44	47

Source: U.S. Department of Agriculture, *Your Money's Worth in Food*, Home and Garden Bulletin No. 183, Washington, D.C.: Government Printing Office, 1974.

parisons. The big chain stores usually offer more variety and better
prices. The small neighborhood stores that offer credit, deliver your

90	95	100	105	110	115	120	125	130	135	140	145	150	155	160	165	170	175	180
47	49	52	55	57	60	62	65	68	70	73	76	78	81	83	86	89	91	94
40	42	45	47	49	51	54	56	58	60	62	65	67	69	71	74	76	78	80
31	33	35	36	38	40	42	43	45	47	49	50	52	54	56	57	59	61	62
40	42	45	47	49	51	54	56	58	60	62	65	67	69	71	74	76	78	80
30	32	33	35	37	38	40	42	43	45	47	48	50	52	54	55	57	59	60
28	30	31	33	34	36	38	39	41	42	44	45	47	48	50	52	53	55	56
39	41	44	46	48	50	52	55	57	59	61	63	66	68	70	72	74	76	79
31	32	34	36	38	39	41	43	44	46	48	49	51	53	55	56	58	60	61
40	42	45	47	49	51	54	56	58	60	62	65	67	69	71	74	76	78	80
31	33	35	36	38	40	42	43	45	47	49	50	52	54	56	57	59	61	62
51	54	57	60	62	65	68	71	74	77	80	82	85	88	91	94	97	99	102
47	49	52	55	57	60	62	65	68	70	73	76	78	81	83	86	89	91	94
30	32	33	35	37	38	40	42	43	45	47	48	50	52	54	55	57	59	60
28	30	31	33	34	36	38	39	41	42	44	45	47	48	50	52	53	55	56
38	40	43	45	47	49	51	53	55	57	60	62	64	66	68	70	72	74	77
35	37	39	41	43	45	47	49	51	53	55	57	59	61	62	64	66	68	70
50	52	55	58	61	64	66	69	72	75	77	80	83	86	88	91	94	97	99
23	25	26	27	29	30	31	33	34	35	36	38	39	40	42	43	44	46	47
53	56	58	61	64	67	70	73	76	79	82	85	88	91	94	96	99	102	105
46	48	51	53	56	58	61	63	66	69	71	74	76	79	81	84	86	89	91
31	33	35	36	38	40	42	43	45	47	49	50	52	54	56	57	59	61	62
48	51	53	56	59	62	64	67	70	72	75	78	80	83	86	88	91	94	96
40	42	45	47	49	51	54	56	58	60	62	65	67	69	71	74	76	78	80
46	48	51	53	56	58	61	63	66	69	71	74	76	79	81	84	86	89	91
32	34	36	38	40	42	43	45	47	49	51	52	54	56	58	60	61	63	65
31	33	35	36	38	40	42	43	45	47	49	50	52	54	56	57	59	61	62
23	25	26	27	29	30	31	33	34	35	36	38	39	40	42	43	44	46	47
41	43	46	48	50	53	55	57	59	62	64	66	68	71	73	75	78	80	82
32	34	35	37	39	41	42	44	46	48	49	51	53	55	57	58	60	62	64
28	30	31	33	34	36	38	39	41	42	44	45	47	48	50	52	53	55	56
38	40	42	44	46	48	50	52	54	56	58	60	62	65	67	69	71	73	75
41	43	46	48	50	53	55	57	59	62	64	66	68	71	73	75	78	80	82
41	43	46	48	50	53	55	57	59	62	64	66	68	71	73	75	78	80	82
50	52	55	58	61	64	66	69	72	75	77	80	83	86	88	91	94	97	99

groceries, and cash your checks and the convenience stores that stay open long hours usually charge more for most items. If the extra convenience is worth the cost and you can afford it, shopping in these stores may be suitable. For cost and variety the supermarket is to be preferred.

Compare the prices in stores that offer trading stamps and "special gifts" and consider the value of these extras to you. Learn where you will generally find the best values on particular items. But remember that driving around town for a single item can be an expensive bargain hunt. Save on transportation by limiting the number of stores at which you shop.

Your own time schedule and the availability of transportation partly determine when it is best for you to shop. Some stores offer specials, especially on weekends. There are often worth considering in your food plan. It is also wise to shop when the grocery store is not crowded, when shelves are well stocked, and when perishables are freshest. Pick a time when you are not in a hurry and when small children, if you have any, may be left with someone else. When children accompany you on your shopping trip do not be influenced by their desires for items they have seen advertised on TV. It is good practice to encourage children to learn to make choices in the marketplace, but adults should be the final authority in terms of cost, nutritional adequacy, and total family preferences.

Comparing Prices

Meats Compare meats by cost per serving, not by cost per pound. Fat and bones are not edible and this fact should be considered when buying. Table 7.2 shows the costs of three-ounce servings of various types of cooked lean meat at specified retail prices.

The latest national food-consumption survey by the U.S. Department of Agriculture (USDA) shows that United States families spend more than one-third of their food money for meats. There is great variation in the cost of meat, so careful selection of cuts can bring worthwhile savings. Poultry, one of the most popular main-dish foods, is usually less expensive than the meats shown in Table 7.2. How much less expensive is determined by the form in which it is bought. Whole chicken is usually a better buy than chicken parts. Also, compared to meats, certain types of fish may be lower in price, depending on the geographic area.

When buying meats, don't forget to compare the costs of different USDA grades. USDA "Choice" and USDA "Good" are the grades most often found in retail stores. USDA Good beef contains more lean and is not quite as juicy and flavorful as USDA Choice, but it is lower in price.

The way in which meat is cooked makes a tremendous difference in its flavor, and cooking meat at too high a temperature causes excessive shrinkage. By improving your skill in meat cookery you can lower the amount of money you spend for meats while still serving main dishes that are adequate, tasty, and satisfying.

Milk and Milk Products Compare the costs of various forms of milk: nonfat dry milk, evaporated milk, skimmed milk, 2 percent fat content milk, and whole fluid milk. The higher the fat content, the greater the cost. Nonfat dry milk powders can be substituted for whole milk in baking. Evaporated milk can be used in creamed sauces, casseroles, and gravies. There are many other ways to cut costs in your milk bill, such as mixing equal parts of reconstituted and fresh fluid milk. It may be well worth your effort to change your habits in using milk. Make comparisons for yourself.

Fruits and Vegetables The search for the best buy in vegetables and fruits extends to several departments in the store, including the sections for fresh produce, canned goods, frozen foods, and dehydrated foods. The prices of fresh vegetables and fruits are influenced by season and supply. The prices of canned, frozen, and dehydrated fruits and vegetables vary widely by item, grade, type of processing, and packing and seasoning. The type of product you select should be determined in part by the way you intend to use it. Consider buying fresh fruits and vegetables at the peak of the season and freezing or canning some for later use. Your home economist with the U.S. Department of Agriculture County Extension Service can provide you with instructions and booklets which will help you do the job correctly.

Breads and Cereals   In the bread and cereal group there are many ways to control cost. Bake some bread and compare the cost, taste, and texture with a similar product from the store. Note the various kinds of rice in the store, and compare the prices. You can probably buy some kinds of rice for as little as $.29 per pound; on the other hand, you can pay as much as $2.00 per pound for "wild rice."

There is a wide choice of cereals in the supermarket. Don't buy by cost alone. Read the labels and select those products that give you the most nutrition. Sugar-coated cereals cost disproportionately more than plain cereals. You can add your own sugar at a considerable savings. Cereals that you cook are more nutritious and cost less per serving than most ready-to-eat ones.

Convenience Foods   If you cannot afford a maid (and most of us can't), you can buy "maid service" built into many convenience foods. Cleaning, peeling, mixing, and cooking services are built into many of the foods we buy. You should realize that most of these foods cost more than ordinary ones. Price comparisons in supermarkets have revealed that some convenience foods cost three times as much as the ingredients needed to prepare similar dishes from family-type recipes.

One study, for example, showed that frozen waffles heated in a toaster cost three times as much as homemade waffles; on the other hand, canned biscuits, ready to bake, cost only one-third more than homemade biscuits. Some ready-to-eat brownies and sugar cookies cost about the same as those made at home, but may have less nutritional value.

Some brands of frozen ready-to-eat main dishes cost more than other brands because they contain more meat. Check the amount of meat you are getting in less expensive prepared dishes. On breaded items, note the amount of breading in relation to the amount of meat. Many convenience foods have fillers, extenders, and a considerable amount of water. Consumers Union found that many prepared pot pies had little meat, few vegetables and were heavily laden with starch and water.

How does one decide generally whether or not to buy convenience foods? Convenience foods, even with their higher cost, may be a suitable buy if you have limited time or lack cooking skills. A person living alone may find that some dishes require too many ingredients to justify preparation at home. Some people may prefer to use their time for activities other than cooking. You should evaluate the built-in maid service of convenience foods in the light of your time, your cooking skill, the cost, and your personal priorities. In comparing the costs of home-prepared and commercially prepared foods, be sure that the servings you are comparing are of equal size and quality.

Some Additional Tips to Help You Get the Most Value for Your Food Dollar

Buy the store brands, since they are usually cheaper.

Don't shop when you're hungry or tired. Surveys have shown that when you are hungry you spend more!

Know a "special," and recognize "loss leaders" (items advertised at very low prices to induce people to shop at a certain store) and "quick markdowns." If a store is out of a special ask for a "markdown" or "rain check."

Buy fresh fruit and vegetables in season when they are plentiful.

Check the bottom shelves, because higher-priced items are usually put at eye level.

Avoid impulse buying. Resist picking up and examining items not on your list. You'll buy them five out of ten times when you do pick them up. Stick to your shopping list.

Watch for costly mistakes. Observe the scales where food is weighed and watch the cash register at the check-out counter.

Pay attention to grades in making food purchases; choose the grade suited to your cooking method. For example, use a lower grade of fruit or vegetable if you plan to cut it up or cook it in a casserole or mixture.

Avoid foods with fancy extras like sugar syrups or sauces that you can add yourself.

Buy food in the form (fresh, frozen, or canned) or package that gives you the most servings for the money.

Since most foods should be used in a reasonable time after processing, rotate the foods on your pantry shelf. Otherwise, you may have to discard them because of spoilage or deterioration in flavor.

Remember that nonfood items are not a part of your food bill. Keep the budget for laundry supplies, cosmetics, hose, magazines, and other such items that you buy in the supermarket separate from your food budget.

Careful shopping—planned in advance—cuts your food waste and controls food costs. You will be able to eat the foods you like and pay less for them. The extra dollars may be used for more food or something else you want.

Unit Pricing

For the past several years, consumers have been complaining about the difficulty of comparing various brands, containers, and packages to determine the most economical product to buy. Recently *unit pricing* has been advocated as an aid to more intelligent shopping. What does unit pricing involve?

Unit pricing refers to the exact cost per unit of measure: cost per ounce, pound, gallon, quart, dozen, or other standard unit. Unit pricing has long been used on many items, such as meat, butter, and cheese (priced by the pound), milk (priced by the quart), and eggs (priced by the dozen). Unit pricing can be a very useful tool for comparing identical products: two brands of sugar, two different-sized cans of the same type of shortening. However, it would be unfair to compare brand X, labeled "pure vegetable" shortening, with brand Y, labeled merely "pure shortening." Different fats may have been used to make the two shortenings; hence there may be a legitimate difference in the price. The label "pure vegetable shortening" means that only vegetable oils have been used. But the product labeled "pure shortening" may contain a combination of vegetable and animal fats, and this would result in a lower price.

Many chain stores are already using some type of unit pricing. The most common form is a shelf tag printed by a computer. Information regarding the cost per unit of measure of the product is included in addition to its total price. This procedure is relatively inexpensive for the big chain stores that have computer services available. For the small grocer who does not have computer services the cost is prohibitive.

The following should be kept in mind regarding unit pricing:

1. It does not measure the relative values of products. For instance, it doesn't distinguish between extra fancy, fancy, and standard pack.
2. It does not measure the drained weight of a wet pack. For example, the cost per ounce of corn with liquid may be lower than the cost of corn with no liquid even when you are getting the same amount of corn for the same money.
3. It does not take into account the cost of making the product ready for table use. For instance, some cake mixes require the addition of eggs and/or butter while others do not.
4. It does not reflect differences in ingredients: for example, the difference we mentioned between pure vegetable shortening and pure shortening.

Unit pricing (left) and universal product code (right)

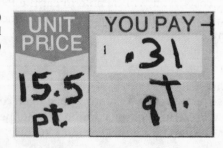 

PERSONAL FINANCE FOR CONSUMERS

The list of confusing relationships that unit pricing does not reveal could become long indeed. The important thing to remember is that the unit price of food is one thing but quality is another. Both need to be considered when you are deciding what to buy.

Open Dating

Trying to interpret the meaning of dates on food in the marketplace can be very confusing. You may find a code number or even a date but what do these markings mean? Most food processors have always used a system for dating along with symbols for variety, product, plant, shift, and so on. Now demands are being made on processors to date products in ways that shoppers can understand. Consumers want fresh products, and open dating will enable them to see for themselves just how fresh the food is.

The phrase "open dating" refers to the use of any date on a packaged food product that can be read and understood by the shopper. The following terms are used in open dating.

1. The *pack date* refers to the date of processing or final packaging.
2. The *pull date* is the last date on which a retail store may offer the food for sale. This dating allows a reasonable time for the customer to store and use the product at home without fear of spoilage.
3. The *freshness date* is the last date on which the product will be at its peak of quality or freshness.
4. The *expiration date* generally is a date after which the product should not be eaten. This is the most difficult to determine and is not widely used.

For the present, open dates are used mostly on perishable and semiperishable foods. Look for the open dates and use them as buying guides. But remember that the open date is no guarantee of continued freshness unless you take care of the product in getting it home and storing it. Storage temperature and handling methods influence the quality of food more than time.

Universal Product Code (UPC)

A revolutionary development is being tested; known as the Universal Product Code (UPC), it is designed to benefit the consumer, retailer, manufacturer, and wholesaler. The UPC consists of a standard ten-bar code which can be printed on a package and read by an electric scanner. Each product is identified by a particular variation in the code. At the check-out stand the coded items pass over the counter scanner and the prices flash on the computerized cash register. It is estimated that with the UPC check-out will be 30 to 50 percent faster and be far more accurate than with the present system.

The UPC will lead to more efficient inventory control, more uniform product ordering, and less frequent out-of-stock conditions. The use of this new system will eliminate the expense of price marking every item or of making price changes on each item. The price will appear on the shelf or bin along with the unit price, and will be stored in the computer's memory. Fewer employees will be needed to mark goods and to operate the supermarket.

Since manufacturers are printing new labels to comply with FDA nutrient-labeling requirements, some are already adding the Universal Product Code. This will save the time and money of further change-overs. It is predicted that by 1979 most major supermarkets will have switched from conventional cash registers to the UPC system to reduce their operating costs and create savings for their customers.

SUMMARY

Plan your meals for the week.   Begin with the main dish for each day, then add the foods necessary to complete the meal. Consider your family's likes and dislikes. Buy nutritious food, not food that merely looks attractive in its package. Use the basic four food groups or a similar guide when planning your meals.

Make a shopping list.   Write down what you intend to buy, deciding on the basis of your "stock on hand" and your needs. List the quantities. Check the ads for the best buys.

Use your eyes when shopping.   Look at the labels. Compare prices, nutritive values, and quantities. Check the quality and freshness. Watch the scales and the cash register. Don't be persuaded to pay more for so-called "health foods."

Store food properly.   Food spoilage wastes money. Proper storage preserves food and flavor.

Shop where you get the best values.   Prices vary in different stores. Compare prices at stores convenient to you. Consider the features and prices at each.

Shop at the best time.   Find the best time of day and day of the week to shop in your locality. Generally more food items are on sale on weekends, but stores may be most crowded at these times. Buy foods in season when possible. Don't shop when you're hungry or tired.

GLOSSARY OF NEW TERMS

Basic four food groups A classification of foods according to equivalent nutritional values; a pattern or guide for an adequate diet.

Convenience foods Products that have been fully or partially prepared for eating.

Food and Drug Administration (FDA) A federal agency that carries responsibility for food and drug safety and develops guidelines to fulfill its mandate.

Health foods Foods grown without chemical fertilizers or the use of pesticides.

Loss leader An item advertised at a very low price to induce people to shop in the store.

Open dating The process of marking a packaged food product so that customers can determine its freshness.

Recommended dietary (or daily) Allowances (RDAs) The daily quantities of nutrients believed to be needed for all healthy persons in the United States. Percentages of the FDA's version of these allowances are shown on new food labels.

Unit price The cost per unit of measure of a given food item.

Universal Product Code (UPC) A group of ten bars that appear on food labels; the code can be read by an electric scanner and the information fed into a computer.

QUESTIONS FOR DISCUSSION

1. Identify the four basic good groups. List the recommended servings for an adult and name three good food sources in each group.
2. How may USRDAs affect our food-buying habits?
3. List factors that influence one's choice of foods.
4. List some convenience foods and compare their cost to that of similar products made at home.
5. Give two tips for controlling food costs when buying each of the following: meats, fruits and vegetables, breads and cereals, and milk products.
6. Explain the importance of making a shopping list.
7. List some "dos" and "don'ts" in food shopping.
8. How does the cost of foods sold in health stores compare with the cost of foods in regular supermarkets? Is the difference justifiable? Explain.
9. Explain nutritional labeling, and the information that must appear on the label. What are the advantages of this type of label?
10. How can unit pricing be used advantageously? What are disadvantages?

SUGGESTED STUDENT ACTIVITIES

1. Identify a number of foods available in your community that you and your family enjoy, and list them in Worksheet 7.1 according to the basic four food group to which each belongs. List the most nutritious ones first.

WORKSHEET 7.1
Your Meal-Planning
Chart

Milk and Milk Products	Meats and Meat Substitutes	Fruits and Vegetables	Breads and Cereals

MANAGING FOOD MONEY

You can refer to your list to make sure you choose foods from each group when planning your menus and making a shopping list.

2. Plan a week's menus for yourself or your family and make out a shopping list, keeping in mind the information you have learned in this chapter.

3. Check the price you would have to pay for your week's groceries in your local stores at the first of the week. Review the food section in the Wednesday evening or Thursday morning local newspaper, and note the items on sale. Compare the costs and check to see if the products on sale are of the same quality as those you normally buy. How much could you save by shopping at the end of the week? Assuming that this is a typical week, figure your savings for a month's and for a year's groceries.

4. Compare the cost of ready-prepared cereal with the cost of oatmeal, Ralston, or Cream of Wheat; note the difference in cost per serving. List factors other than cost that should be considered. Calculate the cost of sugar in sugar-coated cereals.

5. Identify some prepared or convenience food often used by you or your family. Explain what has been done to the food, and compare the price of the food in its natural form with the cost of the product that has the "maid service" built in. Is the convenience worth the difference to you? Explain.

6. Collect food labels and learn what is meant by the information on them.

7. Explore some ways in which families can reduce the cost of their food supply by growing and/or preserving food. Prepare a written report of your findings.

8. Select one food item (for instance, tuna, stew beef, brownies). Visit three different food markets and determine the number of forms available, the package sizes available, the number of brands, and the unit costs. Summarize your findings in a chart, and discuss how the variations in cost are related to form, brand, package size, convenience, and place of purchase.

9. As a variation of activity 8, visit three markets at three different times over a time span of six to eight weeks. Make a graph of price changes for the food item you have selected.

10. Visit a food market. Observe the layout, the arrangement of food items on the shelves, the location of specials, and the location of come-ons (candy, household aids, and so forth). Explain how the merchandising techniques you have observed affect a customer's selection of food items.

FOR ADDITIONAL INFORMATION

Boyd, Jacque. "Food Labeling and the Marketing of Nutrition." *Journal of Home Economics*, May 1973, pp. 20–24.
    Presents a discussion on food labeling, between the assistant editor of the *Journal of Home Economics* and representatives of the FDA. A summary of nutrition labeling regulations is also presented.

Cascioli, Donna Marie. "Checking Out the UPC." *What's New in Home Economics*, March 1974, pp. 15–16.
    An informative article on the revolutionary Universal Product Code, its implications for consumers, retailers, manufacturers, and wholesalers.

Durden, Ellington. "Sense and Nonsense About Health Foods." *Journal of Home Economics*, December 1972, pp. 4–8.
Presents a bit of history behind the notion of health foods, and facts and fallacies regarding a number of items that "ring up" considerable profit for operators of health-food stores.

Fletcher, Adele Whitely. *How to Stretch Your Dollar*. New York: Benjamin Co., 1970.
Points out ways to save on your food dollar and explains some cooking techniques that help conserve energy and money.

Food and Nutrition Board, National Research Council. *Recommended Dietary Allowances*, 8th rev. ed. Washington, D.C.: National Academy of Sciences, 1974.
Explains the recommended dietary allowances and includes additional information on foods needed for adequate nutrition.

Gmur, Ben C., John T. Fodor, Litta Glass, and Joseph J. Langan. *Making Health Decisions*. Englewood Cliffs, N.J.: Prentice-Hall, 1975. pp. 64–77.
This book attempts to help the consumer understand and solve health problems. Chapter V, on developing sound nutritional practices, provides suggestions on what to eat and why. Contains good charts on nutrients and their function in the body. Considers dieting, weight reduction, and organically fertilized food. Glossary included.

How the Shrewdest Shoppers Buy and Use Meat, Dairy Products and Eggs. St. Louis: Ralston Purina Company, 1974. Pamphlet.
Concise suggestions for buying meat, dairy products, and eggs.

Margolius, Sidney. *The Great American Food Hoax*. New York: Walker, 1971.
Shows that food prices have risen but levels of nutrition have declined. Includes analysis of consumer pitfalls and advice on sensible shopping.

Money Management Institute. *Your Food Dollar*. Chicago: Household Finance Corporation, 19.
Suggests a plan for evaluating your food dollar. Meal planning and practical nutrition are emphasized. Shopping hints and buying guides for all types of food are included.

"Nutrition Labels: They Help You Buy Wisely, Eat Better." *Changing Times*, December 1974, pp. 41–43.
Explains how to use information that will appear on more and more packages.

Taylor, Eileen F. "Unit Pricing and Open Dating." *Family Economics Review*. Hyattsville, Md.: Consumer and Food Economics Research Division, ARS—USDA, June 1972, pp. 3–6.
An explanation of unit pricing, open dating, and code dating. This publication is free to librarians.

U.S. Department of Agriculture. *Food Is More Than Something to Eat*. Home and Garden Bulletin No. 72. Washington, D.C.: Government Printing Office, 1974.
Explains the nutritive value of foods and the functions of food other than satisfying hunger.

———. *Shoppers' Guide: The 1974 Yearbook of Agriculture*. Washington, D.C.: Government Printing Office, 1974.
Contains valuable information on shopping for food.

———. *Your Money's Worth in Foods*. Home and Garden Bulletin No. 183. Washington, D.C.: Government Printing Office, 1974.
Explains how to shop so as to make the best use of your food money.

Check with your local USDA cooperative extension home economist for other helpful publications available from the Department of Agriculture.

"Vegetables You Grow Yourself Taste Better." *Changing Times,* April 1974, pp. 46–47.

Stresses the value of the home garden.

Warmke, Roman F., Eugene D. Wyllie, and Beulah E. Sellers. *Consumer Decision Making: Guides to Better Living.* Cincinnati: South-Western, 1972.

Presents guides for getting the most for your food dollar.

"Which Cereals Are Most Nutritious?" *Consumer Reports,* February 1975, pp. 76–82.

Presents data from research study using rats as to the nutritional value of a wide variety of cereals.

8

Managing Clothing Money

8

There are probably as many reasons why people buy clothing as there are places to buy. For some, clothing is to protect and cover the body for work, play, or leisure. For others, clothes elevate their spirits and make them feel important. Some just enjoy the change and variety that new clothes can bring to their lives.

Whatever the purpose for which you spend your clothing money, you want to get the most for the money you spend—the most in value and the most in satisfaction. In this chapter you will learn how to develop a total clothing plan so that your clothes buying isn't a hit-or-miss affair. You will learn about regulations for flammable fabrics designed to provide greater safety for individuals and homes. You will learn how to shop for clothing, and you'll come to understand the factors that influence clothing choices.

Clothing is an individual matter.

Read the account that follows. As you read about Norma and Pat, try to put yourself in their place. What would you have done? Before making a final judgment, read the rest of the chapter.

THE CLEARANCE SALE

The sign in the window read: "SALE—20 to 50% Off on Men's and Women's Clothing."

Norma and her husband Pat were on their way home from work. It was late in September but the fall weather had not yet set in. In fact, it was almost like a hot July day. They glanced at the sign in the window.

"Let's go in," said Norma. "We've both been paid today and there might be some good buys. Your mother won't mind taking care of Artie for a few extra minutes."

Pat began looking for a winter suit and Norma went off in the direction of the dresses. Neither of them liked to ask the other's opinion about clothes because they never could agree; individual shopping prevented arguments. They had decided long ago that whenever they went into a store together there would be no interference. In the past when one had listened to the other they had ended by buying nothing.

Pat couldn't find a winter suit that he liked but he did see a summer suit that appealed to him. Since the suits were on sale, he decided to buy one, figuring that he could get some use from it if the hot weather continued.

Norma found an elegant party dress. It bubbled like a glass of champagne. The sale price was "50% off" the regular price. Like Pat's suit the dress was suitable only for summer, but Norma too thought she'd be able to get some use from it while the hot weather persisted.

"Do you want to try the dress on?" asked the clerk.

"How much time do we have, Pat?"

Pat was busy talking to the salesman about alterations that had to be made on his suit. During the sale, alterations were not included, and Pat was wrestling with his conscience because the suit suddenly was going to cost him more than he had planned on spending.

"Couldn't you fix these pants for me, Norma? Cuff them and take in the waist about an inch? The jacket fits fine."

"I suppose I could," said Norma. "Do we have time to try on this dress?"

Pat took a good look at the dress for the first time and said, "Where are you going to wear that?"

"It's a party dress," replied Norma. "I'm going to wear it to a party. Where did you think I was going to wear it?"

"We don't have time for you to try it on now," said Pat.

"Mother will be getting fed up with Artie. We better get going."

They paid for their purchases and hurried home with their respective packages. When they got home they began to have misgivings about what they had bought. Norma tried on the dress and found that it was too big, although it was marked size 14, which was her size. Pat didn't bother to try on his suit again. The forecast was for cold weather. This was sobering news. It reminded him that he still needed a winter suit.

They decided, together this time, to take the clothes back. The decision was a sensible one, of course, but it was too late. They would find out when they tried to return their clothing that all purchases were final during the sale.

The Total Clothing Plan

Much money can be wasted if clothing purchases are made without thought of the total clothing plan. The plan allows you to evaluate where you are now and where you are going. To develop such a plan you need to answer the following questions for yourself or for your family.

1. What influences your clothing choices?
2. What should be included in your wardrobe?
3. What is available in your present collection? What can be altered and made usable?
4. What should you buy?
5. How much of your financial resources can be allocated to clothing expenses?

Influences on Clothing Choices

Clothing is an expression of one's culture, social inheritance, customs, morals, and religion. It is interesting to study the styles, types of fabrics, and raw materials by which people in various cultures and periods of history have protected themselves from the elements and expressed their lifestyles. Much can be learned about people by a study of their clothing.

An individual's choice of clothing is influenced by the occupational and social activities in which he engages and how he feels about himself; by his status in life; by his need for identification with a particular group and his desire for recognition and approval. A factory worker will want to dress differently from a government official, for psychological as well as practical reasons. Moreover, the purchase of a new suit or dress is sometimes used as a means of satisfying basic needs which are not met in other ways. There is nothing wrong with this: How a person feels about himself is important to his success in life. Money spent on a new garment to boost one's ego is sometimes a wise investment. However, the frequency with which a person allows himself this type of reinforcement should be a matter of concern.

The environment in which a person lives and works possibly has the greatest influence on his choice of clothing. Think of the people you know who live in different climates and whose occupations require that they work indoors, out-of-doors, and in various types of environments; consider the different kinds of clothing they need to protect them physically. Although air-conditioned and climatically controlled buildings and modes of transportation have made clothing choices more uniform, environment is still an important factor.

An individual's tastes in clothing are also conditioned by the values he holds. Values—the things that are of importance to the individual—help him in weighing alternatives and making choices in

Clothes should match the job.

clothing. As a person grows older, values and activities change, and these changes are reflected in clothing choices. The process is not automatic, however; frequently we need to take stock and clarify for ourselves the things that are most important.

What the Wardrobe Should Include

The kind of work you do regularly, the places you go, and the activities you engage in need to be considered when you decide what to include in the wardrobe. Individual taste and the effect clothing has on one's self-esteem should not be overlooked.

Select each item on the basis of its intended use. Children may need different kinds of clothing because of their activities and rapid growth. It is generally better to fit children at the time of purchase than to buy clothes for "when they grow up." Selections for each person in the family should be made so as to get full benefit from each article before it is out of style. If you select clothing with a simple style and good design, it will have a longer usefulness and usually greater durability than clothing that is highly decorated or styled in an extreme way.

What the Present Wardrobe Contains

After deciding what each individual in the family needs for work, for school, for play, and for social events, take a good look at what is already on hand. Decide whether the clothing you have is wearable just as it is. Does it need some alteration, cleaning, or mending to put it into use—or should it be discarded or given away?

When these decisions have been made, it is easier to determine which additional items are needed for the family. Then you can establish priorities—what is needed immediately and what can be deferred until later.

What You Should Buy

Plan your purchases of clothing on the basis of the priorities you have set. Too often "needs" develop suddenly or something appeals to us because we think it is a bargain. Such impulse buying is a danger to the spending plan for clothes.

It takes advance planning and some reliable information to shop wisely. If purchases are planned, sales can be used to greatest advantage. When a store advertises an item on your "needed" list, that is the time to go and see it. In January you usually find pre-inventory sales. July is the time for the end-of-spring and early-summer clearances. The end-of-summer sales are in August and September.

For most of us the amount of money we have to spend limits our freedom in making clothing decisions. When family size increases, the use of the clothing dollar must be planned especially carefully to provide for all members. Generally expenses increase as the children get older. Priorities for clothing must be set by the family as a whole—and adhered to. You must decide how much you should spend on the basis of your own family's needs and your own money plan. Great savings can be made if a member of the family can sew.

Shopping for Clothes

Clothing can be bought at many different types of stores. The large department stores and specialty shops are probably the best known. Among these there are many variations in the quality and style of merchandise, the groups or individuals to whom the store caters and the status the store is accorded.

In addition, there are wholesale outlets, retail outlets, discount stores, and mail-order houses. Usually fewer services are provided in discount stores than in other shops. These stores are frequently located in areas where rent is low and large spaces are available for the display of merchandise. The continuous help of a salesperson is often foregone. You may be on your own in determining the fit and quality of a garment. Alterations are frequently left to the shopper. Returns or exchanges may not be permitted. If you can judge quality, fit, and workmanship and are sure of what you want, a considerable savings may be had by shopping at discount or outlet stores.

The following tips should be considered when shopping for clothing.

Compare quality and price.

1. Before going on a shopping trip, decide on a price limit for each item. This saves time and helps to cut down on overspending.
2. Shop in stores that have reputations for good quality and fairness to customers.
3. Be alert to what is available and to trends in style.
4. Spend time in comparing quality and price in different stores. The best quality at your price is the best buy for you.
5. Know the store policies regarding exchanges, guarantees, and complaints.
6. Get acquainted with salespersons in stores where you shop frequently. If they know you and what you like they can be more helpful. They may also call you when items you need go on sale.
7. Look for signs of good workmanship.
   a. Seams should be wide enough to allow for letting out and should be finished to prevent fraying.
   b. Machine stitching ought to be short, continuous, straight, and securely fastened at the ends.
   c. Hems and facing should be firmly attached but not showing through to the right side of the garment. The hems should also be wide enough to permit lengthening.
   d. Zippers ought to be smooth and flat, securely stitched, and of the correct length and weight; the zipper should remain closed at the top when stress is applied.
   e. Buttons, hooks and eyes, and snaps should be firmly attached and in the correct places.
   f. Look for reinforcement of weak points or points of stress.
   g. Buttonholes should be smooth, firm, evenly stitched, properly placed, suitable to the size and type of garment, and without loose threads.
   h. Linings should be smooth, properly fastened to the garment, and of the appropriate texture and weight for the outer fabric. A pleat in the center back and at the bottom helps to extend the fabric when you are bending or using your arms.
   i. Check for sagging, binding, and pulling when you are trying on a garment.
8. Garments are made of cotton, wool, silk, flax, and synthetic or man-made materials. Get to know about fabrics and the advantages and disadvantages of each. Become acquainted with the different textile finishes, mothproofing, and water-repellant and wrinkle-resistant fabrics. Is the fabric suitable for the style, design, or purpose of the garment? Reading tags and labels can help. Ask questions. There is considerable literature available from your home economist with the U. S. Department of Agriculture County Extension Service in your locality and from pamphlets and bulletins prepared by textile manufacturers to improve your knowledge of fabric and its appropriate use and care.

9. Consider how the garment is to be cared for. Be sure to read the laundering instructions on wash-and-wear apparel. Garments are now required to have a permanently attached tag or label that states the fabric content and instructions for washing or cleaning. If you make your own clothes be sure to ask for a permanent care label when you buy the material so you can sew it in yourself. Merchants who sell yard goods are required to have these available and to give them to customers. However, they sometimes neglect to provide them unless you ask. Also remember that the cost of upkeep is greater for clothes that have to be dry-cleaned, and fabrics that require special handling during laundering will take more of your time. Consider whether you want to spend your time in this way.

10. The fit of a garment is most important. A correctly fitted garment gives longer wear and of course looks better. Extensive alterations of an item that doesn't fit may be expensive and may raise the cost beyond what you planned to spend.

11. Accessories should complement your wardrobe. Properly selected, they can be used for several outfits.

Safety in Clothing

While significant progress has been made in protecting individuals against an unreasonable risk of fabric fires, there is still a long way to go. Three groups among the population are most likely to suffer severe burns or death as a result of their clothing's catching on fire: the aged, children, and the handicapped.

Aged people often do not see well and do not recognize the danger of an open fire or source of combustion. Their lack of mobility makes it difficult for them to escape the enveloping flames. Children are often burned while playing with matches, lighted candles, or cigarette lighters, or when they are around an open fire. They fail to recognize the danger and are often unable to protect themselves. Handicapped persons, whether young or old, are generally not able to move quickly and are less able than other people to extinguish flames.

Although a Flammable Fabrics Act was passed by Congress in 1953 and amended in 1967, evidence continued to accumulate that regulations needed to be improved and made easier to enforce. In 1972 the Consumer Product Act was passed by Congress and the Consumer Product Safety Commission which administers the legislation was given broad authority to issue and enforce safety standards for more than 10,000 products. The flammability of children's clothing came under the commission's jurisdiction.

Any garment worn primarily for sleeping (pajamas, nightgowns, and robes) in size 0 to 6X, manufactured on or after July 28, 1973, is covered by the flammability standard and must be flame-resistant. A label to that effect is not required, but some manufacturers are including information about flammability voluntarily. The law requires that the flame-retardant characteristics of the garment must remain through fifty launderings.

A problem with the flame-resistant sleepwear is that it will lose its resistance if laundered with detergents that do not contain phosphates. Use of a detergent without phosphates permits a kind of buffer to build up. This coating soon interferes with the action of the fire-resistant finish.

Additional standards are now being considered by the Consumer Product Safety Commission for sleepwear up to size 14, children's dresses, upholstered furniture, curtains, and draperies.

SUMMARY

To plan your clothing needs, answer the following questions.

What influences your clothing choices? What does the clothing worn by the people you associate with tell you? How does it affect what you want to buy? How should your clothing choices be related to the environment? Consider how your values relate to clothing.

What should be included in your wardrobe? What are your needs for work and leisure? Consider this in terms of who you are and what you do.

What do you have available? Evaluate the clothes on hand in terms of your needs. Do they require cleaning or mending, or should they be discarded? Is it worth putting them into usable form?

What do you need to buy? Establish a set of priorities for yourself and each member of the family. Who gets what first? Stick to your plan, and avoid impulse buying.

How much should you pay? Base this decision on your own needs and your own budget, not merely on what seems a "good buy." Set a price limit on the items you've decided to buy. It saves time and prevents overspending.

Shop in stores that have reputations for quality and fairness. Buy basic styles that you expect to wear for several seasons. Buy specials when they're on your "needed" list. Get acquainted with salespersons. Spend time in comparing quality and price. Consider safety when selecting clothing, and look for good workmanship.

Read the labels and tags. Learn about the fabrics and how to care for them. Examine and remember the instructions for cleaning on the permanent care label. Consider the cost of upkeep. Ask for permanent care labels when choosing fabric to make a garment.

GLOSSARY OF NEW TERMS

Discount store   A type of retail store that operates on the principle of reduced prices and lower markup to stimulate greater sales.

Flammable Fabrics Act A law passed in 1953 to regulate the manufacture of highly flammable clothing. A 1967 amendment provided more comprehensive fire-safety regulations. The act is administered by the Consumer Product Safety Commission. Standards have been established for children's sleepwear, carpets and rugs, and mattresses and mattress pads.

Permanent care labels Labels permanently attached to garments that inform the purchaser about regular care and maintenance.

Pre-inventory sale A lowering of prices so that stocks may be reduced prior to taking inventory for accounting purposes.

Retail outlet An organization formed to sell a manufacturer's goods directly to the consumer, without the usual middlemen.

Specialty shop A retail shop that restricts its stock to a particular class of goods, such as men's wear, ladies' sportswear, or maternity fashions.

Wholesale outlet An organization that sells to retailers only, generally in multi-unit lots and may sell directly to consumers.

QUESTIONS FOR DISCUSSION

1. Consider what clothes do for an individual besides protect the body.
2. List factors that must be considered in planning and buying clothes for oneself or one's family.
3. Explain what is meant by "impulse buying." Analyze one clothing purchase you have made by this procedure and state your satisfaction or dissatisfaction with it.
4. Discuss when and where to buy to get more for your clothing dollar.
5. Discuss the advisability of buying one good-quality, well-constructed garment instead of two garments of poorer quality and construction for approximately the same amount of money.
6. Explain how laundering and dry cleaning influence total clothing cost.
7. List some indications of good workmanship.
8. What three groups in the population suffer the most accidents from clothing fires? Explain why, and discuss what should be done to prevent accidents of this type.
9. Explain the Flammable Fabrics Act, who administers it, and what garments come under its provisions.
10. Why do you think it was necessary to require permanent care labels?

SUGGESTED STUDENT ACTIVITIES

1. Analyze the lifestyles of people at different times and in different cultures. Collect pictures to illustrate how lifestyle influenced the apparel worn.
2. Make an inventory of the wearable clothing you have on hand. Make a clothing plan which provides for your needs for the next three months. Calculate the cost of additional clothing needed.
3. Calculate the clothing needs for a year for one of the following: a preschool child, a child between six and twelve, a teen-ager, a young adult, and a retired adult. Using a Sears, Penney's, or similar catalog, determine the cost

of the clothing. Consider the activities the person will be engaged in. Share your report with the class.

4. Formulate a list of "dos" and "don'ts" for buying clothing.

5. Make a collection of labels. Find out what the information on each label means. Investigate to find out what information is required by law.

6. Take two garments of comparable cost, one that must be dry-cleaned and one that can be washed by hand. Consider the life of the garment, and figure out how much dry cleaning will increase the cost of the garment over its total span of usefulness.

7. List the different types of stores in your area which sell clothing and give the advantages and disadvantages of shopping at each type.

8. Interview local clothes merchants to find out the extent of theft and of customer damage to their merchandise. Also find out who pays this bill. Report to the group.

9. Identify the kinds of storage space needed to protect one's clothing adequately. Find pictures of well-organized storaged space. Analyze your own storage and develop a detailed plan for improvement.

10. Write to the Consumer Product Safety Commission for copies of the latest regulations on items covered by the Flammable Fabrics Act. Study the materials obtained and share your information with the class.

FOR ADDITIONAL INFORMATION

"At Last! Permanent Care Labels." *What's New in Home Economics,* September 1972, pp. 86-92.
　　Excellent information on permanent care labels. It explains the labels and the care that should be taken in laundering or cleaning.

"Good News for the Consumer. . .Permanent Care Labeling." *Forecast for Home Economics,* May-June 1972, pp. F44–F45.
　　Explains permanent care labels. Charts are included to illustrate symbols and explain the care of various fabrics.

Holloway, Irmagene, and Betty J. Houston. "The Flammable Fabric Issue." *Journal of Home Economics,* March 1974, pp. 17–20.
　　Explains the fabric flammability standards and the need for additional regulations. Considers clothing and furnishings. Gives two case histories of people whose clothing caught fire.

Keil, Sally Van W. "Setting the Pace in New York's Fashion World." *Money,* January 1975, pp. 28–32.
　　Although the article's focus is on the successful career of a woman in fashion merchandising, it provides insight into the buying and selling of clothes.

"Men's Raincoats." *Consumer Reports,* March 1975, pp. 186–189.
　　An evaluation of two styles of men's raincoats. Garments were tested for water repellency, durability, construction, convenience, and comfort. The report gives recommendations for the best value.

Money Management Institute. *Your Shopping Dollar.* Chicago: Household Finance Corporation, 1972.
　　Presents simple and practical guidelines to help the reader learn to dress well and at the same time stretch the clothing dollar.

Newton, Audrey. "Clothing: A Rehabilitating Tool for the Handicapped." *Journal of Home Economics*, April 1973, pp. 29–30.

Emphasizes the importance of clothing for the consumer and how it can provide freedom of movement and comfort even to the physically handicapped.

"Nine Commandments for Smart Shoppers." *Changing Times*, December 1973, pp. 6–10.

Considers impulse buying, places to buy, quality, labels, merchants, brand names, buying calendar, and advertising.

U.S. Department of Commerce. *Fibers and Fabrics*. Publication No. C13:531. Washington, D.C.: Government Printing Office, 1970.

Information about natural and manmade fibers, about fabrics to meet specific needs, and about proper care and use of fabrics.

Warmke, Roman F., Eugene D. Wyllie, and Beulah E. Sellers. *Consumer Decision Making: Guides to Better Living*. Cincinnati: South-Western, 1972.

Offers a good delineation of points to consider in buying clothing and planning a wardrobe.

9

Buying Protection: Life and Disability Insurance, Social Security, and Pensions

9

It has been well established that what we all want most is security. All of us look for ways to protect ourselves against the hazards that threaten our ways of life. We need to identify those hazards that are most likely to impinge upon our security and take measures against them. Decisions about which protection you buy should be based on your own feelings about life's hazards and how much you are willing and able to pay to protect yourself.

Elsewhere in this book we consider protection for your car, your home, and your health. Here we want to examine the measures you should consider to protect your family against the effects of your premature death or disability. In this chapter you will learn:

1. The purpose of life insurance and the kinds that are available to you;
2. How to select the right kind of life insurance;
3. How to decide about disability insurance;
4. How the Social Security Act protects you;
5. The role of pension plans in your security program.

Life Insurance

The purpose of life insurance is to provide a cash reserve or income for dependents upon the death of the major wage earner. When the breadwinner dies the family is usually faced with burial expenses and debts that were incurred before death, and with the need for funds to meet the family's living expenses until new income arrangements can be made. Life insurance should be bought for the primary wage earner, never for children, and for the spouse or secondary earner only if the situation justifies it.

Life insurance is not primarily a savings plan or an investment plan, nor should it be used as a plan to send children to college. Although life insurance is often sold for these purposes, there are better ways in which one can achieve the objectives of saving and investment.

Types of Life Insurance

No matter how many different frills or variations are offered by insurance companies, there are only four basic types of life insurance policy: (1) term, (2) straight life or ordinary life, (3) limited-payment, and (4) endowment. Term insurance policies provide pure protection while the other types have savings features built into them.

Term Life Insurance   As the name implies, this type of insurance provides protection for a stated term, usually one, five, ten, or twenty years. At the end of the term, protection stops; there is no cash value to the policy. There may be an option to renew at the end of the stated term, and if so the policy is called a renewable term policy. The premium rate is increased at each renewal because the rate is based on the age of the insured; but the policy owner does not need to pass any physical examination other than the one he takes when he first signs up.

This type of life insurance gives the greatest amount of protection for the least cost (see Table 9.1). There are no savings or investment features—just protection. Coverage can be increased or decreased as needs dictate. For example, when people marry and have dependents the amount of insurance can be increased. When potential survivors become financially independent the coverage can be decreased.

People who want to get as much protection as possible and who are able to plan their own savings and investment program select term insurance. They need to be able to discipline themselves to adhere to their savings plan. If they cannot, they should resort to a form of life insurance with savings built in.

By saving or investing the difference in cost between term insurance and the more expensive types you can build up a larger cash fund than you would with a savings type of life insurance. Alternatively, you can use the difference in cost to purchase more insurance. For example, on the basis of Table 9.1, a term-to-age-sixty-five life insurance policy for the face amount of $12,000 would cost a young man of twenty-five $88.80 per year (12 times $7.40), or a total of $1,776 after twenty years. He would receive $12,000 of protection during the twenty-year period. On the other hand, a twenty-year endowment policy for the same face amount of $12,000 would cost $498 per year (12 times $41.50). The endowment policy, besides insuring him, would pay him $12,000 if he survived after the twenty years; for this money he would have paid only $9,960 in premiums. However, if this same young man had set aside $30 per month ($360 per year) in a passbook savings account that paid an interest rate of only 5¼ percent, he would have accumulated his $12,000 in twenty years and he would have had $138 a year left over ($498 minus $360); with this money he could have purchased approximately $18,650 worth of term insurance. With the same amount of money invested, and the same return after twenty years, he would have had half again as much insurance.

	Kind of Coverage	Cost
TABLE 9.1 Annual Life Insurance Costs per $1,000 of Coverage at Age Twenty-Five*	10-year renewable term	$ 4.20
	Term to age sixty-five	7.40
	Straight	12.70
	20-payment	24.20
	20-year endowment	41.50

*Figures are from a randomly selected insurance company.

BUYING PROTECTION

Straight or Ordinary Life Insurance   This type of insurance pays a stated amount, the *face value*, at the death of the insured. It is a combination of term insurance and built-in savings. A portion of the premium for the insurance is set aside by the insurance company in some sort of investment. In time this savings portion of the premium accumulates and builds up a cash reserve or *cash value* which the insured may withdraw or borrow. Naturally the longer the period of time over which premiums are paid, the greater will be the cash value. But at no time will the cash value exceed the face value of the policy.

Premiums for straight life are constant during the life of the policy but are higher than for term insurance, in order to provide the company with the funds with which to build up the cash value. At the time of death the insured's beneficiary receives only the face amount of the policy, not the face amount plus accumulated savings. But if the insured survives he may cash in the policy at any time and receive the policy's cash value, at which time the policy is terminated. A person may also borrow the cash value of the policy from the insurance company, in which instance he pays a nominal rate of interest on the loan and the protection of the policy remains in force. However, the benefits that the insured's survivor will receive in the event of death will be reduced by the amount of the loan.

Limited-Payment Life Insurance   This sort of insurance is comparable to straight life, except that premiums are paid for a stated number of years or until the insured reaches a certain age, such as sixty or sixty-five. For example, a twenty-payment policy provides for premiums to be paid for twenty years, after which it is "paid up" and the protection remains in force until the insured dies or cashes in the policy. As with straight life, the face value is not paid unless the policyholder dies, but he may always withdraw the cash value, at which time the coverage ends. Loans may also be made against the cash value.

Premiums for limited-payment life are higher than for straight life because the policy is fully paid up within a given number of years. Such policies are generally recommended for persons or families who have high incomes in their early years but whose incomes might decrease later. Limited-payment life insurance is not a suitable form of insurance for most young couples starting a family, because they generally would not be able to afford to buy adequate protection in this way. Term insurance and straight life will give much more protection at lower cost.

Endowment Life Insurance   Savings are the primary emphasis in the endowment policy, but there is of course some protection provided. The basic purpose of this type of policy is to build up a certain sum of money in a given period of years. If the insured dies before the term of the policy has ended, the beneficiary receives the face value of the policy. If the insured lives to the end of the stated period, the face value is paid to him. The protection is small compared to the cost.

Endowment insurance can be purchased for ten, fifteen, twenty-twenty-five, or thirty years, or to "mature" and be cashed in at a stated age. When the policy matures, the cash value has built up to the face value. Premiums for endowment policies are of necessity much higher than for other types of policies because the emphasis is on savings. As shown earlier, other savings programs can achieve the same cash accumulation much more efficiently.

Which Life Insurance for You?

When considering life insurance you need to evaluate the product you are about to buy just as you would any other purchase. Many people who are selected as "prospects" let themselves be "sold" by neighborhood insurance agents or by friends or relatives who work for insurance companies. You should establish your own insurance program that meets your needs, on the basis of the following considerations.

1. What type of insurance do you need and when do you need it?
2. How much insurance do you need?
3. From whom should you buy life insurance?

What Type of Insurance Do You Need and When Do You Need It? In general your needs depend on the extent of your financial responsibility to others. Young single adults with no one dependent upon them need no life insurance. However, an unmarried adult may have responsibilities to a parent or relative, in which case he or she would be inclined to buy some protection for them. Young marrieds, when both partners are working, should concentrate on establishing a savings program rather than on protection, since dependency is not a prime consideration.

The real need for life insurance usually begins when the first child is expected. If the mother soon will be giving up her job, the young husband needs to provide for mother and child in the event of his death. If the wife has reasonably good earning potential the main concern should be for the child's future. Term insurance will give the best protection at this stage.

As the family size increases, more protection is needed in the event of the father's death. The wife is less likely to go back to work while the children are young. At this stage in life, the couple may decide that they need a house of their own. Now the husband must consider his responsibilities as a homeowner as well as a father and his insurance protection must be increased. Mortgage insurance, which is term insurance on the life of the homeowner for the amount of the mortgage and which decreases as the mortgage decreases, is a good investment at this point. At this time decisions also need to be made

"Congratulations!
You have two more
tax deductions—and
you'll need more
insurance."

concerning the whole family's future goals. Usually this is the time when people choose straight life insurance to take advantage of the forced savings features. However, a combination of term insurance and your own savings plan is more efficient—if your family can maintain its discipline and adhere to the plan.

When children have grown and have become financially independent, life insurance can usually be reduced.

How Much Insurance Do You Need?   Since the actual date of a person's death can't be predicted, a definitive answer to this question is almost impossible. One consideration is that if you need insurance at all, you generally need as much as you can afford. Another way of answering the question is to calculate how much your family would need if you died now.

Take an inventory of your current assets and liabilities to make an assessment of your insurance needs. The assets of your survivors would consists of:

1. The total of all life insurance benefits if you were to die now—less any loans against the insurance;
2. Social Security benefits to survivors;
3. Death benefits from your employer for your survivors;
4. Benefits from pension plans;
5. Cash on hand in savings and checking accounts;
6. Equity in real estate (present value less mortgage balance);
7. Assets such as jewels, artwork, coin collections, stocks, antiques, and other items which have a market value.

Your survivors' liabilities would consist of:

1. Immediate expenses that have to be met, such as medical bills, funeral expenses, mortgage payments, and other uninsured debts (remember that Social Security pays a limited amount toward the funeral costs of the deceased);
2. The living needs of the family.

In considering the family's living needs, ask yourself how much will be necessary for such things as food, shelter, transportation, clothing, and health protection. How much will the family need to meet future goals, such as education and retirement?

Social Security payments are available to children under eighteen when a parent dies; the benefits are extended to age twenty-two if the child goes to college. Widow's benefits are payable while the widow is caring for dependent children and from the time she reaches sixty-two. Provision should definitely be made for income to fill the gap between the time the last child becomes eighteen (or twenty-two, if in school) and the time the widow attains age sixty-two and becomes eligible for her own or her husband's retirement benefits. But even when Social Security benefits are available, as we will see later in the chapter, they are seldom enough to enable your survivors to maintain their lifestyle. Knowing how much is available to your dependents through Social Security and your other assets enables you to calculate the difference that needs to be provided by means of life insurance. In effect, when you buy protection for your dependents you are deciding how much income should be provided by your insurance to make up the difference between what is available to them from your current resources and what is needed to sustain them in the years after you are gone. Your family's goals if you survive should also be taken into consideration when you decide on how much of your current earnings should be set aside for protection. Often it is not possible to buy enough insurance to provide the protection you would like. But having examined all of the factors that go into the decision enables you to make a rational one —one which you can be comfortable with now, and which you can revise as your income and situation change.

From Whom Should You Buy Life Insurance? When you purchase insurance you want to buy from a company that is well established and licensed to do business in your state. The giant insurance companies do not necessarily offer the most reasonably priced insurance. Shop around for the company that offers the best buy, remembering that in comparing prices you should use figures based on your own age and your own insurance needs.

In comparing insurance costs you should be aware that there are two types of insurance companies—stock companies and mutual companies. A stock company, like any other corporation, is owned and operated by the stockholders. A mutual life insurance company is owned by the policyholders; it has no stock and no stockholders. Each policyholder has a vote in the management of a mutual company just as each stockholder has in a stock company.

All mutual life insurance in the United States pay dividends but not all stock companies do. Mutual companies give a refund to their policyholders when they do not use all of the fund set aside from premiums to pay death benefits or when favorable investment and operating procedures result in a profit. Policies under these circumstances are called *participating*. In order to compete with mutual companies, most stock companies also sell participating policies that in effect give the policy holder a rebate at the end of the year. Premium payments are so set that there is enough left over to pay a dividend at year's end. *Nonparticipating* policies do not pay a dividend but are generally lower priced to begin with.

Unfortunately, it is not possible to say whether the net cost of insurance will be less for a participating or nonparticipating policy, or for a stock versus a mutual company. When buying insurance you should understand that the *net* annual premium (premium payment less dividends) is only an estimate. Some years dividends are high; other years they are low.

Friends or relatives may advise you about agents who represent companies that have given them satisfaction. You should, however, realize that the types of policies that suited your friends may not necessarily meet your needs.

Beware of the agent who insists that only some high-priced combination policy will suit your family's needs. It may make you "insurance poor" while the agent gains a good commission. You should also shun the agent who wants you to drop your present policy to buy his. Always call first upon your original insurance company for help in evaluating your situation; then you can decide if a change in company is justified.

There are several good ways to buy insurance without dealing directly with a commercial insurance company. In the states of Connecticut, Massachusetts, and New York savings banks sell life insurance at minimal rates. Fraternal, professional, and alumni associations offer

"Trust me!
Just sign here."

their members group plans underwritten by insurance companies at low rates. Some group plans have the additional advantage of not requiring a physical examination before the policy is issued. Many private employers provide group plans to their employees; these are often excellent buys, since the company may pay all or part of the premium. Buying insurance protection from these sources saves you promotional costs, advertising costs, and agents' commissions.

You have the responsibility to choose the kind and amount of life insurance that most adequately meets your and your family's needs. Compare your alternatives carefully before you make your final decision.

Disability Insurance

Disability insurance protects you against loss of income through disability arising from sickness or accident. Payments are made to the insured at a stated monthly rate for a certain period while he is totally or partially disabled. Generally these payments do not begin until the insured has been disabled for a specified length of time, called the "elimination period" or "waiting period." In some policies benefits for total disability are different from those for partial disability.

You may be protected by some form of disability insurance under an employer's plan, under the laws of your state (workmen's compensation for "on-the-job" injuries), or under Social Security. Therefore, before buying any plan, check the extent of your current coverage.

The protection you get from this type of insurance depends on how your insurance company defines "disability." Total disability may

"Unfortunately, the insurance company says you aren't totally disabled. You can still move your toes."

be considered to exist only when you are "confined to bed" or "unable to leave your home." In other policies total disability is defined as incapacity to engage in your usual work, or as incapacity to do any type of work. Naturally, how you are compensated and whether you are compensated at all depend on which definition the company uses. Know what you are buying before you commit yourself.

Some policies have shorter elimination periods but higher premiums. You should select the waiting period that is consistent with your needs. It is unwise to choose a short waiting period that you pay for in higher premiums if you have sufficient reserves to carry you over a longer period.

The following questions will help you to decide about the disability insurance that will fit your needs.

Is there a waiting period before benefits begin? How long is it?

Does the waiting period differ for sickness and accidents?

How is "total disability" defined?

Will the company pay for partial disability, and how is that defined?

What is the weekly or monthly benefit?

How long will benefits be paid for illness? How long for accidents?

Can the policy be renewed?

What are the exclusions and limitations of the policy?

Will income from workmen's compensation or Social Security or disability income from your employer affect benefit payments?

Get the facts—before you buy.

Protection Through Social Security and Pension Plans

Most people have protection through the provisions of the Social Security Act, and many are protected by private pension plans provided by the companies for which they work. The benefits that are available from such sources need to be recognized and considered when you buy protection. The protection you buy should be supplemental to that provided by the other sources.

The Social Security Act

Since the 1930s the United States government has provided a program of benefits under the Social Security Act which insures those people who are eligible of income when earnings stop and when a family member retires, dies, or becomes disabled. During your working years you and your employer contribute to the Social Security fund which forms the basis for these protection payments. Under the act, as amended in 1974, contributions are made according to the schedule shown in Table 9.2.

Part of the money collected goes for retirement payments, payments to survivors, and disability benefits. Some of the Social Security fund goes to pay for hospital bills when workers or their families reach age sixty-five. Some of the money is for persons sixty-five and over who elect to contribute to a medical insurance fund. The common name for the hospitalization and medical insurance programs is Medicare.

TABLE 9.2
Contribution Rate
Schedule for
Employers and
Employees*

Year	Total	Retirement, Survivors', and Disability Insurance	Hospital Insurance	Maximum Annual Tax on $14,000 of Earnings
1975–1977	5.85%	4.95%	0.90%	$819
1978	6.05	4.95	1.10	847
1981	6.30	4.95	1.35	882
1986	6.45	4.95	1.50	903

*The amounts are expressed as percentages of the taxable base income, which was $14,000 in mid-1975 but which is allowed to rise as necessary to keep pace with increases in payments. The percentages shown are contributed both by the employer and by the employee.

Benefit payments under the Social Security Act depend on the level of earnings of a covered worker during his working years and on the contributions he has made to the fund prior to becoming eligible for benefits. Your local Social Security office will calculate the exact amount for you.

Now we should look at each type of benefit in more detail.

Retirement Income   A person who is eligible for Social Security retirement benefits may receive up to $341.00 per month after the age of sixty-five. If this person has a spouse who is also aged sixty-five they could receive as much as $511.50 per month. If he likes, a person can begin to collect his retirement benefits at age sixty-two. But in that case he receives only 80 percent of what he would have been entitled to at sixty-five. For each month that the retirement benefits are collected before age sixty-five, there is a reduction in amount of five-ninths of one percent. For example, if you take your benefits at age sixty-four you lose twelve times five-ninths of one percent, or 6.7 percent of your monthly payment.

Survivors' Income   There is a lump-sum payment for funeral expenses of $255.00 upon the death of an eligible worker. How much additional his surviving spouse and dependents, if any, would receive depends on the age at the time of death, the person's income since age twenty-two, the age of the spouse, and the number and ages of the dependents. For example, a man who has been earning $800.00 per month dies at age forty-five and leaves a forty-five-year-old widow with two children aged fifteen and ten. His wife and children will each receive $141.70 per month, or a total of $425.10. If there were only one child the survivors would each receive $180.70.

Disability Income   Persons covered by the Social Security Act are eligible for disability income if they will be disabled for one year or more. They may receive their first check for disability after five months. How much they receive depends on age and previous earnings, but it is possible for a disabled person to receive a maximum of $466.00 per month.

Hospitalization Insurance for the Elderly   Persons sixty-five or over are eligible for up to 90 days of government-paid hospital care (except for the first $92.00 worth). They are also entitled to up to 20 days of post-hospitalization care in an extended-care facility or a convalescent home. In addition, the government will handle all but $13.00 per day for an additional 80 days for each illness. In the 365 days after release from a hospital or nursing home, elderly patients are eligible for 100 visits by nurses or health workers.

Medical Insurance for the Elderly   Persons over sixty-five may buy medical insurance from the government for $6.70 per month, or a total of $80.40 per year. This provides 80 percent reimbursement for reasonable charges of physicians and surgeons, less a $60 deductible. Members of this program are also entitled to outpatient hospital care, hospital services for diagnosis, and home health visits up to 100 per year, even without hospitalization. Other services such as diagnostic tests, and purchase or rental of medical equipment such as wheel chairs, are also included.

Pension Plans

Many employers have established for their workers pension or retirement plans which are supplemental to Social Security benefits. In some instances pension plans have provided sufficient income for retirees to maintain themselves without Social Security. However, because of a number of abuses in private pension plans, Congress in 1974 enacted the Pension Reform Act, which is having a tremendous impact upon all employees and their retirement plans.

Under the act, standards have been established for participation in pension plans and for their vesting and funding. These standards provide protection to those who depend on pension plans for their retirement income.

Participation   Under the rules an employee must be eligible for a plan once he or she has put in one year of service and has achieved the age of twenty-five. However, a plan that provides for 100 percent vesting after three years may defer participation until an employee has three years of service behind him. Furthermore, employees who start employment within five years of retirement can be excluded from participation.

Vesting   Once an employee's rights to benefits become *vested*—that is, nonforfeitable—only death can take them away from him. Under the prior law, pension plans were not required to provide vested or nonforfeitable rights until actual retirement. As a result, if an employee switched jobs, lost his job, or left the company for any other reason, he lost all of the rights he had built up under the plan, regardless of the number of years he had participated in it. Under the new law a plan must provide an employee:

1. Complete vesting, or complete rights to the normal retirement benefits, on reaching normal retirment age.
2. Complete vesting of all accrued benefits to which he is entitled because of his own contributions to the plan. In other words, if he leaves the company after ten years, he must receive the benefits to which his ten years of contribution have entitled him, whether he is of retirement age or not.

3. Complete vesting of all accrued benefits to which he is entitled because of his *employer's* contributions to the plan, under one of the following alternatives:
   a. Graduated fifteen-year vesting: After five years of service the employee has a vested right to 25 percent of the benefits accrued from his employer's contributions. For the next five years each additional year of service brings him an additional 5 percent, and for each of the five years after that he receives an additional 10 percent. Thus after fifteen years he is fully vested.
   b. Ten-year vesting: Employees with ten years of service have the right to 100 percent of the benefits derived from their employer's contributions.
   c. The Rule of Forty-Five: An employee with at least five years of service has a nonforfeitable right to at least 50 percent of the accrued benefits derived from his employer's contributions when the sum of the employee's age and his number of years of service reaches forty-five. For each succeeding year of service, the percentage goes up ten points, so that after an additional five years the employee has a 100 percent vested interest in his accrued benefits.

Funding   In the past some retirees have found that, although they were entitled to substantial benefits, the pension fund had no money to pay them. Rules have now been established so that an employer's contributions to a plan will be sufficient to provide not only for the normal costs of the plan, but also for past service costs and expense losses. Thus retirees under private pension plans will have the assurance that there are adequate funds to provide them with the benefits which they were promised.

The new Pension Reform Act also establishes specific rules for computing years of service and accrued benefits and sets forth record-keeping requirements that protect the rights of employees. In addition there are a number of other rules and regulations to protect workers who leave the employer as well as those who retire under the terms of the plan.

If you work for an employer who maintains a pension plan, whether or not you make individual contributions, you should know all the rights and benefits to which you are entitled. Your employer is required to file an annual report with the Secretary of the Treasury which states the names of all participants who have left employment in that year along with their accrued benefits. The employer must also advise each participating employee who has left of his accrued benefits. The plan administrator must furnish a statement of the benefit rights to any participant who requests it. So the information is available to you. It is your own responsibility to learn the facts and be aware of your rights.

The Secretary of the Treasury transfers reports received from your employer to the Social Security Administration so that the information is in your file and can be made available to you or your beneficiaries at death or retirement.

The law also provides that an individual who is not covered by an employer's retirement plan can establish his own plan by setting aside a tax-free sum of up to 15 percent of his earned income, to a maximum of $1,500 per year. If a husband and wife both work they may each set up their own plans. Persons who are self-employed may establish their own so-called Keogh plans which enable them to set aside 15 percent or up to $7,500 of their income each year for retirement. Individual plans and Keogh plans can take the form of savings accounts, mutual funds, stocks, retirement annuities, or retirement bonds.

If your employer does not have a retirement or pension plan to which you can belong, or if you are self-employed, you should contact your banker, a trust officer at your bank, a reliable investment adviser, or an insurance representative in whom you have confidence for specific details as to how to establish a retirement plan that matches your own individual needs.

GLOSSARY OF NEW TERMS

Cash value   The dollar value of a policy that has been built up through payment of premiums. Also known as "cash surrender value."

Disability insurance   Also referred to as "income insurance," this provides for weekly or monthly benefits to the insured in the event of a disabling accident or illness.

Endowment life insurance   A type of insurance that covers the life of the insured while building up a cash reserve payable to the insured if he lives to the end of the term. This type of policy emphasizes savings rather than protection.

Face value   The amount for which a policy is written (usually in multiples of $1,000). Also referred to as "death benefit."

Limited-payment life insurance   A type of life insurance in which the payments are limited in number. Once the last payment is made, the policy remains in force until the insured dies or withdraws its cash value.

Participating policy   A policy that provides for a refund of excess premiums.

Pension or retirement plans   Programs that may be funded by employers, employees, or both to provide for retirement benefits.

Social Security   A program of benefits mandated by Congress that provides for retirement, survivors', and disability income, as well as hospitalization and medical payments (Medicare) for the elderly.

Straight (or ordinary) life insurance   This type of life insurance provides coverage for as long as the insured cares to continue it. The policy also incorporates a savings plan that builds up a cash value.

Term life insurance   A type of pure life insurance that is written for a specific period of time.

Vesting   A process whereby a participant in a pension plan receives nonforfeitable rights to the benefits of that plan.

QUESTIONS FOR DISCUSSION

1. Name the four basic types of life insurance and state the unique features of each.
2. Which type of life insurance affords the greatest protection for a family with young children at the least cost? Explain why this is so and how the program is set up.
3. Which types of life insurance include a "savings" feature? Consider the advantages and disadvantages of accumulating savings through investing in insurance.
4. Discuss borrowing money on an insurance policy. On what types of policy can one borrow money, and how is the amount determined?
5. Explain how the need for life insurance varies according to the family's stage in the life cycle.
6. Explain how Social Security fits into the family's protection plan. For what period would a widow be without Social Security benefits should the "breadwinner" die?
7. Discuss the characteristics of a reliable insurance agent and how to select an agent.
8. What is meant by "disability insurance"? Explain the disability coverage provided by law in your state.
9. Discuss the provisions of the Pension Reform Act.
10. Explain how a self-employed person can set up a pension plan and how much he or she is permitted to contribute yearly to the plan.

SUGGESTED STUDENT ACTIVITIES

1. Compute your family's financial need should the "breadwinner's" pay cease because of death or disability. Use a table like Worksheet 9.1. Figure out how much will be needed yearly and the total number of years the need will exist.
2. If you are considering purchasing insurance, ask a reliable agent to review your computation of insurance needs and explain the various types of coverage, along with the cost and advantages or disadvantages of each plan. Summarize the information you have obtained.
3. Consult a representative from the Social Security Administration to determine the benefits your family would receive in case of your death or disability. Find out about changes in Social Security laws, anticipated increases in costs, and the length of time the coverage would extend.
4. Review your present insurance program to determine whether you are overinsured or underinsured. Also analyze your coverage to see if you are getting the maximum coverage for the money spent.

WORKSHEET 9.1
Your Family's
Financial Needs
If the Breadwinner
Dies or Becomes
Disabled

Burial expenses and cost of administering
   estate $_____

Uninsured debts   _____

Living expenses   _____

Educational fund for children   _____

                                    Total $_____

5. Examine your insurance policy, or a policy on a member of your family, to see if it has a cash value. If it does, determine the current value. Contact your insurance agent or banker to find out if you can borrow against the cash value and the rate of interest you would be required to pay.

6. Secure a copy of an endowment insurance policy; analyze the amount of insurance coverage and the savings benefits. Consider providing the same protection through term insurance and investing the money you save from the lower premium in bonds, a credit union, or a savings and loan association. Calculate the amounts of money you would save by the various plans over a twenty-year period.

7. Check the telephone directory to determine the various insurance companies in your community. Visit four different companies and compare the costs of policies of the same type from the competing firms. Prepare a chart of your findings.

8. Investigate the laws in your state concerning workmen's compensation. Find out how to apply for benefits should you be injured on the job.

9. Talk to the personnel directors from three local firms to find out their plans for compensating persons injured on the job. Explain your findings to the class.

10. Interview the person in charge of administering the pension plan for a major corporation in your area. Find out how employees qualify for retirement benefits, how benefits are funded, and how the retirement fund is managed. Ask about the investment policy of the managers and the changes (if any) caused by the Pension Reform Act.

11. Talk with someone who is self-employed and find out what type of retirement pension plan he has set up, if any. If he does not have a pension plan, explain the Keogh plan to him and suggest sources of additional information about the plan.

FOR ADDITIONAL INFORMATION

Bailard, Thomas E., David Beihl, and Ronald W. Kaiser. *Personal Money Management*. Chicago: Science Research Associates, 1973, pp. 41–44.

Provides information on determining the amount of insurance needed and on evaluating insurance rates and various types of insurance policies. Case problems are included.

"Buy Insurance Like the Experts and Save." *Changing Times*, January 1974, pp. 21–23.

Identifies and explains the basic principles followed by professionals who buy insurance for business firms. These principles can be applied to life, property, or health insurance, or to whatever other kind of policy you're buying.

Comarow, Avery. "Six-Figure Life Insurance for Three-Figure Premiums." *Money*, March 1975, pp. 67–70.

The author shows how term policies can be fashioned to fit the tight budgets of young families who need insurance most.

Concise Explanation of Pension Reform Law. Englewood Cliffs, N.J.: Prentice-Hall, 1974.

A paperback publication that provides a wealth of information on pensions and the Pension Reform Act.

Degener, Jo. "How to Scale Down Insurance Costs." *Money*, April 1975, pp. 68–72.

Points out how to trim unnecessary coverage—by raising some deductibles, for example, and by shopping for insurance bargains. Covers auto, homeowner's, health, life, and disability insurance.

Denenberg, Herbert. *The Shopper's Guidebook to Life Insurance, Health Insurance, Auto Insurance, Homeowner's Insurance, Doctors, Dentists, Lawyers, Pensions, Etc.* Washington, D.C.: Consumer News, 1974.

A former commissioner of the Pennsylvania Insurance Department attempts to inform the public about important facts not otherwise available. A good source of information to help you save money when buying insurance.

Dreyfus, Patricia A. "How to Be Your Own Pension Manager." *Money*, May 1975, pp. 64–66.

The author explains who is eligible to establish a private pension plan under the Pension Reform Act of 1974 and suggests ground rules to follow in setting up a plan.

Federal Trade Commission. *Mail Order Insurance*. Consumer Bulletin No. 1. Washington, D.C.: Government Printing Office, 1971. 8 pp., single copy free.

Describes deceptive practices used by companies in selling insurance by mail.

"A Guide to Life Insurance." *Consumer Reports*, January 1974, pp. 35–66; February 1974, pp. 135–150; March 1974, pp. 219–250.

A special series in three parts that provides concrete aids to help the consumer in shopping for life insurance.

Institute of Life Insurance. *Pension Facts 1974*. New York, n.d.

An information source on pension matters. A bibliography of selected readings on pensions is included.

"A Life Insurance Policy That Costs Less." *Changing Times*, January 1975, pp. 23–24.

Explains a new kind of whole-life policy that is now available at an amazingly low premium.

Main, Jeremy. "How Much Life Insurance Is Enough?" *Money*, January 1974, pp. 31–36.

An exceptionally interesting answer to the question posed by the title.

Worksheets and models are included to aid the reader in determining his own need.

Mumey, Glen A. *Personal Economic Planning.* New York: Holt, Rinehart and Winston, 1972, pp. 189–231.

Clear explanations of Social Security, workmen's compensation, and various types of insurance are presented in this text.

"Sizing Up the Agent Who Sells You Life Insurance." *Changing Times*, October 1974, p. 39.

Lists criteria to use in sizing up an agent.

Stillman, Richard J. *Guide to Personal Finance: A Lifetime Program of Money Management.* Englewood Cliffs, N.J.: Prentice-Hall, 1975, pp. 175–213.

Contains helpful material on Social Security and retirement.

"A Three-Part Report on the 1974 Pension Reform Law." *Changing Times.* Comprised of: "The New Pension Law Could Be Good News for You," December 1974, pp. 7–10; "No Pension Plan? Now You Can Write Your Own," January 1975, pp. 37–39; "Self-Employed? Build Yourself a Better Pension," March 1975, pp. 31–33.

These three articles explain in layman's language the new pension law.

10

Spending for Health and Recreation

10

We cannot derive satisfactions from the money we spend unless we have good health to enjoy our spending. Every money plan needs to provide funds to maintain proper physical, mental, and emotional fitness and to take care of unexpected illness. Recreation and sound health practices should be a part of every person's program for living. Money spent to maintain the best possible health and enjoy the most satisfying recreation, consistent with an individual's lifestyle, is a sound investment.

You know how important it is to plan your spending for food, clothing, and other things. Planning for health expenses is equally as important but is more complicated because health costs are not as predictable and regular as are other expenditures. It is much more difficult to make provision for health care than it is to make decisions about some of the other items in your money plan.

In this chapter you will learn how to establish a spending plan for expected and unexpected medical expenses, how to keep in good health, and where to get professional advice and health treatment to meet your needs. You will also learn how to decide about recreational costs in your money plan.

Planning for Health Costs

The cost of medical services varies for different individuals and different families, according to their needs. To establish a spending plan to meet these needs, consideration must be given to the size, age, and sex of family members, as well as to any individual health problems. Small children and aged parents have special health needs as do persons with identified health disorders. Furthermore, health care costs have become so expensive in recent years that they can seldom be met out of current income. In order to provide for health care costs, you will need to establish a reserve in your money plan should the need arise. The cost of medical services in your community and the health service agencies that are available need to be taken into account when you are establishing your plan; so do your income, your goals, your values, and the other items in your money plan.

With all of these factors in mind, you can establish a spending plan for health care that will adequately provide for all your health needs. Your plan should include:

1. Health insurance to protect against unexpected and major health expenses as well as prolonged illness;
2. A reserve fund that covers those items not included in your insurance, such as drugs.

Health Insurance

Health insurance protects you against the expenses that occur as a result of sickness or accident. This insurance is presently provided through private insurance companies and nonprofit associations such as Blue Cross and Blue Shield. There is considerable discussion in the Congress for establishing a program of national health insurance, and many predict that government-sponsored or -regulated health insurance will be available before 1980. This type of insurance may cover part or all of the expenses for hospitalization, laboratory work, X rays, surgery, physicians' examinations, prescribed drugs, and nursing care. Coverage is sometimes available for individual categories of expense, and sometimes as a "package" that includes a variety of items.

It is often very difficult to sort out the facts in order to make decisions about the coverage you want to buy, because health insurance contracts are complex and detailed. If you consider the following six questions you will be more able to decide what is best for you.

Who Is Paying for the Coverage?   Many people have health insurance available through their employers, their unions, or other organizations to which they belong. In these group-plan insurance programs the types and amounts of coverage may be fixed, and employees or members may not have options available. In many instances the employer pays all or a portion of the premiums for the health insurance coverage. That portion of the premium that the employee pays is generally deducted from wages. Group protection usually provides more comprehensive coverage at a lower rate than do individual policies.

Under Medicare, which we discussed in Chapter 9, some of the health expenses of many older persons are paid for by the government. The Social Security Administration handles the Medicare program. For details concerning the program and eligibility for it, ask for a free copy of *Your Medicare Handbook* at the Social Security Administration office in your area. If you are eligible for Medicare, you will want to know its benefits so that you can calculate whether you need additional coverage.

What Types of Expenses Are Covered by the Insurance?   Every policy explains the kinds of expenses it covers and the conditions under which the company will pay claims. Hospital coverage, which is the simplest form of health insurance, will often pay only a fixed amount for the room and other services while you are in the hospital. Outpatient treatment is generally not included. Coverage for costs other than those incurred in a hospital is available, but you need to have exact information about what types of expenses the policy covers and under what conditions. Get the details before you buy! Are you willing to buy insurance for all hospital costs, or will partial coverage be sufficient? Do you want coverage for visits to your doctor's office and for laboratory tests? The

Know your coverage
before you need it.

choice should be yours, not that of anyone else, and your decision should be based on what you want and what you are able to afford.

How Much Will the Policy Pay? You need to know the limits and restrictions that are written into each policy. You may have seen glowing advertisements that promise "$52,000 extra cash" when you are in the hospital and "$250 tax-free each week." To get $52,000 at the benefit rate of $250 per week you would have to be hospitalized for four years. The average hospital stay is eight days; even among persons with the highest rate of hospitalization the average is only twelve days.

To be sure about what the policy does and does not cover, get a copy of it and read the fine print as well as the large print. Find out what the limits and restrictions are. If you do not understand the policy ask the company representative to explain the items you do not comprehend. Again, get the details before you buy!

Is There a Waiting Period Before Benefits Go into Effect? Usually individual policies (in contrast to group plans) have a clause which states that you cannot collect during the first two years for an illness you had before you enrolled. Sometimes you may not receive benefits even though you did not know the condition existed when you bought the policy. In some policies there may be more than one kind of waiting period. Know the coverage you are buying.

Is the Policy Renewable? If a policy is stated to be "noncancellable" the company cannot cancel until the premium period ends. That is, the company cannot cancel the policy during a particular premium period as long as you have made your payments. However, the company can refuse to renew the policy once the premium period has ended. Few companies offer a truly noncancellable policy—that is, one which stays in force as long as you continue to pay the premiums. This is important, since your insurability may change over a period of years because of accidents or illness.

When reading the policy you will generally find that the company can cancel, refuse renewal, or raise premiums if it does so for all "policyholders of the same class." A "class" may mean all people of the same state with the same coverage, or all people in the same age group. Some companies will guarantee renewal but maintain the right to raise premiums on a class basis. Once more, get the details before you buy.

Is the Company Licensed in Your State? When considering a given company for health insurance, find out if it is licensed by your own state. If the company *is* licensed in your state, you will be able to take any complaints you may have to the state insurance department, which can initiate proceedings against the company. If the company is not licensed in your state, the state's insurance commissioner has no jurisdiction over it. You can find out if the company you are considering is licensed by contacting your state insurance department.

When putting together your health insurance program, you will need to consider such basic coverage as hospitalization costs, surgery, regular medical expenses, and major medical expenses. *Hospitalization benefits* cover all or part of hospital room and board, operating room charges, laboratory fees, X rays, drugs, dressings, and sometimes special nurses' fees. *Surgical benefits* are paid according to a schedule of surgical procedures that lists the maximum that will be paid for specific types of operations. *Regular medical expenses* include physicians' fees in the hospital, in your home, or at the doctor's office.

Few people can afford to pay the medical bill that will accumulate for serious or prolonged illness, even with the coverage outlined above. *Major medical* or catastrophe insurance serves to cover illnesses that extend over considerable periods of time and require expensive surgery and hospitalization.

An infinite variety of combinations can be purchased that include different benefit amounts and different deductibles for each of the coverages outlined above. You need to decide what coverage you want —and can afford.

Remember that the purpose of the insurance is to protect you against unexpected and excessively large health-care costs. It is not feasible to use health insurance as a source of income when you are ill, nor is its purpose to cover all costs. The more all-inclusive the benefits in your policy, the more you will have to pay for them in premiums.

Once you have decided on a plan of health insurance, you should review your program periodically to see that it is up to date and adequate to meet any changes that have occurred in your needs. All members of the family should be aware of the protection you have. Be sure that they know where the policies are kept. Keep your insurance records up to date, and let your insurance company know about changes in your status or address.

Pay your premiums promptly. If premiums for your insurance are not deducted from your paycheck by your employer, be sure to pay them when they are due. Be sure that you have made the necessary provisions in your money plan. If you lose your job or change employers find out what happens to your coverage. Does it follow you? Does it end? How may it be maintained? Do not assume that your coverage is continued.

A Medical Reserve Fund

Your plan for a medical reserve fund will depend partly on those routine health costs not included in your health insurance, such as expenses for ordinary drugs and medicines that you keep in your home. Office visits to your doctor for illnesses, routine medical checkups, and inoculations must be paid for. Provision should also be made for unexpected health costs. Although these unexpected costs are difficult to predict, some reserve must be set aside for them in your money plan. One way of estimating the size of your reserve fund is to go back and examine your records to learn what you have spent for health care last year. Make a list of your annual noninsured health costs, including your drugs and medicines. Divide the average per year of these past expenditures by the number of pay periods you have each year. The result is the amount you should set aside each payday for your medical reserve fund.

Keeping records of uninsured medical expenses will enable you to plan your future spending for health and will provide you with documentation of medical expenses for possible deductions on your income tax return.

Drugs and Medicines

Drugs and medicines represent a substantial portion of the costs incurred in maintaining good health. Some drugs are available only with a doctor's prescription. Others may be purchased over the counter without a prescription. Over-the-counter drugs should be used only in accordance with directions, and in most instances it is prudent to consult your family physician before using these products at all. While over-the-counter drugs must be approved by the Food and Drug Administration before being placed on sale, and may not cause you injury when used as directed, they often don't help and are a waste of money. Attempting to avoid a physician's fee by treating yourself with over-the-counter drugs is a false and foolish economy.

There is considerable controversy currently taking place about the cost of drugs to the consumer. A large spread in prices exists between advertised, brand-name drugs and the less well-known *generic* drugs. For example, Librium, a well-known branded mood drug, costs almost twice as much as the same drug under its generic name of chlordiazetoxide hydrochloride. Professionals, manufacturers, consumer groups, and legislators have different views which have not as yet been reconciled. Discuss the matter of generic drugs with your physician before he writes the prescription.

Once the prescription is written, the druggist must fill it as the doctor has ordered. You should, however, compare the costs and the services of various pharmacists before you make the decision as to who gets your drug dollar. There is a movement to lift the prohibition on advertising prescription prices. Consumerists maintain that advertising prices will increase competition between pharmacists and reduce prices in the long run. The pharmaceutical professional organizations insist that advertising prices will cause a deterioration in professional services. A few states now permit druggists to display prescription prices in their stores. Whatever the practice in your community, you should shop carefully and compare the prices of prescription drugs. You will find a wide range of prices for the same drug in the same quantities.

Keeping in Good Health

The United Nations' World Health Organization defines health as "a state of complete physical, mental and social well-being and not merely the absence of disease and infirmity." Physical, mental, and social well-being are interrelated and each is necessary for healthful and effective living.

While good health is a basic requirement for every individual, the maintenance thereof is not a simple matter. Doctors and health-care delivery services are important ingredients of a sound health program, but there are other important aspects of health maintenance that should be recognized. Adequate housing, good nutrition, exercise and recreation, sound hygiene, and proper education are probably as important to a good health program as are professional health-care services.

The American Medical Association has outlined the following "paths to fitness."

Proper medical care, including routine examinations and prompt treatment for illnesses and accidents
Good nutrition, based on a proper diet

Keeping in good
health means
working at it.

Good dental care, through routine checkups, regular brushing, and
prompt treatment of dental problems

Physical activity suitable to your physical condition and planned for
own satisfaction

Satisfaction in work, based on good working conditions, a feeling of
accomplishment, recognition, and an opportunity for self-expression

Play and recreation, for fun and to relieve tension

Rest and relaxation, including adequate sleep and enough changes in
routine

Professional Services and Facilities

Physicians, dentists, registered nurses, registered dietitians, and
medical technicians are some of the professionals who help you maintain your health or restore it when you are ill. Hospitals, nursing
homes, and various other tax-supported and private health agencies

are the places where most medical services are available. You should know who can provide the services you need in your community.

Physicians

A *general practitioner*, often referred to as a family physician, is trained to treat a wide variety of illnesses. If he cannot determine the cause of your complaint, he will call on the services of a specialist. If your physician does not refer you to a specialist after what you believe to be a reasonable period of treatment, you should ask him to do so.

A *specialist*, such as a surgeon, is a physician who has had general medical training plus at least two years of concentration in a specific area of medical practice. Table 10.1 lists some of the specialists and their area of interest.

In addition to physicians, referred to as doctors of medicine, there are other doctors who offer services based on special theories of healing. An *osteopath* is a doctor who has had the same number of years of education and who has passed the same state board examinations as medical doctors. Originally osteopaths practiced on the theory that diseases arose chiefly from displacement of bones, causing pressure on nerves and blood vessels. They believed that a condition could be remedied by manipulation of the affected parts. Osteopaths are now permitted to prescribe drugs and practice surgery, may become members of the American Medical Association, and are generally considered to be similar to M. D.'s.

Osteopaths should not be confused with *chiropractors,* who receive a shorter period of education and are not permitted to prescribe drugs or perform surgery. Chiropractors treat illnesses by adjustments through hand pressure and by manipulation of joints, especially in the spine.

A *homeopath* treats patients on the theory that a disease is cured by remedies which would produce in a healthy patient effects similar to the symptoms of the complaint. A homeopath is permitted to prescribe drugs.

A *podiatrist* or *chiropodist* is one who treats feet, usually for corns, bunions, and problems of the nails. Ordinarily a podiatrist is not a physician and does not prescribe drugs.

An *optometrist* is a person who fits glasses. He should not be confused with an oculist or ophthalmologist, described in Table 10.1. An optometrist is generally not a graduate of a medical school. He can test your vision but cannot prescribe drugs.

Another term you may hear is *group medical practice.* This refers to an organizational structure of physicians who act as a team in the practice of medicine, sharing their knowledge and skills as well as office and laboratory facilities. Group medical practices may fall into any one of these categories:

TABLE 10.1	Title	Specialty
Medical Specialists	Anesthetist	Administration of anesthesia during surgery
	Cardiologist	Diseases of the heart
	Dermatologist	Skin ailments
	Gynecologist	Diseases of the female reproductive system
	Internist	Physical diseases, generally of the internal organs
	Neurologist	Disorders of the nervous system, including the brain and spinal cord
	Obstetrician	Pregnancy and childbirth
	Oncologist	Cellular diseases such as cancer
	Ophthalmologist or oculist	Diseases of the eyes and prescription of glasses
	Otolaryngologist	Ear, nose, and throat diseases
	Pediatrician	Children's illnesses and children's health maintenance
	Psychiatrist	Mental and emotional illness
	Radiologist	Treatment of a variety of diseases through radiation
	Surgeon	Surgical operations (some specialize in specific areas of the body or specific types of surgery)

1. *Clinics or medical centers.* These offer a choice of primary physicians as well as the services of other physicians, if needed. The group may treat patients in the clinic or in the patients' homes.
2. *Reference or specialty clinics.* These offer diagnosis or treatment of a particular disease, such as cancer, diabetes, or heart disease. The doctors function as a group only in the clinic and are generally called upon by other physicians for consultation.
3. *Prepaid group practice.* This type of arrangement offers group practice with a *prepayment* plan. Unlike other group services, which are paid for on a "fee-for-service" basis, the services of the prepaid group plan are usually offered for a stated monthly fee. You pay your dues, so to speak, and for them you receive whatever care you need. These groups, often organized by trade unions, communities, or insurance companies, provide preventative as well as curative services in the office, hospital, or patient's home. In some communities these groups are called health maintenance organizations, or HMOs. The charges of these groups vary, depending on the extent of the services offered and who sponsors them.

Dentists are trained to provide care of teeth and mouth, including diagnosis, correction, and repair. They keep their patients in good dental health through regular checkups, necessary treatment, and advice on oral hygiene. When necessary a dentist will recommend that his patient see a dental specialist. Table 10.2 lists the common areas of dental specialization.

Choosing Professional Services
Since competent and reliable medical services are so important, you should choose carefully so that you obtain the type of treatment you want and need. You will want to be under the care of a professional

TABLE 10.2
Dental Specialists

Title	Specialty
Oral pathologist	Diseases of mouth tissue, tumors, and injuries
Oral surgeon	Diseases and defects of jaws and extraction of teeth
Orthodontist	Irregularities in position of jaw and teeth
Pedodontist	Dental care of children
Periodontist	Diseases of gums and tissues supporting the teeth
Prosthodontist	Dental appliances and substitutes such as bridges and dentures
Public health dentist	Prevention and control of dental disease and promotion of dental health through public education

who is qualified to provide the services you need and in whom you have confidence.

Medical and dental professionals should be selected before you actually need them so that you can make your choice without pressure. If you do not have a family physician or family dentist, obtain the names of qualified persons from your local medical or dental society, a local hospital, or knowledgeable friends. Before making your selection

Pick the right professional.

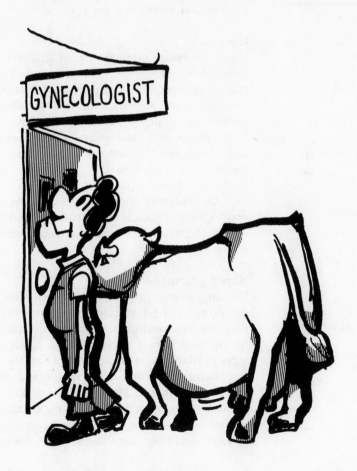

check with your local medical or dental society whether the one you are considering is:

1. A graduate of an approved medical or dental school;
2. Licensed to practice in your state;
3. A member of the local, state, and national medical or dental societies;
4. On a staff of a hospital in your area;
5. A person with a reputation for professional ethics and dependable service.

After checking his credentials, visit the doctor or dentist in his office. An appointment for a checkup is a good way to become established as a patient before any emergencies arise. This will give you an opportunity to talk with him, observe his manner and facilities, and make the decision about a future relationship. While in his office you should discuss fees and how they are to be paid so that you may avoid future misunderstanding and estimate the costs in your spending plan. If you are not satisfied that the professional will meet your needs, keep looking for one who will. Do not just assume that any professional is the one for you.

Hospitals

When necessary your physician will arrange to have you admitted to a hospital in which he has staff privileges or where you may obtain special services. The basic charge for your hospital stay is figured on a day-rate basis and depends on whether you have a private, semiprivate, or multiple-patient room. The day charge includes general nursing care and meals. Charges for operation room, anesthesia, drugs and dressings, laboratory tests, X-ray examinations, and physical therapy are added to the day charge. Fees for physicians' services are billed to you separately.

On entering the hospital you are usually required to establish your credit through an insurance card or other evidence of your ability to pay. Bills for service may be presented weekly or when the patient goes home.

Nursing Homes

Nursing homes provide care to patients who require hospitalization but do not need assistance in carrying on their daily activities because they are recovering from illness or injury or are chronically ill. Costs for nursing homes vary with the accommodations provided, the services available, and the amount of care the patient needs.

Before choosing a nursing home check with your physician or health department. Find out which homes are licensed or registered by local, state, or federal agencies, because these generally provide the proper services. Visit the home you are considering to examine the physical facilities, the food service, the provisions for safety, comfort, and privacy, the standards of sanitation and cleanliness, and the provisions for rehabilitation, recreation, and other activities. Learn which services are covered by the regular weekly or monthly charge, which services, if any, are covered by insurance or Medicare, and which services are charged for as "extras."

Only after you have investigated thoroughly will you be able to decide whether the nursing home is what you want and what you are able to afford.

Spending for Recreation

Recreation is essentially the use of free time to refresh the mind, the body, and the spirit. Such activity can contribute much to a program of health maintenance. Current employment practices, which limit employees to a forty-hour or shorter work week, provide leisure time and give people the opportunity to participate in recreational pursuits. But as the emphasis on leisure time grows, recreation becomes a real expense in the money plan. Sound decisions must be made about spending recreation dollars. You should know your own recreation needs and wants, and should be aware of the recreational opportunities and facilities in your own home and in your community.

Personal Recreation Needs

The kind of recreation you choose will depend, for the most part, on your occupation and lifestyle. If your work requires little physical activity you will probably want to spend your leisure time in active hobbies or sports like swimming, golfing, gardening, and working in a workshop. People who engage in physically strenuous occupations will probably prefer leisure-time activities such as reading, listening to music, and playing cards. Balancing your leisure-time and occupational activities makes it possible to enjoy and develop all of your interests, skills, and abilities.

Select those recreational activities that give you the greatest enjoyment for the money and time you spend. As persons mature their needs change, and they may wish to decide on different recreational activities. Whether you have a great deal of leisure time or only a limited amount available to you, you should plan to use the leisure hours in accordance with your own individual desires and abilities.

Active sports provide vigorous physical activity that promotes health and vitality. The competition of sports helps to develop a sense of fair play and honest effort, and the social contacts build friendships.

Spectator sports provide both emotional satisfaction and relaxation. Spectator sports may also provide the mental stimulation that increases learning and understanding.

Social activities give you the personal satisfaction of building friendships as well as the emotional satisfaction of belonging to a group. You may also develop a better knowledge of yourself and of other people by engaging in this type of activity.

Special activities such as music, painting, and reading enable you to develop your mind and your creative ability and help you build your individuality.

Community service—participating in political or social associations —fills a person's need to be useful and helps to develop a realistic attitude toward life.

Self-improvement activities, such as continuing your education or attending lectures, enrich you through new learning and increased skills.

Gardening can provide both physical activity and a means of contributing to the family food supply, provided you have the space. Gardening is a type of recreation in which all members of the family can participate. You can get a sense of pride and satisfaction from seeing plants grow and sharing their attractiveness or tastiness with your family.

Outdoor or adventure activities, such as hiking, camping, and nature study, bring a better understanding of man and his environment as well as the personally enriching experience of new places and new things.

Recreational Opportunities

There are unlimited sources for recreational activities in your home, in your community, and in your state and region. To plan your leisure time so that you get the most satisfaction, you need to know the possibilities that are available. Look around: There is a wide variety of opportunities within your reach if you will just seek them out.

Your own home has many opportunities for personal and family recreation. Personal hobbies such as reading, painting, workshop activities, and sewing will add to your growth and your enjoyment of leisure time. In your home you can "be yourself" and develop those abilities that free you from boredom and make life interesting. Family activities in the home, such as parties, barbecues, and games, strengthen family ties and improve understanding between family members. Participating in family fun will eventually help children to develop sound, satisfying relationships with others outside the family circle.

The home is also a good place to develop recreation inexpensively. Equipment for sports, games, or hobbies is a good investment that pays off in real enjoyment. Even the planning together for the purchase of home equipment can be a source of family fun and enjoyment.

In your community, too, there are countless opportunities for recreation. There are probably facilities for active participation in sports, for spectator activities, for social activities, and for self-improvement and community service. You can get information about facilities from your newspapers, chamber of commerce, friends, schools, park and recreation departments, and churches. Find the recreational activities that satisfy your needs and fit your money plan.

Throughout your section of the country you may also find many opportunities to enjoy your leisure time. Museums, parks, historical places, art centers, and any number of other interesting and exciting resources can be found within your own region. These regional leisure-time places provide inexpensive destinations for weekend vacations or day-long trips. Plan the activity so that you, or your friends and family, find the satisfaction you seek. You can get information about regional recreational opportunities from friends, local chambers of commerce, tourist bureaus, state conservation departments, newspapers, regional magazines and road maps.

Planning Vacations

Planning your vacation can be a source of pleasure in itself, but it also enables you to get the most satisfaction for the money you spend. Decide what you really want to do and how much you have available in your money plan for this type of activity. If you vacation alone, you have only your own desires to satisfy; but if the vacation includes friends or family, the plan should include activities that all can enjoy.

You may want to vacation at home and take advantage of the facilities in your community. Vacations spent at home provide inexpensive enjoyment. So, too, do camping trips on which groups can enjoy the pleasure and challenge of outdoor living.

Visits with friends or relatives with whom you are compatible and who want to accommodate you during your vacation are often a source of pleasure. Visiting enables you to renew and strengthen relationships.

Resorts at lakes, seashores, or other places can also be fun for those who like the activities offered and who enjoy meeting other people. The costs for this type of vacation may be reduced by taking advantage of "group" or "off-season" rates.

Visiting a new city can be a source of vacation satisfaction for those who can afford what the city has to offer. Accommodations, food, and entertainment for such vacations may be expensive. Smaller hotels and lodgings outside the high-rent center of a city may offer the most reasonable rates. College dormitories are available in some cities for vacationing visitors.

Group or package tours can be convenient and economical ways to travel. Such plans may be available through clubs or organizations to which you belong or through travel agencies.

You can obtain information that will help you plan your vacation through:

Auto clubs, chambers of commerce, travel associations, state tourist offices, government travel bureaus;
Airlines, steamship lines, train, bus, and gas stations;
Travel books and travel sections of newspapers and magazines;
Travel agencies.

To get maximum enjoyment and the most satisfaction for the money you spend, avoid the hazards of exhaustion, overeating, sunburn, and lack of sleep. Planning helps you get the most out of your vacation, but do not make the mistake of overplanning. Leave some flexibility in your plan so that you can rest, relax, and do some things spontaneously.

Plan the kinds of clothing and equipment that you will need for the activities that are associated with the places you go. Keep your wardrobe and equipment simple and essential. Handling excess baggage is not fun.

A Total Recreation Plan

Spending for recreation must of course fit into your total money plan. Since recreation is a flexible expense, it can be adjusted up or down depending on your other expenses and your own priorities. How much you spend depends on how much you can afford and on your decisions about what you enjoy.

Whatever the amount you spend for leisure-time activities, you will get more for your money if you make a plan. Be sure to include all leisure-time activities in the plan. Allocate the money you have to spend to the various activities—sports, hobbies, short trips, vacations, and so on. Include day-to-day activities, special events, and future recreational goals. Do not overlook the cost of special clothing, supplies, and equipment you will need. If other members of the family are to participate, be sure to involve them in the decision-making process. Day-to-day recreational expenses are usually paid for as they arise, but you will need to set aside money each pay period to handle larger expenses. Adjustments will probably need to be made as your personal interests and income change.

To gain greater enjoyment from your leisure hours, decide which recreational activities give you the most satisfaction and eliminate those you don't really like. To stretch your recreational dollar, use your imagination to find leisure-time activities at little cost. Free or inexpensive activities include reading books from the library, visiting parks, zoos, and museums, and attending free concerts, exhibits, and lectures. Gardening, hiking, and working with community organizations are other possibilities. You may be able to use your hobbies to earn extra money by making salable items, growing vegetables or flowers for sale, or developing salable skills.

There are many ways to enjoy the free time that contributes to sound mental, physical, and social well-being. Include in your program as many enjoyable activities as you can. Rising medical costs and the availability of increased leisure time have placed new emphasis on sound decision making for recreation. Wise management is needed to build a balanced recreational program that relieves stress and makes your life happier and more satisfying.

GLOSSARY OF NEW TERMS

Basic coverage Medical insurance that provides for at least some portion of hospitalization, surgery, and physicians' costs.

Clinic A gathering of physicians, students, and patients for the study and treatment of disease.

Fee-for-service A system currently in practice in which the patient pays for medical services as they are utilized.

Generic drugs Drugs that belong to a large class or family of drugs, as distinct from a special brand-name drug.

Health maintenance organization (HMO) A health-care organization that provides a complete range of medical services, all from the same source. Clients pay one fee in advance for all necessary health services.

Major medical plan A type of insurance coverage that provides benefits for catastrophic illness or accidents, in which the insured pays a certain amount—$50 or $100—before the insurer pays anything (deductible clause) and which requires the policyholder to pay part of the bill—20 or 25 percent—that remains after the deductible amount has been subtracted (coinsurance clause).

Prepaid group practice A name used to describe health maintenance organizations.

QUESTIONS FOR DISCUSSION

1. Define "health." Explain the requirements for good health maintenance during various stages of the family life cycle.
2. Discuss procedures one might use to select a competent and reliable physician or dentist.
3. Identify charges other than the cost of the hospital room that are added to the total bill when one is hospitalized.
4. What questions should be considered in selecting health insurance?
5. Consider some ways to cut the cost of the family drug bill.
6. Why has recreation received more emphasis recently?
7. Consider several different recreational activities and explain how an individual or family might make an intelligent selection from them.
8. Consider the advantages and disadvantages of one long vacation as opposed to several short vacation trips.
9. Where can one obtain information and help in planning a vacation?
10. Explain how one should set up funds for recreation in an overall spending plan.

SUGGESTED STUDENT ACTIVITIES

1. Review your records for the past year and add up all the funds that you paid out for health care. Be sure to include fees for visits to your physician, dentist, and oculist and the cost of the prescriptions and other medicines. Divide the total by your number of pay periods to find the average amount needed per pay period. Make a decision, based on this amount and your anticipated future needs (taking into account costs), as to how much to save in each pay period for health care.
2. Consult a hospital administrator in your community about the cost of hospitalization. Develop a chart showing the charges for private, semi-private, and multiple-patient rooms. Also list the charges for other services required while one is in the hospital. Find out how much the costs have increased in the past several years and the reasons for the increases.
3. Make a list of five or more common prescription drugs. Check the costs of these with as many pharmacists as possible. Make a chart to show how the charges for the same drugs vary.
4. Make a survey of recreational opportunities within fifty miles of your home. Consult travel agents, chambers of commerce, cooperative extension services, departments of parks and recreation, and so on. Prepare a bulletin or mimeograph of your findings and distribute it to interested persons.
5. Identify some creative kinds of recreational activities that appeal to you. Organize the ideas according to various types of activity: crafts, gardening, and so forth.
6. Prepare a list of the benefits of a sound recreational program.
7. Make a list of tips for travelers. Include advice on such things as getting information; selecting and staying in motels; making reservations; traveling by plane, train, bus, or car; eating in public establishments; selecting clothes and packing. Try to think of everything the traveler does.
8. Prepare a written account of a decision that you or your family made about vacation plans (where to go, what to do, and so on).
9. Report on some recreational activities or hobbies that can contribute to a person's income or lead to a full-time occupation.
10. Formulate a list of safety precautions one should take when camping, boating, biking, or traveling.
11. Prepare a report on a person's civic responsibility for protecting the environment when vacationing.
12. Interview the chairman of your city council or board of county commissioners to find out what portion of your tax dollar is spent to provide recreational opportunities. Also find out what plans are being considered for future developments. If possible, record your interview and share it with the class.

FOR ADDITIONAL INFORMATION

Blue Cross Association. *Generation in the Middle.* Chicago, 1970.
    Provides helpful suggestions for keeping fit after forty.
————. *Stress: Blueprint for Health.* Chicago, 1974.

A paperback, containing a series of articles by various doctors and others, that suggests ways to cope with stress and to learn to live successfully in today's world.

Boroson, Warren. "Diagnosing Your Health Insurance." *Money,* September 1974, pp. 39–51.

The need for adequate health insurance is forcefully presented, along with guidelines as to what constitutes adequate coverage. Advice from professionals on buying individual policies and a discussion of how to analyze a policy are included.

Bryant, Shari G. "Your Health and Recreation Dollar." Chicago: Money Management Institute, Household Finance Corporation, 1971.

This pamphlet tells how we can get the most from our recreation dollar by knowing our recreational needs and wants, by being aware of the recreational opportunities and facilities in our community, by planning vacation time, and by including recreational costs in overall financial planning.

Daley, Margaret. "Vacation Insurance: Are You Covered?" *Better Homes and Gardens,* July 1975, pp. 35, 38, 39, 98.

The author discusses coverage for sickness abroad and for auto liability, insurance on rented vehicles, and so on.

"How to Develop a Local Directory of Doctors." *Consumer Reports,* September 1974, pp. 685–691.

Offers guidance for groups interested in preparing a local directory of personal physicians. Information is also included on how to judge a hospital.

"How to Find a Doctor for Yourself." *Consumer Reports,* September 1974, pp. 681–684.

This article explains how to interpret a doctor's credentials and affiliations.

"How to Judge a Dentist." *Consumer Reports,* July 1975, pp. 442–448.

Provides statistics on dental diseases and areas of specialization within the dental profession. Lists fourteen points to consider in choosing a dentist.

"How to Pay Less for Prescription Drugs." *Consumer Reports,* January 1975, pp. 48–53.

An informative discussion on the varying costs of drugs. Gives points to consider to help you cut costs.

Mead, William B. "Fly Later, Pay Less." *Money,* May 1975, pp. 68–70.

Explains how to reduce air fare by 20 to 66 percent.

"National Health Insurance: Which Way to Go?" *Consumer Reports,* February 1975, pp. 118–124.

Explains the national health insurance proposals in Congress. The article considers the extent of insurance coverage, the method of financing, and the mode of administering, and explains what the different plans mean to consumers.

"The New Low-Cost Motels—Where to Find Them." *Changing Times,* May 1973, pp. 7–11.

Explains what to expect when choosing an economy motel, and the differences between these motels and conventional ones. Contains a directory of locations in various states.

"Outdoor Recreation" series. Washington, D.C.: Government Printing Office.

The following pamphlets provide helpful information: *Bicycling for Recreation and Commuting,* 1972; *Federal Assistance for Outdoor Recreation,*

1970; *National Scenic and Recreational Trails*, 1970; *Wild and Scenic Rivers*, 1970.

"A Practical Guide to Family Bicycle Touring." *Better Homes and Gardens*, July 1974, pp. 91–96.

This article tells the many things to consider when taking a bicycle tour, including safety, clothes to carry, bicycle repair, and types of foods to carry.

"Train Travel Is Back and Getting Better." *Changing Times*, October 1974, pp. 25–28.

Suggests how to save money and help combat the ever-impending energy crisis by traveling by train.

U. S. Department of Agriculture. *Consumers All: The 1965 Yearbook of Agriculture*. Washington, D. C.: Government Printing Office, 1965.

This yearbook contains information on recreation, camping, outdoor life, gardening, and cookouts.

Wilhelms, Fred T. "From Pieces to Patterns." *The Consumer Educator*, June 1973, pp. 1–4.

Describes ways in which the individual can make the most creative use of his dollars for leisure-time pursuits.

11

Saving, Investing, and Estate Planning

11

Saving is setting aside money from present earnings to use in the future. When you postpone spending and retain your money for use at some later time, you are saving.

Investments are a way of getting a return on your savings. Investments are income-producing assets established for the purpose of receiving interest, dividends, rent, profit, or some other return.

Estate planning is a way of providing for the disposition of your assets after death. Most people tend to avoid this unpleasant task, but proper planning can serve to make things less traumatic for your survivors by eliminating painful problems and reducing expense.

In this chapter you will learn why people save, where savings may be placed, how much you should save, the role of investments in your money plan, and how to plan for disposition of your estate.

Saving

Why should a person save? Nowadays, practically anything you may want is available on credit. You can "enjoy now and pay later" with such items as clothing, appliances, cars, travel, education, and medical services. You can even pay your taxes through a credit plan. Why then should you deprive yourself of immediate satisfactions by setting aside money for future use?

Why People Save

It is true that you can enjoy many satisfactions through credit. It may seem foolish to wait until you have accumulated the money to buy the things you want. As long as current income continues and payments can be made as agreed, everyone can enjoy the "buy now and pay later" way of life. But what happens when illness or accident or economic conditions over which you have no control cut off your regular earnings? That's when savings are important. As long as people are subject to human frailties and the uncertainties of life, they cannot rely solely on current income to provide for all of their needs. Savings provide security and protection against the unexpected.

Just as savings can protect you financially if something unexpected happens, savings can also help you *make* things happen. Savings can give you the means to fulfill planned objectives, a way to buy the things you and your family have established as "future goals" in your money plan. Short-term savings can bring you something in the near future, such as a car, an appliance, a vacation trip, or a down payment on a home. Long-term savings can provide for college education for children, for investment in a business, or for retirement income.

You need to have a purpose for saving. Saving just for the sake of accumulating money does not provide the challenge and excitement

Saving helps to make things happen.

that can be found in saving for a specific objective. When saving is directed toward a goal which all family members share, there is a greater incentive for saving.

Planning—setting goals and establishing priorities—helps you place the proper emphasis on each of the purposes for which you wish to save. Your savings goals should provide for your immediate and long-range needs and should be attainable within your current income.

Where to Place Your Savings
Once you have decided on a savings plan, you need to find a place where your money is safe and secure, where it is readily available if needed, and where it earns interest or dividends while you are waiting to use it.

There are a number of different places to save money. Each has its own characteristics. Your decision about where to put your savings should be based on what you want to achieve and how long a time span is involved. Are you planning to use your money next year or in ten to fifteen years? One thing is certain: The sooner you start a savings pro-

Savings should grow with safety.

gram, the greater the number of years you will have to build up your savings and meet your objectives.

Bank Accounts, Savings Associations, and Credit Unions

A bank is a financial institution which receives your money and that of other customers and performs a variety of services.

Commercial banks, owned by shareholders, provide checking accounts, savings accounts, loans, safe-deposit boxes, investment and trust services, and collection services. They sell and redeem United States savings bonds and issue traveler's checks.

A savings account at a commercial bank permits the depositor to make deposits or withdrawals at will, although banks can legally require thirty days' notice for withdrawals. Your passbook serves as a record of your account, duplicating the one kept by the bank; it shows deposits, withdrawals, and earnings credited to your account. Such earnings are called *interest* in commercial banks. Commercial banks also issue *certificates of deposit*, by which the bank pledges to pay the face amount of the certificate after a certain period of time, plus a stated rate of interest during that time. The period might, for instance, be six months, one year, two years, or ten years. When the time is up the certificate is said to have reached *maturity*. CDs, as these certificates are called, are usually issued in amounts of $1,000 or more. Because of the time factor, certificates of deposit pay a higher rate of interest than savings accounts. However, there is usually a penalty for early withdrawal. You should investigate the regulations if you think you will need your money before the certificate reaches maturity.

Mutual savings banks are owned by the depositors, not by stockholders as are commercial banks. Mutual banks specialize in savings accounts and use most of their deposits for investment in real estate mortgages. Earnings on accounts are called *dividends* rather than interest and are generally higher than the earnings distributed by commercial banks. This is because mutual banks operate at lower costs, chiefly due to the fact that they are not paying stockholders a return on their investments.

Savings and loan associations are mutual associations, formed by people who wish to pool their savings and lend their money to other people who wish to buy or build homes. They do not perform the usual banking functions, but operate similarly to mutual savings banks. Savings and loan associations offer savings accounts and certificates of deposit similar to those of commercial banks.

Credit unions are cooperative organizations established to encourage thrift among members and to provide them a source of credit. Membership is limited to persons who have a common interest through occupation or some form of association or who live in a well-defined community or neighborhood. Credit unions vary from small groups with a few thousand dollars in assets to large groups with millions of dollars in assets. Directors, drawn from the membership by election, are responsible for the general policy of the credit union; separate committees of members handle loan applications, conduct education programs, and supervise the credit union's operations. Often offices and equipment, and in some instances clerical help, are donated by the sponsoring organizations. Credit unions are exempt from federal income tax. All of these factors make it possible for credit unions to offer their members higher interest rates on deposits than commercial banks and to charge their members less for credit.

In selecting where to place your savings you should seek answers to the following questions.

1. *Are my deposits insured?* Commercial banks and most mutual savings banks may insure deposits up to $40,000 through the FDIC, the Federal Deposit Insurance Corporation. Savings and loan associations are federally chartered, and their deposits are insured by the FSLIC, the Federal Savings and Loan Insurance Corporation. Credit unions do not have federally sponsored insurance, but are closely supervised and have a good safety record.

2. *How much will my savings earn?* The rate of interest that banks and other institutions pay varies from place to place and time to time. Find out if your savings will be earning compound interest, and whether the interest is paid daily, quarterly, semiannually, or yearly. In compound interest during the first period interest is paid only on the amount deposited. During the next period interest is paid on the principal plus the interest earned during the previous period. Each periods. The shorter the interval of time between interest determination, the greater the growth. The time interval and the method by which interest or dividends are figured affect the amount of money your savings earn.

3. *What services are offered?* Find out what services are available and evaluate their importance and cost. It does not make sense to pay for services you do not use.

4. *How convenient is the location?* If you deposit or withdraw money frequently, location can be important. Many banks provide mail service as a convenience. Who pays the postage for this service?

Before making your selection, shop around and make inquiries of several institutions in your community. Select the one that best meets your needs.

The next question is how much to save. Before we discuss it, read "The Samsons" to get some idea of the considerations involved.

THE SAMSONS The Samson family includes the father, Joe Samson, aged forty-six, employed as a skilled mechanic at the Aero Electric plant; his wife, Alice, aged thirty-nine, a high-school graduate; and three children:

Jack, eighteen, a senior in high school, Jean, aged twelve, and Harry, aged ten.

They have just moved to this city so that Joe Samson could take a foreman's job at a substantial increase in wages. They have enough furniture for a three-bedroom home or apartment, and they completed the payments on their car before they moved. At this time they have their furniture in storage and are looking for housing. The company is paying their moving expenses.

Up until now the family has been able to keep itself free of debt and has accumulated $5,000 in savings bonds through the payroll deduction plan at the place Joe used to work. He has a life insurance policy for $5,000 on which he pays $112 a year.

You've met the Samsons through mutual friends, and when they learned you were knowledgeable in personal money management they asked you to help them plan their living expenses and savings. They want to save some more money for educating their children and for retirement.

Joe's take-home pay will be $193.35 each week. His firm deducts money for Blue Cross, Social Security, and federal income taxes from his weekly pay. Jack has been promised a part-time job that will give him $22 per week. The family has no other sources of income.

Before you decide on what advice to give the Samsons, read the material that follows.

How Much to Save
Needs vary for different individuals and families, as well as during the various stages of the life cycle of the same family or individual. There is no set pattern of saving or investing. Young people may be interested in saving in order to train for a job or profession. After marriage, saving to establish a home may become important. At another stage in life, when children arrive, goals change and family needs expand. Money is invested in durable goods and family protection, and expenses of this sort may limit the opportunities of saving for long-range objectives. Saving and investment objectives change again when children are grown, leave home, and become financially independent. This is the time when parents may concentrate on their present needs or build retirement plans.

The decision that a person needs to make is not whether to save but rather how much to save. The decision depends on a person's own goals. What seems important to one person may be frivolous to another. But whatever the goals, everyone should save something. The amount set aside may be small, may even seem insignificant. However, money set aside at compound interest grows appreciably, as shown by Table 11.1.

	Interest Rate	Number of Years for Money to Double
TABLE 11.1 Doubling Time of Money at Different Rates of Interest Compounded Annually	2%	35
	3	23.5
	4	17.5
	5	14.35
	6	12
	7	10.25
	8	9
	9	8
	10	7.25
	11	6.6
	12	6

As income increases and the need for capital goods and house furnishings decreases, more money may be set aside for savings and investment. How much should the Samsons save? It depends on what goals they have set themselves. What do they want now? What later? What proportion of their current flexible expenses are they willing to set aside to meet these goals? How much can they set aside? Answers to all of these questions and many more need to be given before anyone can advise the Samsons as to how much they should save.

As an exercise in planning, make your own assumptions about the Samsons' future goals and establish a savings plan for them.

Investments

Investments are made in order to increase the earning capacity of savings. Investments entail risk and should be considered only after the following have been established:

1. Adequate insurance to care for dependents;
2. A cash reserve in a savings account;
3. Educational funds for children;
4. A basic retirement plan;
5. In some instances, a mortgage-free home.

When adequate provision has been made for these aspects of financial security, then, and only then, should consideration be given to investment in securities or real estate. At no time should money needed for daily living be used for investment purposes.

This is not the place to provide the expertise necessary to make sound investments in securities or real estate. However, some basic principles will be outlined so that you will understand the nature of investments and the role that they play in the money plan.

Each of the different types of income-producing investments has separate characteristics. You need to understand the risks and potential earning capacity of each type in order to make rational decisions about which to use.

Kinds of Securities

Securities include stocks and bonds, which corporations and government agencies issue in order to raise money to operate. Stocks and bonds offer a return on investment in the form of dividends or interest, as well as a possible increase in value.

When you buy stock in a corporation you purchase part-ownership of the business. If the company prospers, you share in its success through the dividends paid to shareholders or through the increase in value of each share. On the other hand, if the company does not succeed, it may pay no dividends, the value per share may decrease, and you may even lose your entire investment. There are two types of stocks, *common* and *preferred*. A corporation may offer both types or only common stock.

Common stock pays dividends when they are declared by the board of directors of the company. If earnings are good the dividends may be high and the value of the stock may increase. But when company earnings are poor, or when the economic future is uncertain, there is no assurance that dividends will be paid or that the value of the stock will not decrease.

Preferred stock has a prior claim on the assets of a company; that is, if the company can pay dividends to only some of its shareholders, those who have preferred stock come before those with common stock. However, neither group is paid until the claims of bondholders and other creditors have been satisfied. Preferred stock pays a fixed dividend, whenever any dividend is declared. *Cumulative* preferred stock has this additional feature: Dividends not paid in prior years must be paid to the holders of cumulative preferred stock before any dividends can be distributed to holders of common stock. If the preferred stock is *participating*, the holder will share in earnings in excess of the stated dividend rate. *Convertible* preferred stock may be exchanged for a given number of shares of common stock, generally within a specified time limit.

Bonds represent money lent to their issuer. The issuer promises to pay (a) the stated face value, or principal, at a definite future date (the date when the bond *matures*), and (b) a stated amount of interest, at specified times. Because interest, principal, and maturity are fixed, bonds tend to be more stable in price than other securities. However, bonds do fluctuate with interest rates. When rates rise bond prices fall. When interest rates fall you will pay more for them. Bonds may be issued by the federal government, by local governments (state, city, or county), by corporations, and by foreign governments and companies. Bonds issued by state and local governments have an advantage in that interest earned is free from federal income tax. Bonds of all types are rated as to quality or safety. The higher the quality of the bond, the lower the return; the lower the quality of the bond, the greater the risk and the greater the return. United States federal bonds, having the highest quality, pay the lowest rate of return.

Safety, Income, and Growth

Before investing in securities you should ask yourself what your investment objectives are. They will depend on your current income, accumulated funds, long-range goals, and values. How important to you is each of the following?

1. Safety—the reasonable assurance that you will regain the full amount of your investment
2. Income—the regular and uninterrupted payment of dividends or interest on your investment
3. Growth—the increase of the value of your investment over time

Of course, you would like to have all three of these objectives fulfilled when you make an investment, but that is not possible with any one investment. Typically stocks and bonds have the relative characteristics shown in Table 11.2. You should try to develop a portfolio or group of investments of different types that gives you the blend of characteristics that most nearly approaches your own investment objectives. Having decided on the objectives that best suit your needs, you should look into the various industries and the companies within each industry that you believe will serve your purposes.

How to Buy Securities

Securities are purchased through an *investment dealer*, a *brokerage firm*, or an *investment company*. You will have to search out the source that most adequately meets your needs.

Investment dealers and brokerage firms buy and sell securities through stock exchanges. They also deal in "over-the-counter" securities—that is, ones not listed on any exchange. You pay the broker or dealer a standard commission for purchasing or selling a security for you. Some brokerage firms offer a monthly investment plan under which you buy stock on a periodic basis. You sign an agreement in which you state the amount you want to invest regularly over a definite period and your choice of stock. Each time you make a payment your broker buys the number of full and fractional shares which your pay-

	Type of Investment	Safety	Income	Growth
TABLE 11.2 The Relative Characteristics of Securities	**Common stock**	Least safe	Most uncertain	Larger
	Preferred stock	Safe	Regular	Smaller
	Bonds	Most safe	Most regular	Smaller

PERSONAL FINANCE FOR CONSUMERS

ment will allow, and these shares are credited to your account. You pay the regular price for the shares of stock and the standard rate of commission. Before entering into such an arrangement you should examine the commission cost, since you are buying small amounts and paying brokerage charges on each purchase. Would it be more economical for you to save enough to buy a larger number of shares at once and thereby reduce the brokerage commission?

In the face of recent increases in commission charges for small purchases of stock, some companies are offering their stockholders the opportunity of purchasing additional shares by reinvesting dividends and of making outright stock purchases periodically. The costs are minimal, since commission rates are *prorated*—that is, a portion of the cost is paid by each person in proportion to the amount reinvested. Some banks are seeking to provide a similar service to their customers and are waiting for legal interpretations of their right to do so.

Here, as in other buying and spending activities, you need to investigate to learn the best buys at the least cost. Investing periodically and regularly, however, does have an advantage, in that it permits you to engage in *dollar averaging*.

In dollar averaging you periodically put the same fixed amount of money into the same stock no matter what the current price. Your money will purchase more shares when the price is low and fewer shares when the price is high. Over a period of time, as a result of this process, the average cost of all the shares you have bought will be lower than the average price at which shares were sold in the market. If this seems confusing, look at Table 11.3, which shows an example of dollar averaging. At the end of the fourth quarter the hypothetical investor has purchased twenty-two shares at an average cost to him of $18.18. The average market price during this period was the sum of the various prices per share divided by four: ($20.00 + $25.00 + $12.50 + $20.00) ÷ 4 = $19.38. In other words, the investor saved $19.38 minus $18.18, or $1.20, per share.

Investment companies, also referred to as investment funds or trusts, give you the opportunity to invest in a variety of securities to minimize your risk through diversification. They offer the services of investment specialists to manage your money for you. All you do is

TABLE 11.3 How Dollar Averaging Works	1st Quarter	2nd Quarter	3rd Quarter	4th Quarter
Amount invested	$100.00	$100.00	$100.00	$100.00
Price per share	$20.00	$25.00	$12.50	$20.00
Number of shares purchased	5	4	8	5
Number of shares owned	5	9	17	22
Total invested	$100.00	$200.00	$300.00	$400.00
Average cost per share	$20.00	$22.22	$17.65	$18.18

SAVING, INVESTING, AND ESTATE PLANNING

buy shares in the investment company itself. The company uses the funds it obtains from you and others to make investments in a variety of ways—in bonds and in common or preferred stocks, in varying amounts depending on the company's objectives. Some funds limit their investments to certain industries or certain countries. Some concentrate on securities with the potential of growth, others on income or safety of the principal. Generally there is a ready market in which you can sell your shares if you choose to.

There are two types of investment companies. *Open-end* companies, also known as *mutual funds,* issue new shares whenever an investor wishes to buy them. The number of shares outstanding varies from day to day. In buying or selling these securities you deal directly with the investment company or with a licensed broker. The price of the shares is calculated by dividing the assets of the company by the number of shares outstanding on the day of transaction. This is called the *net asset value.* When you buy these shares a charge of 6 to 9 per cent is usually made as a sales commission. However, some investment companies, dealing directly with the investor, do not charge a sales commission; they sell their shares at the net asset value.

Closed-end investment companies have a fixed number of shares outstanding. You buy or sell these securities through an investment dealer or broker just as you buy or sell corporate stocks. You pay the standard commission charges when you buy or sell. The price of the shares is determined by the action of the market, just as for any other company. Some shares of closed-end companies sell at more than the net asset value and some at less, depending on how the market evaluates the future potential of the investment company.

To make your own evaluation of an investment company you should obtain a prospectus from the company or from a broker which gives you a complete history of the company and its plan of operations. The prospectus should give details about all phases of the company's operation, its management, its objectives, its expenses and performance. These facts will enable you to make an informed buying decision.

Whether you build a portfolio of your own selection or invest in an investment company, you should consider the following:

1. Is the dealer or broker well established? Do you have confidence in him?
2. Does the investment meet your investment objectives? Does it offer the security, income, and growth potential that meet your needs?
3. Have you spread your investments to provide the diversity that will minimize risk?
4. Have you kept yourself informed about the current economic condition, the quality of management, and the financial stability of the company you are investing in? What is the earnings record? How

have the shares fluctuated in price? Is the company seasoned or a new venture? What is its potential? Did you get all the facts or are you acting on a "tip" or "hunch"?

5. What are the fees that you will have to pay to buy or sell?

6. Have you the temperament to wait for a return on your investment? Or do you expect to make a quick "killing?" If the value of the shares declines, will you have the financial and emotional resources to wait for a recovery in value? Or will you have to sell no matter what the loss?

There are ways to gain investment experience while risking little or no money. You may "follow the market" by selecting certain securities and watching their progress without investing money in them. Keep a record as though you had actually bought and sold them. Over a period of years you will gain knowledge, and when the time comes to invest you will know how to go about it. Another way is to form or join an investment club, a group organized to learn the fundamental principles of sound investment procedure. Each member contributes a definite monthly amount, generally $10 or more. The funds are pooled and invested regularly after various opportunities have been studied. The investment decisions are made by majority vote of the members. The earnings are reinvested. Information about investment clubs and how to form them is available from the National Association of Investment Clubs, 1515 E. Eleven Mile Road, Royal Oak, Michigan 48067.

Courses on investment are available in high schools, colleges, and adult education centers. Brokerage houses, as a public service, also conduct seminars and lecture series on investments.

Facts about investments can be found in business magazines such as *Forbes, Fortune*, and *Money*; newspapers such as the *Wall Street Journal*; reports from trade and professional organizations; and industry surveys made by government, educational institutions, and investment firms. Some of these resources are available in public libraries or from your broker; others are available from individual firms. For some publications you may have to purchase subscriptions. See the section "For Additional Information" at the end of this chapter for a few good sources of general information.

Investing in Real Estate

Elsewhere in this book the subject of buying a home has been discussed in detail. Investment in real estate, as covered in this section, refers to buying property for rental purposes or as a means of asset appreciation. Such real estate includes commercial and residential property as well as farm acreage. *Improved* real estate is land with buildings, and *unimproved* real estate is vacant land. Improved property may give an immediate return in the form of rent and an increase in value over time. Unimproved property is usually purchased for long-term investment, in anticipation of the land's increasing in value.

Real estate has been an attractive means of investing because of the traditional belief that land values always appreciate over time and because of the feeling of stability that owning land can bring. Moreover our tax laws offer benefits to land owners through depreciation and capital gains taxation. Investing in real estate, though, is not an activity for amateurs. In order to make money in real estate, you need experienced guidance in making selection and in carrying out sound management practices. When investing in real estate you should follow these recommendations:

1. Acquire a knowledge of property values and of local conditions which may affect the future value of property in the area where you plan to invest.
2. Use the services of a competent, reliable real estate agency in finding suitable property. If in doubt about the value of the property in

which you are interested, employ a real estate appraiser, who will assess the property's value.

3. In buying improved real estate consider the amount of your initial investment as well as future investments you may be required to make to maintain the property in a suitable condition. Compare your estimated total expenses with your expected income. On unimproved property consider whether the rate of interest and the taxes you have to pay offset the potential increase in the property's value.

4. Invest only money you will not need for an extended period of time. Be prepared to hold on to your property for some time in order to realize an increase in value or profit from rentals.

5. Do not take on so large a mortgage on improved property that you must strain your finances to meet the mortgage payments.

6. Have your attorney investigate all matters concerning the purchase and sale of the property. Be sure the title is clear and obtain title insurance.

Recently many small investors have been given the opportunity to invest in real estate through *real estate investment trusts* (REITs). A REIT is similar to a mutual fund, except that the holdings consist of real estate rather than stocks and bonds. The attraction in REITs is that they may, if successful, pay a higher rate of return than is available through the purchase of stocks and bonds. Some of the income derived through REITS may be tax-free, another point which makes this type of investment attractive. However, you ought to remember when considering this type of investment that it is a business which depends on borrowed money to generate income; it requires sound management, and intelligent use of depreciation and leverage principles, to be successful. Shortly after the federal act of 1960 which changed the tax status of these investment trusts, they were quite successful and were rewarding to many individuals who invested in them. But with the tight money situation and high interest rates in the early 1970s, many REITs were caught with overextended development plans and mortgages that caused them to suffer considerable losses. It remains to be seen whether REITs can serve as a secure investment medium during varying market conditions. Therefore amateur investors should be extremely cautious about putting funds into a REIT.

Estate Planning

Contrary to popular thinking, estate planning is a necessary process of everyone's financial mangement. For rich or poor, death is inevitable. The disposition of your assets in accordance with your wishes and to the benefit of your survivors is an integral part of your money plan. The larger the estate, the more complicated it may be, but having a small estate is no excuse for not planning its disposition, just as having a small income is no excuse for not planning how to spend it.

Getting Advice

Planning for the disposition of your estate after death or during your lifetime should be done with trust officers of banks, accountants, lawyers, and properly trained insurance agents. It is not a do-it-yourself activity, but rather one that requires expert knowledge and a thorough understanding of state and federal laws concerning estates and trusts. Your assets may be distributed while you are still alive through trust arrangements or by planned gift-giving. We will consider here the disposition of your estate in the event of death.

Whatever the eventual size of your estate, the professional who counsels you will want to know (a) what assets you have now, (b) your present income, and (c) your responsibilities and goals. Knowing these your adviser will examine alternatives and suggest ways in which your estate may be distributed in accordance with your wishes and within the framework of the laws of your state. Your adviser will also make provisions to protect your beneficiaries from unnecessary costs and annoying problems.

Making a Will

A will directs the disposition of your property after you die. If you die without a will, the state law determines who shares in the estate. Leaving this decision to the state is unsatisfactory because the laws—which vary considerably from state to state—may require that your assets be given to people whom you did not wish to benefit, or may deny a share of your assets to people whom you did wish to include. Yet almost 70 percent of those who have died in this country have died *intestate*—without a will. Responsible financial management requires that a will be drawn to eliminate ill-feelings and legal entanglements.

A warning is due at this point: *Do not draw your own will.* Many people write their own wills and believe that they have fulfilled their responsibilities. This is not so. They are leaving their designated heirs open to legal squabbles that may continue for years. The fee for hiring a lawyer who is familiar with the laws in your state is not large, and having a lawyer draw your will should eliminate the potential for problems.

A properly drawn will lists beneficiaries; these may include your family, friends, churches, charitable organizations, and any other persons or organizations you desire to have share in your assets. Consideration should be given to your marital status, the number and ages of your children, the possibility of the simultaneous death of both spouses. The executor of your estate should be a person (or bank or corporation) that you believe to be able and willing to administer the estate. In the event that there are minor children, a guardian should be named who will hold, manage, and conserve the property for them until they reach the age of twenty-one.

Review your will periodically to keep it up to date, especially when family relationships change. Check your will if you marry, separate, or are divorced; if your spouse dies; if a child is born, is adopted, or dies; if a grandchild is born or is adopted; if your estate increases or decreases substantially; if you acquire property in another state or abroad; if you move to another state or retire. A lawyer should be consulted when you review your will and want to make changes.

Joint Ownership of Property

Many couples arrange to own their assets jointly so that, upon the death of one of them, title passes to the other with a minimum of legal entanglements and delays. Such jointly owned property passes outside of the will and is not subject to the laws of intestacy that govern property when no will is left. But people who use this arrangement to avoid probate—the process by which a will is validated—or to eliminate the costs of probating a will, or to eliminate the need for a will are ill advised. Joint property, in the event of a common disaster, may pass to people who would not have been named as heirs. Joint ownership should not be used to avoid probate or to avoid making a will.

Joint ownership does not free property from estate taxes either. Under federal estate tax law, it is assumed that all property held jointly belongs to the one who dies first. Even if the survivor is the one who actually paid for the asset, the law assumes that it belonged to the one who died. To avoid taxes, the survivor must *prove* that he or she was the original owner or paid for the property. To avoid the complications arising out of joint ownership, other methods of reducing estate taxes should be used, such as trusts and outright gifts. Professional help is of course necessary.

Your Estate and Taxes

The federal government and all of the states except Nevada levy taxes on the estates of deceased persons.

Federal law grants an exemption of $60,000. If your estate is worth less than $60,000, no tax is due and no return need be filed. If there is a tax due, it is paid by the estate, not by the individual beneficiaries.

Some states levy an estate tax similar to the federal tax, on the entire estate. Others levy a tax on the shares received by the beneficiaries; this is called an inheritance tax. Some states have a combination of both. A state, however, can tax real estate and tangible personal property only within its borders. Intangible personal property such as securities is generally taxed in the state in which the deceased was domiciled at the time of death.

Estimating Taxes In order to estimate your estate taxes your adviser will need to make an inventory of everything you own. This includes cash, securities, mortgages, rights in property, trust accounts, life insurance payable to your estate or payable to others, personal effects, collections, and artwork. Property given away within three years of the donor's death may also be subject to estate taxes, if the gift is judged to have been made "in contemplation of death"; therefore you should include recent gifts in the inventory. If you own property jointly with your spouse, list the entire value in your inventory, unless you have proof that your spouse invested his or her own funds.

When the inventory has been made and a fair market value established for each of the items, your adviser will be able to estimate your taxable estate. If there will be more than $60,000 in your estate after allowable expenses, the estate will have to pay taxes unless arrangements have been made to establish tax shelters. Your professional counselor should be able to advise you on how to minimize taxes.

Marital Deductions   If you are married the law allows you to pass to your surviving spouse an amount up to one-half of your adjusted gross estate, tax-free. The property must be given to the surviving spouse outright. Your lawyer will advise you how to protect your survivor's interest and how to qualify any trust property for the marital deduction.

Liquid Assets for Paying Estate Taxes   An estate may have considerable assets but no cash with which to pay estate taxes. This can create problems for the executor and force the sale of assets the survivors may have wanted to keep. Lack of cash for taxes may also force the sale of assets in an unfavorable market.

By careful planning the amount of funds needed to settle your estate can be anticipated. You should arrange to provide liquid assets in the form of cash or insurance for just this purpose.

Reviewing Plans

No estate plan is ever really final. Your personal situation and economic conditions are always subject to change. For this reason your plan should be reviewed periodically, at the same times when you review your will.

If you plan your estate properly, your survivors will not have to make decisions about the disposition of your assets at a time of emotional crisis. Your survivors should not be required to make these serious decisions without the benefit of your guidance.

Remember that estate planning requires the counseling of a professional with experience and knowledge. Be sure to have one assist you.

GLOSSARY OF NEW TERMS

Bond   An obligation by a business or other legal entity to pay a certain sum of money on or before a certain date, at a specified rate of interest.

Certificate of deposit   A bank's written acknowledgement that a stated sum has been deposited to the credit of the person named.

Closed-end investment company   A corporation that invests money it receives from the sale of its shares in the securities of other companies. It will issue only a limited number of shares when formed and usually no more. These shares sell on the basis of supply and demand.

Commercial bank   A banking institution that offers a full range of banking services such as receiving deposits for checking accounts and savings accounts, granting loans, and maintaining trust departments and other financial advisory services for its customers.

Common stock   A share in the ownership of a corporation. When only one type of stock is issued it is called "common."

Compound interest   The premium that arises from the use of money; it is added at regular intervals to the principal.

Credit union   A cooperative formed by people with the common interest of serving as a nonprofit, member-owned organization that will save collectively and provide a low-cost source of credit to the member-owners.

Dividend   A share of the declared profits of a firm or corporation.

Dollar averaging   A system of buying shares of stock for a fixed sum of money and at regular intervals. This results in the average cost of all shares purchased being lower than the average price at which the shares were purchased.

Intestate   The legal term for a person who dies without leaving a will.

Maturity   In business, the time when a note, loan, or bond becomes due.

Mutual fund   The name applied to *open-end investment companies.*

Mutual savings bank   A type of savings bank that is owned by the depositors rather than by shareholders as in a regular savings bank. They are found in only 18 states, mostly in the Northeast.

Open-end investment company   A corporation that is formed to issue and sell new shares at any time so that the number of shares is always changing. It is also known as a *mutual fund.*

Preferred stocks   A form of share in a company by which the owner receives a share of the profits before holders of common stock, usually at a fixed amount per share per year. These stocks may be *cumulative* in that any dividends not paid for in previous years must be paid in full to holders before any dividends can be paid to common share holders; they may also be *noncumulative* and not have this advantage. Some preferred stocks are *participating*, whereby holders share in any earnings of the company that are in excess of the stated rate of dividend.

Probate   Official proof of the genuineness of a will as ascertained by a judge or other official, usually in a probate court by a judge of probate or surrogate.

Real estate investment trust (REIT)   A type of *mutual fund* that invests only in real estate rather than in stocks and bonds.

Savings and loan association   An institution in which people pool their funds and lend money to others who wish to buy or build a home. It is sometimes known as a building and loan association or a savings association. They do not perform the usual banking functions.

QUESTIONS FOR DISCUSSION

1. List the purposes for which families generally save.
2. Discuss the importance of establishing goals for saving and involving family members in planning for their attainment.
3. How are deposits in most commercial banks and savings and loan associations insured, and for how much?
4. What factors should be considered in selecting a place to keep your savings?
5. Explain the relationship of saving to the family life cycle.
6. Explain why a certificate of deposit can offer a higher rate of interest than a regular savings account.
7. How are credit unions operated, and who can participate in their savings and lending programs?
8. Since most investments involve a certain amount of risk, what five things should one have provided for before investing in stocks or bonds?
9. Define "common stock," "preferred stock," and "bonds."
10. Why do you suppose common stocks are considered a hedge against inflation?
11. Discuss possible advantages and disadvantages of investing through a monthly investment plan, an investment club, and an investment company.
12. What questions should one consider when making a decision to invest in securities?
13. Explain why common stock has a greater risk potential than preferred stock or bonds but the best growth potential.
14. You are frequently told to investigate before you invest. What should be considered in the investigation and where can the information be obtained?
15. Explain dollar averaging and the advantage of using this technique.
16. Discuss the differences between open-end and closed-end investment companies.
17. Why do you think amateurs are urged to be cautious about investing in real estate?
18. What questions would a lawyer or professional legal counselor need to have answered in order to help you develop an estate plan?
19. Explain the purpose of making a will and who should make one.
20. Discuss the possible complications of joint ownership of property.
21. Explain estate taxes, who levies them, who is required to pay them, and ways in which heirs can benefit if the estate was carefully planned.

SUGGESTED STUDENT ACTIVITIES

1. Identify some objectives for which you would like to save a portion of your income. Arrange them in order of importance and according to whether they are "long-term" or "short-term." Use a table like Worksheet 11.1.

WORKSHEET 11.1
Items for Which
to Save

Long-Term Goals	Short-Term Goals
1.	1.
2.	2.
3.	3.

2. Assume that you have $1,000 you want to place in a savings account. Consult various savings institutions in your community, consider the interest or dividend returns from different programs in each institution, and decide where you would place the money in light of your objectives.

3. Figure the yearly interest you would receive on $1,000 at 8 percent when it is computed in the following ways.
   a. Annually
   b. Quarterly

4. Conduct a survey to find out why people save. Interview the following people.
   a. A single man
   b. A single woman
   c. A young married couple with no children
   d. A married couple with young children
   e. A couple with teen-age or college-age children
   f. A middle-aged couple
   g. The head of a one-parent family with children
   Report your findings to the class and make generalizations about why people save.

5. Review your own savings program. Compare the rate of interest you are receiving with the current rate of inflation. Make conclusions as to your net gain or loss.

6. Make out a list of terms which are frequently used in discussing investments and which you do not understand. Look up their meanings and make a glossary of them.

7. Select six common stocks from a daily paper that gives the stock report. Check their closing prices. Make a graph showing the weekly changes for the next eight weeks.

8. Assume that you have $5,000 to invest. Investigate various investment opportunities and then make your decision. Prepare a written justification of your choice. Check your portfolio quarterly for the next twelve months to see how well you did.

9. Visit a stock exchange or brokerage house, and ask the manager to explain how stocks are bought and sold and what is the function of his firm.

10. Talk to a realtor about investing in real estate, both developed and undeveloped. Make a list of questions beforehand, and summarize the realtor's responses after the interview.

11. Review the listing in your local paper of real estate, both houses and farm acreage, for sale. Go to the library and check back issues of the paper to

determine the prices of similar offerings three, five, and ten years ago. Describe the changes you have observed and account for them.

12. Compile the information you need to make a will. Consult your banker or a lawyer and prepare a legal will if you do not have one. If you have a will and it has not been reviewed in the last five years, or if changes have occurred in your family situation since you last looked at it, ask a lawyer to review it with you and make the necessary changes.

13. Prepare a paper on the possible pitfalls of joint ownership of property.

FOR ADDITIONAL INFORMATION

"Are Tax-Exempt Bonds Right for You?" *Changing Times*, February 1974, pp. 42–43.
   This article explains tax-exempt bonds and the points to consider in choosing them as an investment.

Bailard, Thomas E., David L. Beihl, and Ronald W. Kaiser. *Personal Money Management*. Chicago: Science Research Associates, 1973, pp. 275–338.
   These authors, having served both as financial consultants and as educators, present in an easy-to-understand manner helpful suggestions on increasing one's income through various types of investments.

Credit Unions—What They Are, How They Operate, How to Join, How to Start One. Madison, Wisc.: Credit Union National Association, 1973.
   This booklet can be obtained for free by writing to the Credit Union National Association, P.O. Box 431, Madison, Wisc. 53701.

Dreyfus, Patricia A. "Higher Interest on Your Savings." *Money*, March 1975, pp. 91–96.
   This article explains how to maximize the growth of your savings—how to make them yield as much as 12 percent.

Gordon, Leland J., and Stewart M. Lee. *Economics for Consumers*. New York: Van Nostrand Reinhold, 1972.
   The small investor is advised on various types of investments and on making savings grow.

How to Read a Financial Report. New York: Merrill, Lynch, Pierce, Fenner and Smith, 1968.
   A helpful aid in interpreting a financial report. You can get it free by writing to Merrill, Lynch at One Liberty Plaza, New York, N.Y. 10006.

"Is Saving Obsolete?" *Changing Times*, October 1972, pp. 7–11.
   This article explains who the savers are, their purpose for saving, and where they keep or invest their money. The relationship between the state of the economy and savings is explored.

McKitrick, Max O. *Financial Security*. The Contemporary Consumer Series. New York: Gregg and Community College Division, McGraw-Hill, 1975.
   Discusses money investment, banking services, and various methods of saving.

Money Management Institute. *Your Savings and Investment Dollar*. Chicago: Household Finance Corporation, 1973.
   This booklet explains saving and investing to accomplish short-range and long-range goals. The advantages and disadvantages of various places to put savings are thoroughly explored. Investments are explained, and the problems related to buying securities are considered.

"Mutual Funds: How to Find the Best Performers." *Changing Times*, July 1974, pp. 6–10.

This article presents information on selecting a mutual fund and directs the reader to reliable material to use in evaluating funds.

Persons, Robert H., Jr. *The Practical Money Manager.* New York: Charles Scribner's Sons, 1974, pp. 61–163.

Helpful information on investments. Provides rules for buying real estate and stocks and bonds.

Stillman, Richard J. *Guide to Personal Finance: A Lifetime Program of Money Management.* Englewood Cliffs, N.J.: Prentice-Hall, 1975.

This text offers comprehensive coverage of saving, various types of investments, and estate planning.

"To Save and Invest Successfully, Make a Money Plan." *Changing Times*, May 1974, pp. 11, 15–18.

Presents ten basic rules for investing. The focus of the article is on setting goals, diversifying, and checking performance.

West, David A., and Glenn L. Wood. *Personal Financial Management.* Boston: Houghton Mifflin, 1972.

This book contains a thorough discussion of various types of investments, ways to select investments, and how to build an investment portfolio. Saving plans are also considered.

12

Fakes, Frauds, and Advertising

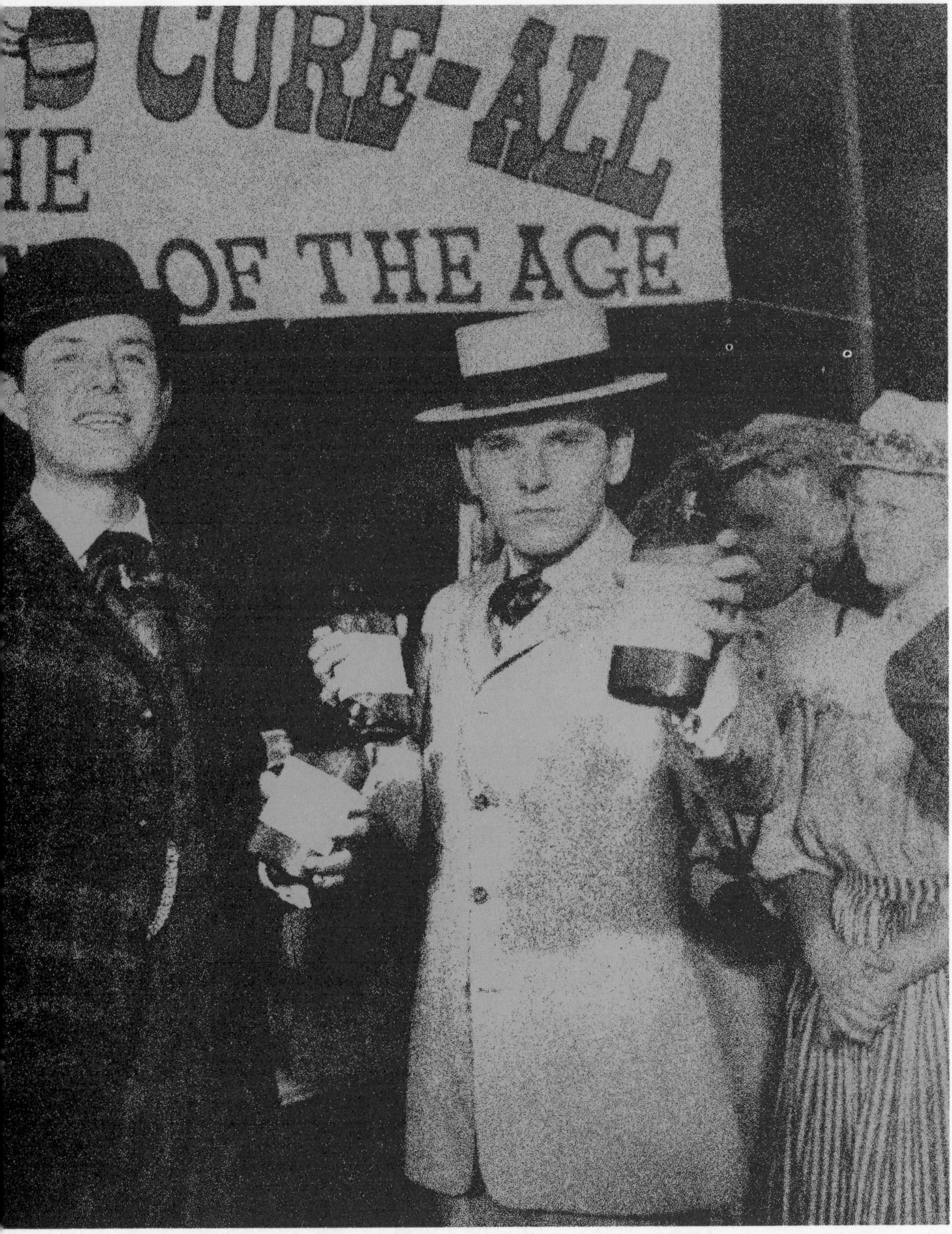
CURE-ALL
HE
OF THE AGE

12

All that you have learned in this book about managing your money will be of little help to you if you are cheated by fakes and frauds. Your efforts to earn, to plan, and to save in order to reach your goals will be wasted if you allow yourself to fall prey to the "gyp" artist.

Most merchants are honest and have built a following in their communities because their customers can depend on them to be fair. There are, however, many schemers who exist on their ability to take advantage of gullible buyers. These perpetrators of fakes and frauds often do not have an established location in the community. They come from somewhere else to prey upon local citizens. This does not imply that everyone who does not come from your own community is trying to cheat you, but it does mean that you need to be careful and alert when you are doing business with someone you do not know.

The schemer knows that most people want to get satisfaction and value for the money they spend. So he promises a great deal of value and a great deal of satisfaction. It is only when he delivers the goods— if he delivers them—that you find out you are getting little of either satisfaction or value.

You need to be able to recognize the tricks of a fake. You should know when someone is trying to swindle you. In this chapter you will learn why people allow themselves to be tricked and how to avoid it.

This chapter will also discuss advertising, which some people consider just a polite form of swindling. You'll learn how advertising is regulated, what some of the justifications for it are, and how it can play a useful role in your life as a consumer.

Why People Let Themselves Be Tricked

Getting Something for Nothing
All the world loves a bargain.

People let themselves be tricked because they want something for nothing, which is the greatest bargain of all—if you can get it. When we think about it and use our common sense, we know that we can't get something for nothing, but we allow ourselves to be convinced by the schemer when he says he will give it to us. We turn off our common sense and allow our wishes to take over.

The records are filled with examples of people who have been swindled while trying to buy high-quality watches, furs, or jewelry at ridiculously low prices. In most instances the victim is approached on the street. The seller tells a sad story about a sick relative and why he is willing to sell the item at a low price to get some cash to buy the life-saving medicine. Or the story he tells may be of inheriting the merchandise from a rich relative; in order to avoid inheritance taxes, he

"It's a family heirloom but I'll let you have it cheap."

says, he is willing to sell the goods quickly, for a low cash price. Sometimes the item is described by the swindler as having been "left in his delivery truck." The approaches for this type of sale are infinite in number. They depend on the creativity of the seller and the gullibility of the buyer. When the victim gets home with his "bargain," he finds that the item is worth much less than what he paid for it.

Another common example is the salesman who comes to the victim's home to make a sales pitch. This does not mean that every salesman who comes to sell you goods at your home is a trickster. Many house-to-house salesmen represent reliable and legitimate companies. The Fuller Brush Company and Avon are but two examples of companies that provide a legitimate service and have built extensive sales organizations based exclusively on house-to-house calls. It is up to you to be sure that the salesperson calling on you is legitimate and reliable.

The scheming house-to-house salesman may be offering books, pictures, household goods, special services, or any one of a multitude of products. His sales talk is designed to convince the victim of the "terrific values" and the "low cost." He completes the fake or fraud in one of the following ways.

Getting the Victim to Sign for More Than the Stated Amount In these situations the seller enters a price on the contract higher than the price he has quoted. He manages to distract the buyer during the conclusion of the sale so that the buyer is unaware of what is happening. Sometimes he even gets the customer to sign a blank agreement, after which the salesman fills in a greater amount than that originally quoted. When it's time to pay, the buyer must hand over the greater amount because he signed the contract.

Delivering Inferior Items   The salesman, after having demonstrated his product and concluded the sale, goes back to his car or truck parked outside the victim's home to get a "factory-fresh" package of the item he has just sold. When the victim opens the package, he finds an item different from the one demonstrated—and inferior. In the meantime the seller has taken off and is nowhere to be found. The buyer is "stuck."

Disappearing with the Victim's Deposit   In these cases the salesman, having convinced the victim of the merits of his product or service, obtains a deposit to consummate the deal. A substantial deposit is necessary, the schemer explains, in order to assure the victim of obtaining the special low price offered. The salesman is very precise about giving the buyer a formal and impressive-looking receipt for the deposit. However, the victim never sees the seller again and is unable to locate the company the salesman said he represented.

In all these instances the trickster is able to accomplish his scheme because the victim thinks he will be getting something for nothing. The victim lets his greed convince him. Furthermore, he does not know with whom he is doing business. The smart trickster will use impressive-looking credentials that, if examined closely, will tell you nothing about whom he represents. Sometimes the name of a well-known organization is used to lure the victim, but on investigation it is found that the seller is not actually an employee.

Getting Rich Quick

In addition to being taken in because they want something for nothing, people let themselves be victimized because they want to get rich quick. These people are fooled by the fake who promises them wealth if they invest their money with him.

In this category can be found those victims who invest in businesses such as vending-machine services, home manufacturing, and animal-raising. The usual approach in such schemes is to offer the victim an opportunity to make a great deal of money by investing in supplies and equipment. Exciting examples are cited of others who have achieved great earnings by getting into the business. In most cases the examples are fictitious. The seller also neglects to tell the victim about the difficulties he will have in finding customers who will buy from him and about the time it will take him to build up a profitable volume of business. In all cases the profit potential is grossly exaggerated.

Vocational-training programs and home-study courses that promise "big-paying" jobs also fall into the get-rich-quick category. After the victim has spent his money for inadequate training, he finds that he is unable to find a job in the field. The so-called training institute has no mechanism for helping him to find one. Blame is generally placed on "economic conditions" or on the victim's supposed failure to have made the proper effort.

Buying Miracles

The natural desire to improve one's health or physical appearance is another reason why tricksters are able to play their games. The "gyp" promises miracles because he knows that's what the victim is looking for. The schemer takes advantages of the victim's needs to separate him from his money.

Cancer cures, skin foods, bust developers, hair growers, and soaps and creams to reduce weight are just some of the products that the trickster sells. Millions of dollars are spent each year by gullible people seeking to buy health and beauty miracles.

The United States Food and Drug Administration (FDA) is the government agency that tries to protect the public from the sale of miracle cures. This organization has been successful in keeping many fraudulent products off the market. However, because so many people are anxious to find these miracle cures, operators continue to function. Sometimes swindlers circumvent the policing powers of the FDA by skipping from one location to another or by skirting the fringes of the regulatory laws. As long as there are people who are seeking miracle cures to improve their health or appearance, illegal and shady operators will find a profitable market for their fakes.

Rules to Avoid Being Gypped

Don't Be Rushed

The trickster wants to prevent your common sense from entering into the transaction, so he tries to rush you into buying. He tries to convince you that the opportunity he is offering is so great that there are hundreds of other people who will grab it if you do not. A legitimate merchant or salesman should be willing to wait until you have had an opportunity to examine the facts and evaluate them. The trickster tries to give you the "rush act" and convince you that you will have missed a golden opportunity if you do not buy immediately. He is trying to prevent you from examining his promises too closely. He wants to take advantage of your weaknesses to accomplish his purpose.

If the opportunity to buy can't wait, then it is not for you. The only opportunities you should consider are those that give you time to satisfy yourself that they are what you want—not what the salesman wants.

Know the Seller and the Product—Investigate

It is very unlikely that an established businessman will try to trick you with a fake or a fraud. He depends on repeat business. The ill will he would create by trying to trick you would affect his reputation and his future business. The legitimate merchant can also be found readily if you have a complaint. The trickster, on the other hand, does not depend on repeat business and makes every effort to hide himself from those he has cheated.

"Mrs. Roberts, this is 100 percent guaranteed by the company."

If you do not know the person or company that is offering you the goods, take time to investigate. A printed card or a fancy certificate doesn't tell you anything useful. It just lets you know that the seller has a good printer.

Ask for references—the names of others with whom the salesman or company has done business in your community. These are excellent sources of information. Contact these people to learn what their experiences have been with the vendor. Don't be taken in by the seller who uses names of prominent people to impress you. Get the names of people like yourself who have bought from him. You can also check with your local better business bureau or chamber of commerce.

No matter how you investigate, do it. Only the trickster will attempt to rush you into buying without giving you time to find out about the company he represents.

Investigate the product too. For instance, if a product is supposed to cure you of some illness or make you more beautiful or attractive, ask your family physician or local health agency about it. The local office of the FDA or your state or city health department can also advise you about "miracle cures." Just because a product is advertised in a reputable newspaper or magazine it is not necessarily a reputable product. Many newspapers and magazines try to monitor the ads they run, but many do not. It is your money that is involved. It is up to you to investigate before you act.

Read Before You Sign

If all else seems to be right and you are asked to sign a contract or a sales agreement or any other printed form—slow down. Read the document. Make certain that the material you are signing agrees with what the salesman told you. A legitimate merchant will allow you time to do so. The trickster will try to convince you that you do not have to do so. You are liable for what you sign, not for what you claim the salesman told you.

Never sign a form that has blank spaces that the salesman will fill in after you have signed it. The trickster will attempt to rush you into signing a blank contract that he can manipulate after you have signed. A legitimate merchant will not. If the salesman is too busy to complete the form or too busy to give you time to read and understand it, run, do not walk, to the nearest exit.

Canceling At-Home Purchases

If you purchase something from a house-to-house salesman that you later decide is not what you want, you can cancel the sale. A Federal Trade Commission regulation applicable to all states allows a three-day cooling-off period for any door-to-door sale in the amount of $25 or more. You have three days in which to advise the company that you've

Investigate before you sign. Read the small print.

changed your mind and want to cancel your purchase. You pay no penalty for canceling.

The government regulation also provides that:

1. The seller must furnish the buyer with a contract.
2. At the time of sale, the seller must provide the buyer with a written notice and an oral explanation of the right to cancel the sale.
3. On cancellation the buyer must make available, at his residence, any goods which may have been delivered.
4. If the goods are not picked up by the seller within twenty days after the sale has been canceled, the buyer may keep them.

5. The seller must pay all expenses in connection with the return shipment of the rejected goods.

Fakes and Frauds: A Summary
People get gypped by fakes and frauds because they want to get something for nothing, they want to get rich quick, and they want to buy miracles. The way to prevent being a victim of a trickster is to remember the three rules to avoid being gypped: Do not be rushed into buying. Know the seller and the product. Read before you sign.

Advertising and the Consumer
Although all advertising is not a fake or a fraud, there are a great many people who believe it is. We need to take a look at advertising to see what effect it has upon you as a consumer.

What Is Advertising?
From the advertiser's point of view, the role of advertising is to inform you about new products, to provide information about product features, prices, and availability, and to persuade you to buy the product. The advertiser uses advertising to win customers away from other products, to maintain the customers he has, and to attract new users of his product.

Until World War II it was believed that ads should use heavy repetition to get the desired action from the consumer. The advertising campaigns of the 1930s for Lucky Strike cigarettes and Pepsodent toothpaste are excellent examples of using constant repetition of brand name to affect sales. More recent research has revealed that ads, as well as products, must be related to customers' needs to be effective, otherwise they will be ignored. Thus advertising must work with the value system of the society within which it is operating and fulfill the needs and wants of its members. No amount of advertising can produce sales over an extended period of time for a product or service that is incompatible with the consumers' way of life. Nor will advertising sustain products that have gone out of style, that are outmoded technologically, or that do not live up to their promises. As evidence, witness the inability of the manufacturers to stimulate sales for the Edsel, luxury cars in today's environment or long skirts as women's daily wear. Advertising is not likely to stimulate the sale of straight razors for shaving nor has it been successful in getting Americans to use seat belts in their autos. Each year thousands of products fail to succeed in the market in spite of heavy advertising because they do not fill a need or live up to their promise. Actually, then, advertising does not have as great an ability to change behavior or to "brainwash" people as is generally attributed to it.

Why Is Advertising Condemned?

Why then is there such a hue and cry against advertising by enlightened citizens and by consumer advocates? Opponents of advertising have maintained that it is an economic waste. They claim that advertising raises prices, creates undesirable wants, and provides unreliable information. The validity of these arguments must be examined.

How much does advertising cost? Food processors spend about 2.5 cents for each dollar of sales on advertising. Motor vehicle manufacturers spend about one cent, and cosmetic and toiletries manufacturers, the heaviest spenders for advertising, about 11 cents. While in total the amount spent for advertising approaches 25 billion dollars each year, the prices of individual advertised items would be reduced very little if advertising costs were entirely eliminated.

Supporters of advertising argue that advertising actually reduces prices of goods because advertising expands the market for many products, permitting more efficient production methods and lower costs that are passed on to the consumer. According to these people, advertising is also the least costly way of promoting goods and providing product information—much less costly than using salesmen, sales clerks, or direct mail. Without advertising, prices might be higher.

As an added advantage, advertising has been shown to have contributed to expanding markets for new and better products. Many of the products we depend upon in our daily living would not be available to us if firms had not been free to develop large markets through advertising.

Another criticism of advertising is that it creates undesirable wants, leading people to desire the things advertised rather than to look for other—and maybe better—products. It is true that we are influenced to spend more on advertised products that fulfill our immediate needs and wants than on social services such as libraries and cultural facilities such as museums and concert halls. It should be realized, though, that consumer wants have meaning no matter where they originate. A want generated in response to an advertisement is not necessarily less important than one which comes from a person's life experiences. Perhaps more emphasis should be placed on the promotion of good nutrition rather than food brands or of good recreational facilities instead of sporting events. But is such advertising the responsibility of industry? Would the elimination of commercial advertising bring forth an abundance of socially advantageous advertising? This is not likely. It should be noted that the advertising profession has worked through the Ad Council to enlist public support by advertising for such things as better schools, protection of the environment, fire and highway safety, and the sale of government savings bonds.

Advertising directed at children that promotes the sale of questionably nutritious products through cheap prizes or super heroes is one of the main targets of criticism. All advertising suffers because of this obviously flagrant abuse of children's gullibility. Action is now being taken by the Federal Trade Commission to eliminate *premium* offers from television ads aimed at children; this move is receiving the support of organizations such as the Society for Nutrition Education. There is no doubt that further steps will be taken by concerned consumer groups to eliminate entirely advertising abuses that affect children.

Probably the greatest reason for the public's adverse opinion of advertising is the industry's failure to live up to its primary purpose of providing information. Dull, boring commercials, sometimes in bad taste, filled with half-truths or outright deceptions, have created disillusion in the mind of the consuming public. Meaningless claims, puffery, and misrepresentation have made people wary of advertisers' activities. A public that is on the average more educated and sophisticated than in the past can no longer be readily deceived by deceptive advertising. People want to know more about the products they buy. *Open dating, open labelling,* and *truth in advertising* are being demanded, for consumers can make intelligent choices only if reliable information is available. They are beginning to insist that advertising either gives them reliable information or be banned from the media.

Regulation of Advertising

The government agency that has major responsibility for regulating advertising is the Federal Trade Commission. The FTC sees to it that advertisers adhere to accepted standards for integrity and reliability. The FTC also has the responsibility of taking action against deceptive claims in advertising. Since 1969 when Ralph Nader and his associates issued a report criticizing the FTC for its ineffectiveness against deceptive advertising, the agency has taken a more active role in attempting to control the dissemination of false advertising. However, the FTC is hampered in its efforts because its power to enforce regulations is inhibited by lengthy and costly court battles. Advertisers can continue questionable practices, possibly for long periods, until the court passes judgment on the merits of the complaint. Recently the FTC has resorted to "corrective" advertising. This requires the advertiser guilty of deceptive advertising to run corrective ads, which serve to dispel false impressions given by the offending ads through provision of accurate information.

The FTC also instituted a program that requires advertisers to substantiate all claims made in their advertising and to make available the data upon which such claims are based. However, the agency is not able to police every advertisement to be certain it adheres to established standards. The tendency is to concentrate on the more flagrant violations and on those that set precedents. The FTC's effectiveness will depend upon the support its efforts receive from industry. The consumers' duty is to maintain a vigilance to assure that both sides are playing according to the rules and that industry pressure does not encourage the FTC to ease up on its enforcement program.

Most states have laws which attempt to regulate against deceptive advertising. However, many such laws are very weak and are not very effective means of regulation and protection. A few states have adopted the Unfair Trade Practices and Consumer Protection Law developed by the FTC. This law, which gives the state attorney general the power to control deceptive advertising at the state level, has the potential, if effectively used, to protect consumers.

With the rising consumer protest against deceptive advertising many businessmen and advertisers have recognized that continuation of such deceptions is not in their interest, and they have taken measures to eliminate this kind of advertising. The National Advertising Review Board, which represents the Council of Better Business Bureaus, the American Advertising Agencies, and the Association of National Advertisers have been established to focus on complaints of deceptive advertising. It remains to be seen whether the self-policing efforts of the industry are effective in putting an end to bad practices. Many individual newspapers, magazines, radio and television stations, as well as the advertising agencies themselves are attempting to screen ads for misleading claims or bad taste.

Advertising and the Spending Plan

How does all of this affect you as the consumer? In spite of all these efforts to eliminate deception in advertising and to make it a reliable information-giving mechanism, the burden still rests on you as the consumer to make rational buying decisions. When you have a plan for spending and an intelligent approach, advertising can *serve* you by giving the information you require to make those buying decisions that meet your needs and satisfy your wants. Advertising can help you to make rational decisions if you are aware of the reliability of the information that is provided. Advertising can tell you the virtues of different ranges, which cars give good gasoline mileage, and which televisions provide the features you seek. However, if you do not have a spending plan, if you are swayed in your buying decisions by your wants of the moment, then advertising only serves to confuse you. You are likely to buy the car whose advertisements appeal to your emotions, the appliance whose promoters satisfy your ego.

Advertising in itself should not be blamed for consumer compulsiveness and inefficiencies. The wise buyer should not be denied the information and the economic benefits of advertising because some consumers succumb to emotional advertising. Instead, consumers should be taught how to make rational decisions that meet their needs. Advertising that is frank and honest will help them to make those decisions. And educating consumers not to respond to deceptive and emotional advertising is the best way to eliminate it.

GLOSSARY OF NEW TERMS

Competition   The act of seeking to gain that for which another is striving; rivalry between business firms.

Corrective advertising   A method whereby an advertiser is forced to run advertisements that counteract a misstatement or deception appearing in previous advertising.

Direct mail   A method of soliciting business through the use of letters sent to prospective buyers.

Expanding markets   Increase in sales, in units or dollars, for a particular item or group of items.

Gyp   A slang term for a swindler.

Open-dating   A method of marking goods so that the buyer can identify the date of manufacture, learn the last day for selling, or gain some other information.

Open-labelling   A method of writing labels for processed food products so that all of the ingredients therein are clearly identified.

Premiums   Trinkets or small toys placed in cereal boxes to encourage youngsters to ask for the product.

Promotion   Any technique used to persuade people to buy a product.

Ralph Nader   A young attorney who has won fame for himself as an advocate of consumers' rights.

Sales pitch   A slang expression to describe a salesperson's sales presentation.

QUESTIONS FOR DISCUSSION

1. Identify three reasons why consumers allow themselves to be tricked by fakes and frauds.
2. Name and explain three techniques used by unscrupulous salesmen to trick the consumer.
3. Discuss the three basic rules to follow to avoid being gypped.
4. Explain what a consumer can do if he purchases an item (costing more than $25) from a door-to-door salesman and decides the next day he does not want to keep it.
5. What agencies, organizations, and individuals help to guard against fraudulent advertising?
6. Discuss the advantages of advertising.
7. What are some ways in which advertising might be wasteful or inefficient?
8. Discuss the types of advertising that you think would be most beneficial to consumers.
9. Suggest possible differences in the ways an "educated consumer" and an "uninformed consumer" would be influenced by advertising.
10. Discuss the types of advertising that you think are most harmful to consumers.

SUGGESTED STUDENT ACTIVITIES

1. Describe in writing an incident, in your own life or that of someone you know, in which a house-to-house salesman used one of the following techniques. Tell what you or your friend did, and evaluate the action.
   a. Making a gift
   b. Stating that the company is underselling others
   c. Playing on the customer's sympathy
   d. Claiming that the goods can't be bought in a store
   e. Attaching a string to the sale—such as "money off" for each sale made to a person named by the customer
2. Secure an item sold by house-to-house salesmen and compare its quality and price with those of similar goods available in local stores.
3. Interview a representative of one of the following organizations to find out the type, number, and working pattern of the fakes or fraudulent operators frequenting your community.
   a. The local chamber of commerce or better business bureau
   b. The sheriff's office or police department
   c. The Legal Aid Society
   d. The local newspaper, post office, or radio station
4. Make slides or posters or a flip chart showing various sources of consumer help in your community. Explain the purpose of the various agencies and organizations and how to contact them for help with consumer problems.
5. Prepare the script and videotape a scene of a person trying to say "no" to an aggressive house-to-house salesman. Present it to the class for viewing and analysis.
6. Collect articles from the newspaper concerning examples of fraud, extortion, profiteering, or other disreputable schemes. Discuss what was done and what should have been done to protect the consumer.
7. Prepare a list of "dos" and "don'ts" to protect the consumer from frauds.
8. Collect examples of advertising that is: (a) beneficial to consumers and (b) deceptive or misleading. Share your collection with the class and see if the others agree with your analysis.
9. Interview five people. Ask them about their three most recent purchases and how they were influenced to buy each particular item or brand. Summarize the role of advertising in the sales.

FOR ADDITIONAL INFORMATION

Aaker, David A., and George S. Day, eds. *Consumerism.* New York: Free Press, 1974.
  This book covers deceptive advertising and where to turn for help. It also treats warranties, product safety, and ecology. The articles are written by such notable consumer advocates as Ralph Nader, Senator Warren G. Magnuson, Jean Carper, and Mary Gardiner Jones.

"Before You Sign Up with a Vocational School." *Changing Times*, March 1975, pp. 21–23.
  This article points out that some so-called vocational schools can be fraught with hazards, the chief one being that promises of a job may be false. A checklist is included for sizing up a school.

Bober, Gerald F. *Protection and the Law*. The Contemporary Consumer Series. New York: Gregg and Community College Division, McGraw-Hill, 1975. A paperback module designed to provide a basic understanding of the protection available to the consumer. It suggests how this protection may be used to prevent fraudulent and deceptive practices.

Federal Trade Commission. *Don't Be Gypped*. Consumer Bulletin No. 8. Washington, D.C.: Government Printing Office, 1972.

———. *Guard Against Phony Ads*. Washington, D.C.: Government Printing Office, n.d.

———. *List of Common Deceptions*. Washington, D.C.: Government Printing Office, n.d.

———. *Protection for the Elderly*. Consumer Bulletin No. 9. Washington, D.C.: Government Printing Office, n.d.

———. *Unordered Merchandise*. Consumer Bulletin No. 2. Washington, D.C.: Government Printing Office, n.d.
All of these publications by the FTC can be secured free.

"Guide for the Responsible Consumer." *American Association of University Women,* Spring 1972.
An excellent exposé of common frauds and deceptive practices. Explains ways to protect yourself as a consumer, legislation that protects you, where to turn for redress, the consumer's code of ethics, and how to reconcile consumption with ecological concerns. Reprints of this twelve-page article can be ordered from the AAUW Sales Office, 2401 Virginia Avenue N.W., Washington, D.C. 20037. A single copy costs 35 cents.

Howard, John A. "The Role of Advertising." *Penney's Forum*, Spring/Summer 1971, pp. 6–7.
A professor of marketing discusses in question-and-answer form the influence of advertising on consumer behavior. (There are also other informative articles on consumer behavior in this issue.)

Margolius, Sidney. *The Responsible Consumer*. Public Affairs Pamphlet No. 453. New York: Public Affairs Committee, 1970.
This pamphlet explains that a new awareness of your rights and needs as a consumer stems from the realization that how you spend your money is almost as important as how you earn it. Discusses some of the federal and state laws passed in the late sixties and early seventies to protect the consumer against fraud and deception.

Raines, Margaret. *Consumers' Management*. Peoria, Ill.: Charles A. Bennett, 1973. The author explains how people can save themselves money and disappointment when buying goods and services by being informed and exercising their rights. She points out that the families who can least afford it are often the victims of consumer exploitation. Their needs are greater than those of others, and the something-for-nothing idea is particularly attractive to them. The emphasis is on recognizing and avoiding deceptive practices in order to help put the exploiters out of business.

Rosenbloom, Joseph. *Consumer Complaint Guide 1973*. New York: CCM Information Corporation, 1972.
This publication offers advice for the buyer to consider prior to a purchase; discusses how, where, and to whom to complain; and lists the manufacturers of consumer products and firms offering service to the consumer.

"Sometimes You 'Sign' a Contract and Don't Know It." *Changing Times*, September 1974, pp. 45–46.
An explanation of the various ways in which one makes binding con-

tracts unintentionally, such as by waving the hand at an auction and signing slips of paper without reading them. Discusses how these contracts are interpreted by the law.

"Warning! Some Buying Clubs Are Traps." *Changing Times*, August 1974, pp. 21–23.
Some warnings against outfits that mislead consumers by exaggerating the savings to be had by buying through group plans or clubs.

Young, James Harvey. *The Medical Messiahs: A Social History of Health Quackery in Twentieth-Century America*. Princeton, N.J.: Princeton University Press, 1967.
This book shows how the consumer can be gypped and deceived by medical charlatans even in a day of enlightenment and regulation. It points out the changing patterns of deception and the ebb and flow of regulatory victories and defeats. Consumers Union commends this book as a fascinating commentary on the adaptation of the twentieth-century medicine man to his time.

13

Environment, Energy, and the Quality of Life

13

In the foregoing chapters you have developed an informational base for making decisions about buying goods and services to establish a desired lifestyle. The essentials of a money plan have been explained, and you have seen how to manage your income to purchase appliances, housing, food, clothing, transportation, health care, and recreation. You have learned the importance of credit and how it can be used. You have also learned the wisdom of protecting your assets and putting aside a portion of your earnings for future crises or for when you are no longer earning a monthly income. You have learned the techniques used by gyppers and con artists and how to avoid being "taken" by them.

This chapter will discuss the environment and the energy crisis. In doing so, it will help you to look at yourself as a consuming citizen. It will raise some questions about present trends and the changes appearing on the horizon and will point up the effects that your decisions may have on the world in which you live. You will be encouraged to reexamine your values and to assume your share of the responsibility so that you and others may live in harmony with the environment.

Characteristics of Life About Fifty Years Ago

To gain a perspective on how you live today as a consuming citizen, let's compare the present day with the situation about fifty years ago in rural America. We need not refer to history books for information; citizens who are still living can give us a picture of life as they experienced it. Your grandparents or perhaps your parents, even if they were not rural dwellers, can tell you from first-hand experience how the number of choices in the marketplace has increased and how the role and responsibility of a consumer have changed.

Compared with current practices, life as a consuming citizen in the rural America of the earlier twentieth century was characterized by the following:

> A simpler lifestyle;
> Fewer goods and services from which to choose;
> Greater dependency of individuals and families on the soil;
> Slower and less readily available transportation;
> Recreation centered in the home and the local community;
> A greater feeling of responsibility for the welfare of one's fellow man and a greater trust in people generally;
> Limited availability of mass media and other means of communication.

The simpler lifestyle was a result of the limited availability of goods and services and of resources with which to purchase them. Families and individuals valued the soil and the opportunity to produce food—

fresh fruits and vegetables, meat, nuts, milk, butter, eggs, and cereals. In addition to the food which was produced from livestock and cultivated fields, fish were caught in the unpolluted streams and rivers. Wild game was trapped or killed by hunters, and wild berries, fruits, and green and succulent plants were harvested for eating. Sweets were primarily in the form of honey and syrups made from boiling the juices from various kinds of cane, sugar beets, and the maple tree.

Food that was not needed for immediate use was canned, dried, or cured for use later when fresh foods were not in season. The production of foods was a family affair and the excess was given to neighbors and those in need. Few food items were purchased from the local grocery store.

The simpler lifestyle required a different type of clothing from our present-day wardrobe. First there were work or "everyday" clothes. A person's "Sunday" clothes, which frequently consisted of one outfit, were worn to church and on occasions which required one to dressup. A person had two pairs of shoes: a "Sunday" pair and an "everyday" pair. When the everyday pair wore out, the Sunday ones were taken for everyday use and a new pair was bought for Sunday. Having a pair of shoes to match each outfit was unheard of and certainly not in the realm of possibility for most consumers.

Houses were frequently built by a local carpenter and by neighbors who volunteered to help or to exchange work with the new occupant. The design was generally simple, with small closets (if any), open fireplaces, and a flue for the kitchen range. Few houses had running water or electricity. Windows provided for cross-ventilation, and the porch was a place to rest and visit in the cool of the evening. The older citizens could sit on the porch and view the landscape and the younger members of the family at work. Mothers or grandparents could also keep an eye on the young children at play in the yard.

A well or spring nearby afforded fresh, cool water for the family's household needs. Clothes were washed with homemade soap and hung on a clothesline to dry. A tub or wash basin was used for bathing unless one chose to "take a dip" in a nearby water hole or pond.

Garbage disposal was relatively simple. There were no paper towels, aluminum foil, plastic wrap, and paper or plastic plates and cups. Aerosol sprays were unheard of and soft drinks came in returnable bottles. The deposit required and the shortage of money were sufficient incentives to return the bottles to the merchant. Glass jars were used and reused in home canning. Syrup buckets, lard cans, and earthen crocks were kept in use until they rusted out or were broken. The garbage—table waste, peelings, rinds—was either fed to the animals or put into a compost pile in the garden. This recycling eliminated the need for garbage dumps.

Among children there was less emphasis on receiving things and more emphasis on taking care of the few items or toys available. A little girl took care of her doll and kept it until she was grown. If there were three children, rather than getting three bicycles, they received one and took turns riding it. There were animals to love and space to run and play, trees to climb (in place of gym sets), woods in which to walk, and streams in which to wade. Possibilities were limited chiefly by the imagination and creativity of the individual or group.

Transportation was much slower than today. Few families owned their own cars. Even if there were funds to make the initial purchase, operating the car often took money that was needed for other things. Automobiles were used mainly for essential travel. Trains were used more often than other modes of travel for long trips, but there was the problem of getting to your destination once you arrived at the nearest depot. Therefore most people never traveled very far from their local community. Pollution from automobiles and airplanes was not a problem.

The difficulties of transportation kept recreation close to home. The church and the home were focal points for hayrides, picnics, and community singings. Home parties of various types, including games, ice cream suppers, and cookouts, were frequent. People had time to talk and learn about each other. Associations were cherished and lifelong relationships were formed.

There were no television sets through which to view world happenings and by which to be entertained. Nor were individuals tempted to buy things they did not have by frequent commercials on the "tube." Radios were available in limited numbers but their cost prevented many families from owning one. Some families had telephone service, but none had the wide-area coverage we know today. Many local papers were published either weekly or biweekly, so news of the world outside the local community was meager.

There was no Social Security program and no free school lunch program for the needy. No welfare programs as we know them today existed. Families assumed more responsibility for the welfare of their "kin" and their fellow citizens. When a farmer had a prolonged illness during the planting or harvesting season, neighbors would join together to plant or harvest his crops, chop the wood, and see that he and his family were provided with the basic essentials. Round-the-clock nursing care when needed was often furnished by relatives or neighbors.

People seemed to have greater trust in the honesty and integrity of others. Doors were seldom locked even if they had locks on them. Security systems were unknown and unnecessary. The same sense of trust that was evident among rural folk was also to be seen in city dwellers. The lifestyle we have described for rural inhabitants was characteristic of about 90 percent of the total population. But even the 10 percent that lived in large cities also led a simpler life than today. Before the mass migration of rural workers from the farms to the city factories, and the tremendous growth of the cities, city life had a similarity to life in rural America. Food came from the neighborhood store instead of the family garden, and people lived in rented apartments located in multistoried buildings. But distant travel was rare, transportation was for local purposes, resources were limited, and there was a close-knit relationship among friends, family, and neighbors that differed very little from the mutual dependency in the country.

Consumer Concerns

It used to be fashionable to look back at the past with condescension, to think of how far progress had brought us. But nowadays more and more people are considering the past with nostalgia, convinced that to gain our present-day conveniences and comforts we have sacrificed the "quality of life" that we once had. Much of the recent concern has focused on the environment—what we have done to it in our haste for "progress," and what we can now do to repair the damage. Air and water pollution, noise, and waste have increased so dramatically that they are threats to our physical and emotional health. And we have used our resources so recklessly that we may now be forced to give up some of our material gains whether we like to or not.

We cannot be separate from our environment. The choices we make as consuming citizens affect the larger environment in which we live, and this in turns affects our own health, happiness, and ultimate survival. The search for environmental equilibrium in all spheres of human life must begin in earnest, and it must begin at home where each individual can make a contribution. Earlier approaches to environmental pollution were directed at industry and its technological development. The responsibility for regulation and control was solely in the hands of governmental agencies and political bodies. Now it is becoming increasingly imperative that attention be devoted to the responsibility of the consuming citizen for the environment in which he lives. The clock continues to tick, but there is still time for us to adjust our principles and actions. Electrical brownouts and an earth atmosphere with too many pollutants and too little ozone are vivid reminders of the possibilities that face us. Philosophical musing must be replaced by responsive action on the part of the consuming citizen. We must ask what steps individuals can take to improve the quality of life for all.

Water Supply

The concentration of people and industry is closely associated with the quality of water. Modern life means crowded life and great concentrations of waste water. Informed people believe that finding pure, unpolluted drinking water will be one of the major crises of the late seventies.

As consumers and citizens, we need to be concerned with the pollution of rivers, streams, and even the ocean. When industry dumps waste into the rivers or when pesticides, herbicides, or other chemicals get into streams, fish and marine life are killed. As concerned citizens we should report such action to the proper authorities or join with volunteer groups to bring about remedial action. In addition, we need to actively participate in community efforts to improve sewage treatment facilities.

What additional things can consuming citizens do?

1. Visit your local water-treatment plant and see how water is treated to make it safe for human consumption. If your water is from a spring or well, call the county health department and request that it be tested.
2. Be aware that you may be contaminating water. Since pipes can be a source of contamination, have your home water supply tested, especially if the pipes are lead or galvanized iron and the water is acidic. Be sure that you use one of the pollution-free, nonphosphate detergents.
3. Become familiar with the Public Health Drinking Water Standards, which were established in 1962 and revised in 1972. Find out about fluoridation and the latest conclusions about its value.
4. See if you can reduce your water consumption and still maintain an acceptable standard of cleanliness and sanitation. Check to see how much water you use. Do you wash clothes and linens more often than necessary? Do you operate the dishwasher with a full load? Do you let the shower run continually when bathing? Do you study the weather report and refrain from watering plants when rain is predicted?

Noise Pollution

We are told that the loss of hearing is a greater handicap than the loss of eyesight, yet we frequently overlook the excessive levels of noise to which we are exposed. There is increasing concern about the effect noise has on health—both physical and psychological.

Persons exposed to excessively high levels of noise over extended periods of time may have a slight shift in their hearing thresholds. This can result in permanent hearing loss. Some early signs of the effect of excessive noise are frustration, irritability, muscle tension, headaches, and general discomfort. People vary in their tolerance of of noise. You may have noticed that your parents or grandparents respond differently to the sound level of the radio, stereo, or television than you do.

In the home you can identify many noises to which you are subjected daily. There is noise from the refrigerator, freezer, dishwasher, washing machine, clothes dryer, air conditioner, electric shaver, hair dryer, radio, television, stereo, stove exhaust fan and other cooling or ventilating fans, disposal, vacuum cleaner, and so on. Step outside the house and listen to other sounds.

Consider the sound levels in places where people work. There are sounds associated with our transportation system; there is noise in places where we shop and where we go for recreation and entertainment. Small wonder that people are seeking escape to the quiet of mountains or secluded resort areas.

What can you do to reduce noise pollution?

1. New building codes are being drafted in some areas to require better soundproofing of apartments, homes, and office buildings. Support and encourage these measures.
2. Fans, compressors, and other noisy machinery can be encased to reduce noise levels.
3. Sound-absorbing materials can be used in or on walls and around noisy machinery.
4. Simply reducing the volume on musical instruments or on the television will help reduce the noise.
5. Placing washers, dryers, trash compactors, and the like in areas that can be enclosed or in places away from the family living quarters will eliminate some noise.
6. Whenever possible, schedule the use of cleaning equipment for times when members of the household are away from home.
7. If you work in a high-noise occupation, wear special ear protectors. Even if you have a noise-free occupation, encourage your company to provide ear protectors for those who are exposed to noise.
8. Manufacturers of appliances, machinery, and so forth can be urged to search for ways to reduce the noise level of their products.
9. Replace gutted mufflers or mufflers with defects or holes.
10. Consider just not purchasing noise-polluting equipment and appliances!

Solid Waste

In addition to the kinds of pollution you hear the most about, there is the pollution caused by solid waste and garbage. Litter and junk are probably the most obnoxious of all forms of pollution to most people. Although we may become accustomed to the daily chore of garbage disposal, our anger is being increasingly aroused at the sight of roadside dumps, auto graveyards, and the ubiquitous drink cans or containers. Solid wastes are accumulating at a rate of approximately 1,600 pounds per person per year, and the annual cost for disposal exceeds $2 billion. The need for planning and consumer action is clearly evident.

Solid waste, although not presently as great a threat to human welfare as gaseous and liquid waste, may become the greatest problem of all. The quantity and kinds of solid waste are linked to population growth and technology as well as to economics, geography, and public attitude.

There are three basic methods of disposing of solid waste: dumping, burning, and recycling. Dumping is a primitive method handed down through the centuries, but recently "sanitary landfills" have helped to make it more acceptable. Burning in many cases merely transforms solid waste into air pollutants, but the use of electrostatic precipitators to cleanse smokestacks can partly solve the problem. Recycling is a sophisticated procedure which is beginning to receive widespread attention. Recycling can include, for instance, the composting of raw sewage sludge for use as fertilizer and the use of solid waste as an industrial fuel.

What can you as a consuming citizen do about solid waste?

1. Reduce solid waste at the source by altering the nature of your purchases.
   a. Buy fewer disposable items, such as disposable paper products and nonreturnable bottles and cans. When you must buy disposable containers, look for ones that are degradable—that is, ones that will gradually decompose when exposed to the environment.
   b. Cut down on items that are overpackaged, such as individually wrapped slices of cheese, prepackaged fruits and vegetables, liquids in fancy bottles, plastic-encased products, and so on.
   c. Buy in bulk when possible.
   d. Eliminate extra bags and boxes by providing your own tote bag to carry home your purchases.
2. Reuse or recycle whenever possible.
   a. Return drink bottles and coat hangers to their sources.
   b. Use old newspapers to polish windows, clean ovens, wrap packages, and so on.
   c. Share magazines with friends or give them to institutions.
   d. Give reusable clothing, toys, china, and furniture to charity. (You may claim a tax deduction.)
   e. Take newspapers, aluminum cans, and nonreturnable bottles to recycling centers.
   f. Request recycled paper for your own needs and urge other consumers to do likewise.
3. Work for effective disposal.
   a. Urge the construction of effective disposal systems in your area.
   b. Support tax measures which provide funds for the construction of disposal systems. Proper treatment of solid waste is by no means cheap. Show that you are willing to pay for it.
   c. Support legislation to prohibit the dumping of litter or garbage

Don't litter—
it starts with you.

along the roadsides and on public or private property. Stiff penalties should be set and offenders punished.
d. Keep yourself from littering. And when you can do so tactfully, remind others not to litter.

Pesticides

Pesticides were developed to control or kill insects and rodents that transmit diseases to humans, such as yellow fever, malaria, typhus, and plague. Pesticides have also been valuable in destroying pests that attack and destroy agricultural crops. Their use has made possible a more abundant supply of food, thereby reducing the incidence of

ENVIRONMENT, ENERGY, AND THE QUALITY OF LIFE

rickets, scurvy, and pellagra, as well as outright starvation. However, as consuming citizens we are concerned not only with the benefits derived from the use of pesticides but also with the potential dangers associated with their use.

Pesticides are poisons. Inhalation of their fumes, or accidental swallowing or absorption through the skin, can be harmful. Public health officials are also concerned about the possibility of long-term ill effects from the use of certain chemicals in pesticides. Because the chemicals in pesticides are not readily degradable, they remain active for many years, during which time they may be transported great distances by ecosystem cycling. They can be found on foods, in water, in air and soil. DDT, the chief culprit, can now be found in ocean water as well as on every land mass in the world.

Medical researchers are studying the gradual build-up of pesticides in body tissue. Food and water are also being routinely analyzed. If the residues of pesticides in foods go beyond certain limits, they can no longer be sold in markets and are removed from the shelves.

There is also great concern about the danger of pesticides to wildlife. There have been many instances in which birds, fish, and other living things have been unintentionally killed by the use of pesticides. As a result of the danger to the safety of people and other living creatures, some pesticides can no longer be used. Some states prohibit the use of DDT. All pesticides that are shipped between states must be registered with the Environmental Protection Agency (EPA). If a hazard exists, a shipment can be stopped.

What can you as a consuming citizen do to promote the safe use of pesticides?

1. Work for discontinued use of pesticides that are hazardous to human life and wildlife.
2. Use pesticides only when you are sure that they are needed. Use the most appropriate one for the purpose.
3. Keep pesticides in a safe place, clearly labeled and away from children.
4. Never use arsenic, mercury, or lead as a pesticide.
5. "No-pest" strips using DDVP (vapors) are dangerous. Use them with extreme caution and never in the kitchen.
6. Never use shelf paper treated with pesticides.
7. Never pour pesticides into the sewer system. Use established disposal centers for getting rid of containers and unused materials.
8. Avoid getting pesticides on the skin, and wash your hands throughly after using them, especially before eating or smoking.
9. Be sure to read the directions for using a particular pesticide and follow the instructions.
10. Consider all pesticides dangerous and handle them accordingly.

Air Pollution

Air pollution takes a toll on the health and well-being of humans, animals, and even plants. The social and economic cost of unclean air, caused by technological developments, is mounting daily. The problem of dirty air in heavily populated areas is so great that a reminder of the "particles per cubic centimeter" has become a regular part of the daily weather report.

The worst air pollution is found in areas where there is a heavy concentration of people and industry, where the traffic of automobiles, buses, planes, transport trucks, and trains is heavy, and where there are extensive open fires. The major air contaminant is the carbon monoxide emitted from motor vehicles. There are other pollutants, such as particulates, sulfur oxides, hydrocarbons, and nitrogen oxides. These may be found in smoke, gases, products of combustion, and radioactive matter. There are also the more traditional pollutants: pollen and dust.

Perhaps the most controversial pollutants at present are the fluorocarbons. These are used as propellants in aerosol-spray products and as circulating substances in refrigeration systems. Some scientists say that the fluorocarbons released through aerosol sprays and refrigeration systems may be rising into the stratosphere to break up the ozone layer. Ozone is a form of oxygen with three atoms to the molecule. A thin layer of ozone, lying sixteen to nineteen miles above the earth, shields us from some of the sun's ultraviolet rays. Some experts claim that the damage done to the ozone layer will ultimately cause an increase in skin cancer and a decline in marine life, and will even threaten all life on this planet. Other authorities disagree with these reports. Nevertheless, numerous groups are concerned and are studying the issue. How would you be affected if all aerosols, refrigerants, and foam-blowing agents were banned? Consider the effect on industry.

The economic effects of air pollution are continuing to rise, and the individual consumer is only beginning to be aware of the cost. Pollution results in damage to plants. It makes driving more hazardous because of irritation of the eyes. It is associated with irritation of and damage to membrane surfaces of the body. Hay fever is becoming widespread, and certain kinds of pollen seem to be the principal offenders. Chronic bronchitis, emphysema, lung cancer, and cardio-vascular diseases have been either caused or aggravated by air pollution. There have been a number of episodes in which death has been attributed to air pollution. In London in 1952, where the worst air pollution in history occurred, there was an increase of four or five thousand in the weekly number of deaths, and pollution was a chief suspect.

The cost of air pollution is also reflected in day-to-day living costs. Clothing must be laundered and houses cleaned and painted more frequently because of pollution. Lights must be used for longer periods. The federal regulations concerning emission control on cars have increased the cost of an automobile. You no doubt can think of many additional costs of pollution.

Air pollution control activities are becoming more organized, and efforts to solve the problem have been intensified at the state and national levels. Some local governments have also set up regulations to curb air pollution. Each consuming citizen must share the responsibility for clean air. Following is a list of suggestions.

1. Walk or ride a bike when the distance to be traveled is short and take advantage of mass transportation and car pools to reduce the use of individual cars.
2. Burn unleaded gasoline if your car is equipped to operate on it. Learn the octane and lead requirements of your car from your dealer or by writing to the manufacturer. Older cars as well as the new ones may operate on low-lead fuel. Always be sure to use the lowest octane level your car can run on without knocking.
3. Have regular tune-ups at least twice a year; a well-tuned engine pollutes less. Follow the tips in Chapter 6 for saving fuel; the less fuel you burn, the less you are polluting.
4. Keep up with the research on aerosol products and be prepared to discontinue use of them if evidence warrants it.
5. Avoid setting open fires and burning trash and leaves. Help to combat and prevent forest fires.
6. Call attention to or report industries that disregard air pollution regulations.
7. Refrain from smoking, not only for your own health's sake but for the protection of those around you.
8. Help to destroy ragweed and other plants that give off pollen which contributes to hay fever.
9. Work to see that the burning of fuel oil, coal, and other materials that release pollutants into the atmosphere is controlled.
10. Plant cover crops to prevent dust storms.

These are a few suggestions on which consuming citizens can begin immediate action. It is well to remember that eliminating pollution is costly in terms of both human effort and money.

Energy Conservation

We are all aware of the looming shortages of petroleum products and the electricity produced from oil. We have been doubling our use of electricity every eight to ten years and our entire energy consumption about every fifteen years. We have grown accustomed to thinking of electricity and petroleum products as items of little cost. In fact, until recently, consumers were encouraged to use these resources as though the supply were inexhaustible. Our lifestyle has been shaped by these resources. Think for a moment of all the things in your home that are a result of, or dependent on, electricity or petroleum products. What changes would occur in your lifestyle if these products were no longer available?

The average consumer has the equivalent of about 300 persons as "energy servants." It is a shock to learn that we may have to give up or curtail the use of some of these energy servants. Perhaps one of the most difficult adjustments that will have to be made is the development of changed attitudes and values with regard to electricity and petroleum products. The family unit plays a primary role in the shaping of members' values and attitudes. It is through everyday use and practice that we learn to relate resources to the achievement of desired goals. Consequently the family's behavior will have to change. Our time-honored values of independence, individualism, competition, and mastery of nature—values prevalent in Western society—will need to be reevaluated as we set new standards for energy use.

An accurate assessment of our present energy supply and a projection of future needs for energy are essential. The ambiguities of the past few years have served to confuse, frighten, and even antagonize the consuming citizen. We do not need to hear doomsday predictions or to be told that we will have to return to the lifestyle of fifty or one hundred years ago. Some lessons from the past, though, may help us to cope with present and future problems. Educated, independent, resourceful American individuals and their families will accept the

Will all of these still be available in an energy-short society?

ENVIRONMENT, ENERGY, AND THE QUALITY OF LIFE

challenge and make necessary adjustments when they are fully aware of the realities of the situation. When we know that cooperative efforts are being made by government and other consuming citizens to conserve present resources and seek new or alternate forms of energy, we too will do what needs to be done.

Most people are now aware that driving a car uses a great amount of energy and that our driving habits should be changed. But many people still do not realize that between 20 and 30 percent of all energy used in the United States is used in the home. This does not include energy used by manufacturers to produce items for the home or the energy consumed in producing and operating our millions of cars. It is not hard to comprehend why home energy consumption has increased so rapidly in recent years when we consider the changes and improvements in heating and cooling systems and the proliferation of electric appliances.

Let's look at some uses of energy in the home:

Energy is used to heat and cool the home living space and to adjust the humidity.

Energy is used to heat water to desired temperatures for all the family needs.

Energy is used to prepare, cook, and preserve food.

Energy is used to power household appliances.

Energy is used to remove garbage and waste from the home.

Energy is used to bring light to the home.

Energy is used to keep us in touch with the outside world by means of radio, television, and telephone. These items also provide entertainment and cultural development.

Of all the energy used in the home, the major amount is consumed in heating and cooling the living space. The next largest use of energy is for heating water. Your water heater is the most expensive appliance to operate after the furnace and air conditioner. It accounts for about 15 percent of the utility bill, while the range accounts for 5 to 7 percent. Self-cleaning ovens are large users of electricity, and the frost-free refrigerator requires about 50 percent more energy than the conventional type.

Home lighting consumes only about 3.5 percent of our total energy —so a blackout would do little to conserve energy.

What are some ways you can conserve energy in the home? We discussed some of them in Chapter 4 in connection with appliances. Here are some more:

1. Install or increase insulation.
2. Check for air leakage and install storm windows, storm doors, and weather stripping where needed.
3. Have equipment checked once a year and change or clean filters.

4. In building a house, consider having windows that open to provide cross-ventilation rather than installing an air conditioner.
5. Turn the heat and air conditioning off in rooms that are not used regularly.
6. Repair leaky faucets immediately.
7. Use lights in specific work areas instead of lighting the entire room.
8. Turn off lights when a room is not in use.
9. Substitute fluorescent for incandescent lighting.
10. Eliminate gas lights because of their inefficiency.

Is the Consuming Citizen Changing?

We have mentioned that the energy crisis and the damaging of our environment may require us to adjust our lifestyles. Already there is evidence that such a change is taking place. Millions of people are making do with less these days. Partly this is a reaction to inflation and a result of an unwillingness to spend in a time of economic uncertainty. But partly it derives from a genuine feeling that consumption should be kept under control, that one should not eat the whole hog if half would do.

Individuals are buying fewer cars, and of those sold an increased proportion have been smaller, more economical models. Consumers are turning their backs on high-priced travel by choosing recreation close to home. When they do travel, they go by the most economical route, and the destination is generally selected because of its unique features and reasonable cost. Overseas travel and travel to more prestigious resort areas have declined. Airlines are providing more options, including economy no-meal service.

Today there is more emphasis on the functional use of space. Some families are selecting less costly homes and are omitting such infrequently used space as a separate dining room. One building corporation is encouraging new-home buyers to finish some of the space themselves in order to save money or to get more house for the money spent. Consumers are giving more attention to nondeluxe appliances and are expressing a willingness to tolerate some discomfort in order to save on energy.

One finds that there has been a considerable increase in home gardening and in freezing and canning food for home use. There are indications that consumers are becoming more prudent shoppers; when an item becomes overpriced, they either use less of it or substitute lower-priced items.

There are other, bolder indications of greater frugality on the part of consumers. In some cases one might term their careful spending "ostentatious parsimony." We see it manifest in the wearing of old and threadbare clothes and shoes with holes in the sole. Infrequent haircuts have become fashionable among the younger generation. Young people who have grown to maturity surrounded by an abundance of "things" are turning to a simpler lifestyle. Many of our youth are asking some basic and searching questions about values. These young people are better educated, have traveled more extensively, and are more vocal than any previous generation. They are questioning which things are really important. They want to know what may happen if the world population keeps growing and we keep using natural resources as we have in the past.

SUMMARY

In summary, how does one begin to act as a responsible consuming citizen? Your actions at home, in the marketplace, and in the community can encourage your friends and family to do their part. Small steps by each consuming citizen can create giant steps for mankind. Subtle changes can result in a more wholesome lifestyle consistent with our new circumstances.

What are some of these "small steps" that if multiplied by the millions of people who take them will result in a better life for all citizens?

1. *Recognize that our natural resources are limited and often fragile.* American pioneers discovered a rich, vast country whose natural resources seemed inexhaustible. For the last two hundred years, we have been cutting the forest, draining the swamps, impoverishing the soil, and depleting the ground water. The great natural resources of this country have in many cases been squandered. Much of what remains has been spoiled by pollution. The attitude has been one of conquering nature, rather than of recognizing our dependence on natural resources and our need to live harmoniously with the environment.

    One hundred years is required for a mature forest to develop from an abandoned field. This is just one example of how natural resources are difficult or impossible to replenish. Each consuming citizen must be aware of the effects his decisions have on present and future generations. Steps must be taken to see that our resources are nourished and given proper treatment. They are the sources of future supplies.

2. *Buy wisely; do not overbuy.* There is enormous waste in this country. For example, authorities say that Americans waste 40 percent of their food supply. A reduction of 200 to 500 calories per day per adult would help to build up world food supplies and probably result in healthier Americans as well. Millions around the world are starving because of an inadequate food supply. Food saved by reducing intake could help alleviate the problem.

3. *Make a commitment to assume a fair share of the responsibility for change.* Each person should seek to learn the facts about the quality of life in his own immediate area—the air pollution level, the procedure used to dispose of solid waste, the exploitation of natural resources. Each of us then can join established groups or initiate a citizens' action group to beautify and preserve the local area. If each person would make a small contribution to the improvement of the environment and the preservation of resources, much could be accomplished.

GLOSSARY OF NEW TERMS

Degradable containers Containers made of substances that will decompose when the container has been discarded.

Environmental Protection Agency (EPA) An agency established by the U. S. Congress to watch over the country's environment and take measures necessary to improve it and prevent further deterioration.

Fluoridation The addition of minute amounts of fluoride, a chemical substance, to drinking water in order to protect against the formation of dental cavities.

Fluorocarbons A chemical gas used in aerospray products.

Litter Solid waste scattered on the landscape.

Ozone layer A concentrated band of ozone lying about 15 miles above the earth's surface that serves to filter out some of the dangerous rays from the sun.

Particulates Minute amounts of liquid or solid matter found in the air, caused by smoke and auto emissions.

Quality of life The general satisfactoriness of the life we lead. It involves the interrelationship of physical, mental, social, emotional, and nutritional factors. Adequate services and a community structure are important dimensions of the quality of life.

Recycling A process of reusing waste material—for instance, using discarded glass bottles as a source of new glass products.

Solid waste All waste that is not airborne or waterborne.

QUESTIONS FOR DISCUSSION

1. Identify some major differences in the lifestyles of individuals living in rural America fifty years ago and individuals living in your community today.
2. Discuss the changes occurring in the lifestyles of young families today. To what can these changes be attributed?
3. Explain the adverse effect of technology on the environment.
4. List some ways by which you can reduce the amount of water you use and still maintain acceptable standards of sanitation.
5. Identify ten appliances or pieces of equipment generally found in the home that make a major contribution to noise pollution.
6. Explain how noise in the home can be reduced without altering the family lifestyle significantly.
7. Explain what is meant by "solid waste." Identify three examples.
8. Name three methods of disposing of solid waste. What might be some of the advantages and disadvantages of each method?
9. Discuss ways in which consuming citizens can assume their responsibility for reducing solid waste.
10. Discuss the advantages and disadvantages of pesticides and their relation to the "quality of life."
11. Name five things you can do to promote safe use of pesticides.
12. Identify four contaminants of the air. Discuss the effects of polluted air.
13. List five things you can do to help clean the air and keep it clean.

14. Discuss why the use of energy has increased rapidly in recent years.
15. Identify five things that individuals or families can do to conserve energy in the home.

SUGGESTED STUDENT ACTIVITIES

1. Prepare a two-column chart listing the "pollution" and "antipollution" activities of consuming citizens. Evaluate your own activities daily for one week, making notations in the appropriate column on the chart. Identify the activities that can be changed from "pollution" to "antipollution" and describe the procedures for making the changes.
2. Carry out an energy-conservation project in your home. Record the amount of energy (gas or electricity) used for one month. Then implement your conservation project, and at the end of a month compare the amount used with the data from the previous month.
3. Visit your local sanitation department and find out, from the engineers, what procedures are used for disposing of solid waste. Share the information with other members of the class. (Pictures and a taped interview would be interesting and informative.)
4. Initiate an antilitter campaign. Prepare a bulletin board or exhibits on ways to stamp out litter. Volunteer to talk to groups about beautifying your area by proposed disposal of solid waste.
5. Investigate local and state air pollution controls. Prepare a list of major contaminants in your community.
6. Check the insulation in your home. Find out what is considered adequate, evaluate your home, and suggest changes that should be made to conserve energy.
7. Find out if there are local groups engaged in activities to improve the environment. Prepare a report of your findings, giving the name of each group, its purposes, achievements, and projects under way. If there is a group with which you can identify, join and become active.
8. Select a packaged food (for example, peas, lima beans, or corn), prepare it for eating, and weigh or measure the volume of solid waste. Record your findings. Buy the same food in its natural raw state (for example, corn in shuck, beans in the shell). Prepare the same quantity that you purchased prepackaged. Again weigh or measure the volume of solid waste. Chart your findings. Formulate conclusions from your experiment.
9. Contact the local building inspector to find out the requirements for insulation and soundproofing of new apartments and other new buildings. Prepare a report of your findings.

FOR ADDITIONAL INFORMATION

Concern, Inc. Eco Tips. A series of leaflets. Washington, D.C.
> Leaflets on various environmental concerns. They can be obtained by writing to the organization at 2233 Wisconsin Avenue N.W., Washington, D.C. 20007.

"Conserve Energy and Save Money." *Changing Times*, August 1973, pp. 45–46.

A lengthy list of energy-saving tips culled from many sources to help consumers conserve electricity, gas, coal, and oil.

The Energy Crisis and Home Economics. Journal of Home Economics, December 1973.

This special issue on energy contains a series of articles by various authors on the energy crisis as it relates to the home. Includes suggestions for curtailing the use of energy.

Gmur, Ben C., John T. Fodor, Litta Glass, and Joseph J. Langan. *Making Health Decisions*. Englewood Cliffs, N.J.: Prentice-Hall, 1975.

Chapter 13, on preventing and eliminating environmental contamination, contains valuable suggestions on air, water, and noise pollution, on radiation, and on presticides.

Harris, Robert H., and Edward M. Brecker. "Is the Water Safe to Drink?" *Consumer Reports*, June 1974, pp. 436–443.

The first of a three-part series on making water safe to drink. The authors cite the problems of unsafe drinking water, point to research findings, and stress the urgency of immediate action.

"Less Pollution—More Auto Upkeep." *Changing Times*, August 1973, pp. 19–20.

Simple precautionary steps are suggested to make sure that the anti-pollution equipment on your car is working correctly and to keep it functioning efficiently.

Maddox, John. *The Doomsday Syndrome*. New York: McGraw-Hill, 1972.

A British scientist and editor does a thorough job of analyzing the statements of his fellow scientists on such topics as the environment, ecology, and population. The author recognizes the seriousness of the issues but is optimistic about the future.

Saalbach, William F. *The Consumer and Current Issues*. River Forest, Ill.: Laidlaw Brothers, 1974.

This ninety-six-page paperback, written on the secondary level, contains valuable information on ecology and the economy from which even the postsecondary student can benefit. Suggested projects are included.

Office of Consumer Affairs. *Ways to Reduce Energy Consumption and Increase Comfort in Household Cooling*, No. 0303–0876. Washington, D.C.: Government Printing Office, 1972.

A pamphlet that offers eleven ways to reduce energy consumption in cooling the house. 20 pp.

———. *Ways to Reduce Fuel Consumption in Household Heating—Through Energy Conservation*, No. 0303–01086. Washington, D.C.: Government Printing Office, 1972.

This pamphlet explains seven methods of reducing the use of fuel in heating the home.

Thomas, Dana L. "The Sky Is Falling! Chicken Little Is Alive and Well and Worrying About the Ozone." *Barron's*, March 3, 1975, p. 3.

A provocative article about the danger to the ozone posed by fluorocarbons in aerosols and refrigeration systems. Explains both sides of the issue.

U.S. Department of Agriculture. *A Good Life for More People: The 1971 Yearbook of Agriculture*. Washington, D.C.: Government Printing Office, 1971.

A substantial portion of this yearbook is devoted to space for living. Emphasis is also given to conservation, use of resources, and providing a quality environment in which to live.

Ways to Reduce Energy Consumption and Increase Comfort in Household Cooling, and *Ways to Reduce Fuel Consumption in Household Heating—Through Energy Conservation,* Washington, D.C.: Government Printing Office, 1972.

Two pamphlets, one offers 7 ways to reduce fuel consumption in heating and the other gives 11 ways to reduce energy consumption in household cooling.

"What America Really Thinks About Pollution Clean-Up: A Report of Special Gallup Survey." *National Wildlife,* April 1972, pp. 18–19.

Stimulates thinking about one's civic responsibilities for the prevention and control of pollution.

14

Consumerism and Consumer Services

14

Consumerism and consumer movements in the United States are not new issues. As far back as the latter part of the nineteenth century, efforts were under way to alert consumers to the need to beware in the marketplace. Conditions that arose in the early 1900s and again in the late 1920s also aroused social and political groups to seek reforms on behalf of the consumer. The current consumer movement began in the 1960s, helped in no small measure by the efforts of Ralph Nader and his associates, who challenged a number of accepted practices by large corporations, particularly General Motors.

In this chapter you will learn about: (1) early efforts to protect the consumer, (2) the dimensions of consumerism today, (3) some issues of consumerism, and (4) some of the agencies and resources available to help you. It is well to keep in mind that the consumer is *you*—for as a consumer you have both rights and responsibilities.

Early Efforts to Protect the Consumer

In the 1890s and early 1900s, with the rapid growth of cities and the rise of industrialization, new problems appeared in the United States. Some of these were poor housing conditions, urban poverty, hazardous working conditions, sweatshops, exploitation of child labor, and various classic "consumer" problems, such as adulterated foods and fraudulent trade practices. These or similar conditions stimulated the formation of a variety of reform organizations. The first Consumers' League was formed in New York City in 1891. Its first effort was to prepare a "white list" of shops that paid fair wages and had reasonable hours and decent sanitary conditions. In 1898 the National Consumers' League was organized, and by 1903 it had grown to sixty-four branches in twenty different states.

Early efforts to pass consumer legislation met with stiff opposition. The dangers of adulterated and dyed foods and of unlabeled drugs containing opiates and large quantities of alcohol were publicized by the "muckraker" press, a group of newspapers and journals that exposed abuses in politics and business. The need for pure-food-and-drug legislation was becoming more evident. Theodore Roosevelt urged the enactment of such a law in his annual message to Congress after his election in 1904. But it was not until after the publication of Upton Sinclair's book *The Jungle,* an exposé of the working conditions in Chicago's meat-packing industry, that the Pure Food and Drug Law was passed by Congress in 1906. It took years of effort, a full-blown scandal, and the pressure of a strong president to bring about passage of the bill.

The first consumer movement was not a continuous surge. However, the need for government regulation of the business activities and competitive practices of the rapidly growing railroads and industrial

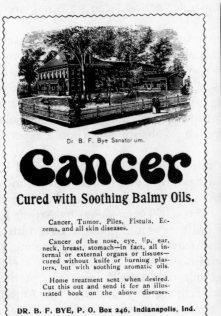

Dr. B. F. Bye Sanatorium.

Cancer
Cured with Soothing Balmy Oils.

Cancer, Tumor, Piles, Fistula, Eczema, and all skin diseases.

Cancer of the nose, eye, lip, ear, neck, breast, stomach—in fact, all internal or external organs or tissues—cured without knife or burning plasters, but with soothing aromatic oils.

Home treatment sent when desired. Cut this out and send it for an illustrated book on the above diseases.

DR. B. F. BYE, P. O. Box 246, Indianapolis, Ind.

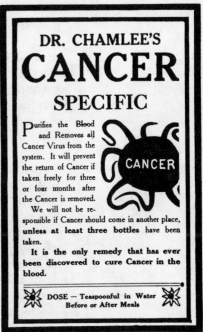

DR. CHAMLEE'S
CANCER
SPECIFIC

Purifies the Blood and Removes all Cancer Virus from the system. It will prevent the return of Cancer if taken freely for three or four months after the Cancer is removed.

We will not be responsible if Cancer should come in another place, **unless at least three bottles** have been taken.

It is the only remedy that has ever been discovered to cure Cancer in the blood.

DOSE — Teaspoonful in Water Before or After Meals

corporations was becoming more and more evident. In 1914 the Federal Trade Commission Act provided the machinery to enforce antitrust laws and to spell out unfair methods of competition, including deceptive advertising.

Following World War I, wages rose, prices remained relatively stable, and consumers' disposable income therefore increased. More goods became available and consumers were besieged with advertising. The general public had not yet been aroused by consumer problems. However, by the mid-twenties educators began to recognize the need for consumer education. Home economists had been concerned with consumer education since the formative years of their national association, founded in 1908. By the mid-twenties the American Home Economics Association, concerned about the limited amount of economics in students' curricula, had stimulated research into consumer problems and into ways to improve teaching in the field.

Discontent continued to grow as new and unfamiliar goods flooded the markets. Except for advertising, consumers had little information on which to base decisions. A 1927 publication, *Your Money's Worth*, By Stuart Chase and F. J. Schlink, attacked advertising and high-pressure salesmanship and called for consumer protection laws, product testing, and furnishing of the scientific information a consumer needed to make decisions. The book became a best seller and led to the formation of Consumers' Research, Inc., a product-testing agency. This revival of consumer concern can be considered the start of a second "movement."

The depression of the 1930s goaded consumers further and made consumer education seem urgent. Budgeting was introduced into consumer education classes, to teach people a means of controlling their expenditures. Consumers were taught to renovate or make do with what they had. Instruction in making cold cream, toothpaste, and soap became a part of the curriculum in many schools. Students were urged to use inexpensive substitutes for more expensive, highly advertised products.

By the thirties, the 1906 Pure Food and Drug Act was outdated because of many new developments in technology; it also had been weakened by court decisions. Franklin Roosevelt's administration, inspired by *100,000,000 Guinea Pigs* by Arthur Kallet and F. J. Schlink, sponsored a bill that would give the government considerable power, including control over labeling and advertising; a new agency, the Food and Drug Administration (FDA), would be created. Concern about the sale of dangerous products, the wasteful proliferation of brands, and fraudulent advertising was growing. The American Home Economics Association and the National Congress of Parents and Teachers urged passage of the proposed legislation.

However, there was strong opposition to the bill, especially to the regulation of advertising and the creation of a grade-labeling system for food. It was not until 1938, after a liquid form of a new sulfa "wonder drug," Elixir Sulfanilamide, was placed on the market without testing and over one hundred people died from its use, that the FDA legislation was passed. The new law updated the government's regulatory powers over foods and drugs. New controls on advertising were included, but the Federal Trade Commission rather than the FDA was given authority in that area. Consumer groups were unhappy with the weakened form in which the legislation emerged; nevertheless, an awareness had been created among teachers, young people, and others which was to keep consumerism alive. The creation of Consumers Union, a voluntary nonprofit organization formed in 1936, can be traced to the "guinea pig" book. Its publication, *Consumer Reports,* survived the Great Depression and today claims over two million subscribers.

The Present Consumer Movement

The present consumer movement emerged in the sixties. President John F. Kennedy can be credited with much of the present concern for consumerism on account of his 1962 State of the Union Address. In this address he proposed a consumer "bill of rights" which included:

1. The right to safety—to be protected against the marketing of goods which are hazardous to life or health;

2. The right to choose—to be assured, whenever possible, access to a variety of products and services at competitive prices;
3. The right to be informed—to be protected against fraudulent, deceitful, or grossly misleading practices and to be given the facts necessary for an informed choice;
4. The right to be heard—to be assured of sympathetic consideration in the formulation of government policy and fair, prompt treatment in the administrative tribunals.

During the current consumer movement a number of significant consumer protection laws have been passed—some of which follow closely the lines suggested in Kennedy's "bill of rights." Among these are the Fair Packaging and Labeling Act (1965), the National Traffic and Motor Vehicle Safety Act (1966), the Federal Cigarette Labeling and Advertising Act (1967), the Wholesome Meat Act (1967), the Consumer Credit Protection Act (1968), the Fair Credit Reporting Act (1970), the Truth-in-Food-Labeling Act (1972), and the Consumer Product Safety Act (1972).

In 1964 President Lyndon B. Johnson appointed the first special presidential adviser for consumer affairs, Esther Peterson. This appointment brought a person to the highest level of government to represent the consumer. The office was later transferred to the Department of Health, Education and Welfare; its responsibility is to advise the president on matters of consumer interest and coordinate all federal activities in the consumer field. Efforts are under way to create a Consumer Protection Agency at the national level to argue the consumer's side of issues before other government agencies. Ralph Nader, the Consumer Federation of America, and a coalition of consumer groups, labor unions, and other organization all support the measure.

Many other pieces of legislation are currently pending. Included in these measures are bills for no-fault automobile insurance and credit reform. The current efforts in the Congress are designed to give citizens more muscle in the marketplace. The recession and inflation of recent years have imposed a sense of urgency on Congress. Because of the state of the economy and changes in legislative leadership, the odds appear to favor congressional action that will benefit the consumer.

Today's consumer is better educated and enjoys a higher income than the consumer of old. He or she is not afraid to speak out. The consumer is encouraged by advocates like Ralph Nader and by the private groups that have been formed to present the consumer's position.

Consumers of past decades were able to take for granted a wholesome environment and "unlimited" resources. Today's consumers have suddenly become aware that their very survival is threatened by unsafe and unhealthy products, wholesale pollution of air, water, and land, and the irresponsible use of scarce natural resources both by commercial companies and by individuals.

The consumer
is beginning to flex
his muscles.

The consumer movement which started in the sixties is unlike earlier movements in that it seems destined to remain a strong force. The earlier movements, to a degree, accomplished their objectives, but soon they lost their momentum. The consumer movement of the sixties and seventies has broadened its base to include questions of ecology, social consequences, and ethics. A more enlightened and better educated citizenry, coupled with a higher standard of living and an increased technological capability, has brought about greater interest in an expanded array of consumer issues. Millions of consumers are responding to the issues in a variety of ways. Government representatives at all levels are hearing from their voters. Manufacturers and business organizations are being made aware of consumer concerns and consumer actions. They now must recognize that it takes more than advertising and a good public relations program to satisfy customers and maintain sales.

The results of the present consumer movement should be a more responsible marketplace, a more responsive electorate, a more genuinely concerned citizen, and a significant improvement in the quality of life for all.

Consumer Education

Educators, businessmen, and other citizens began to recognize in the late sixties that consumer education could not be left to television or salesmen, and plans began to evolve for providing systematic instruction. The Vocational Education Amendments of 1968 included Part F, entitled "Consumer and Homemaking Education," which stipulated that consumer education would be made an integral part of all vocational home economics programs. The Education Amendments of 1972 also included a section on consumer education.

Demands for education that is relevant to current problems of living have been loudly sounded. It is increasingly evident that American society is strongly consumer oriented, yet educators have not given sufficient attention to the development of consumer knowledge and skill. As a result, several states have passed laws mandating courses in consumer education, while others have used a variety of subtler techniques to develop consumer education programs. Some states give priority to in-service education for teachers, while others concentrate on the development of curriculum materials for consumer education. Topics such as financial planning, credit, consumer protection, insurance, the buying of food, clothing, shelter, and transportation, saving and investing, estate planning, and consumer citizenship have been incorporated into the curricula at various levels.

Consumer Issues

Some of the issues that consumers will need to give attention to in the years ahead are already upon the horizon. As good citizens and consumers we should not only recognize these but also learn the proper approaches for dealing with new problems as they occur. Situations are bound to change, but the process of seeking solutions remains the same.

Some issues for immediate attention are:

1. *Values and Beliefs.* Our values, and our beliefs about what is important to us, need to be clarified and sustained. Our choices in the marketplace are influenced by these values and beliefs. Unless we have convictions based on sound principles which we are willing to defend, we may easily be influenced by sales pressure, advertising, or uninformed persons, and in such cases we may act irresponsibly.

2. *The Quality of Life.* As consumers we need to consider the ethics of our consumption. More and more people are living in crowded metropolitan areas. No longer can each person "do his own thing" without considering the effects of his action on others. Noise pollution, water pollution, air pollution, and the accumulation of solid waste influence the quality of life for all consumers. As responsible citizens we must reckon with these issues.

3. *Energy and Other Resources.* Our lifestyle has developed largely from our use of energy and natural resources. It is hard to imagine the changes we would have to make if we could not use the family car, for example. We have not yet come to the full realization that the supply of energy is limited. Yet we must conserve if our supply is

to last and if we are to remain reasonably independent of other countries. The economic and political aspects of this issue must be faced and dealt with.

4. *Expansion and Complexity of the Marketplace.* Although they may be proud of the fact that a great array of merchandise is available, consumers are bewildered by the increasing size and complexity of the marketplace. A multitude of news items make choices difficult. With so many items available from which to choose, and with only limited information, consumers can find the purchase of a single item a real dilemma. What to buy as well as how to buy it poses a real problem.

5. *Service and Maintenance.* New technology has brought new service problems. How long should an appliance last, and what type of service should be provided by the manufacturer or dealer? How well can the consumer make decisions about service costs versus replacement costs? The warranty is often written so that it is difficult for the consumer to understand. In many instances the supplier is protected at the expense of the buyer. Service, maintenance, and warranties are issues that need to be resolved.

6. *Legal Rights, Arbitration Courts, and How to Complain Effectively.* With the increase in complex contractual agreements, there is more need to understand consumers' legal rights and obligations. The consumer needs to know what channels of recourse are available and how to make his or her dissatisfactions known. Voluntary arbitration boards, in convenient locations, are one way to resolve the differences between customers and businesses. Some trade associations have set up regional or national arbitration panels that are usually binding on members. The Major Appliance Consumer Action Panel (MACAP) is a good example. Adequate recourse for consumers is a real concern.

7. *Health and Funeral Costs.* Medical and hospital costs continue to rise. The poor and the elderly suffer from more illnesses than the average American, but frequently it is the middle-income family whose lifelong savings are wiped out by a major illness. If health is a basic right of all citizens, finding equitable means of financing health costs is a consumer issue that needs to be resolved. National health insurance, now being considered by Congress, is one possibility.

Another issue, along with health costs, is the high cost of dying. Funeral expenses frequently consume a sizeable part of the estate at a time when it is most needed by the family. Consumers need to be protected from unnecessary services and excessive charges at a time of great emotional stress.

These are only some of the issues that are worthy of consumers' attention. As you become more aware of your role as a consuming citizen, you will identify many additional issues. As you read the daily newspaper or current periodicals, try to identify issues of concern to consumers. Consider joining a volunteer action group and working to bring about changes on the local or state level to benefit consumers. Contact your elected representatives to let them know your position on matters affecting you and others. Remember that an informed citizen is in the best position to make intelligent decisions and to avoid costly mistakes.

Where to Get Assistance

As consumers we want the government to assist us in making sounder decisions about the multitude of new products and services that are constantly coming on the market. The increased variety and complexity of goods and services makes rational consumer decisions much more difficult. Consumers are looking for the government to supply them with (1) the reliable information they need to make sound decisions about the many products being offered, (2) standards of quality for consumer products and strong enforcement of these standards, (3) protection against unfair and unsound business practices, and (4) re-

Consumers seek protection through government services.

course for abuses against consumers. The various levels of government attempt to fulfill these expectations by means of consumer agencies.

Federal Consumer Agencies

There are about fifty different federal agencies and bureaus performing some two or three hundred functions affecting the consumer. Some of the more important ones are named in the following list. For a more complete catalog of agencies that provide consumer assistance, refer to the sources listed under "For Additional Information" at the end of this chapter.

The Office of Consumer Affairs of the *Civil Aeronautics Board* is concerned with customers' complaints about airline services.

The *Consumer Affairs Section* of the Department of Justice is responsible for processing cases referred to it by other agencies.

The *Consumer Marketing Service,* part of the Department of Agriculture, tries to regulate, improve, and protect the nation's food-marketing system.

The *Consumer Product Safety Commission (CPSC),* established in 1972, has sweeping powers to regulate the production and sale of potentially hazardous consumer products.

The *Environmental Protection Agency (EPA)* is concerned with the development of programs to improve the quality of our environment.

The *Federal Trade Commission (FTC)* is the agency that protects the public from unfair marketing procedures and deceptive practices.

The *Food and Drug Administration (FDA)* protects the health of consumers by seeing that foods are safe, pure, and wholesome; that drugs and therapeutic devices are safe and effective; that cosmetics are harmless; and that all of these products are honestly labeled and packaged.

The *Food and Nutrition Service* of the Department of Agriculture provides citizens with information on nutrition and on food programs, such as the school food service, the food stamp program, and special milk programs.

The *Health Services and Mental Health Administration (HSMHA)* is the agency that provides the leadership for health programs and services. It is concerned with the development of comprehensive health-care maintenance systems.

The *National Bureau of Standards* of the Department of Commerce is the nation's laboratory for measurement and product and safety standards.

The *National Business Council for Consumer Affairs*, part of the Department of Commerce, encourages business firms to meet their responsibilities to the consumer.

The *Office of Consumer Affairs* in the Department of Health, Education and Welfare analyzes and coordinates all federal activities on behalf of consumers. It serves as a focal point in the government's effort to help people.

The *Securities and Exchange Commission (SEC)* is responsible for establishing regulations to protect the public against fraud in investments.

As of this writing (in 1975), Congress is considering a bill to create a *Consumer Protection Agency (CPA),* which would operate independently of all other federal agencies. The CPA would serve as the consumer's representative at all formal and informal hearings of federal departments and bureaus. The administrator of the CPA could enlist the support of the courts to enforce his right to attend informal hearings. He would also have the power to conduct his own investigations. There is a strong possibility that the bill will receive congressional approval in spite of strong business and administration opposition.

State and Local Consumer Agencies

Generally, in the past, state and local agencies, where they existed, have been negligent in providing consumers with protective services. However, there is now evidence of greater legislative efforts, stimulated in no small measure by consumer demands.

States usually regulate such matters of consumer concern as banking, credit and insurance, utility rates, milk and agricultural products, real estate sales, sales of alcoholic beverages and tobacco products, and burial services. At the city and county levels we find concern for such consumer interests as weights and measures, sanitation in restaurants and markets, and building and construction standards.

Consumer protection in most states is the responsibility of the state attorney general; consumer protection staffs operate out of the attorney general's office. Some states, however, have consumer affairs and consumer protection offices directly responsible to the governor. State departments of agriculture, education, and commerce are also often active in the consumer area.

A growing number of states, in response to consumer demands, are establishing consumer affairs or consumer protection agencies, as well as strengthening legislation to control unfair and deceptive practices. At least thirty-six states now have laws patterned after the Federal Trade Commission Act.

At the city and county level, local statutes, ordinances, and codes offer consumer protection. We are also beginning to see more and more "ombudsmen" who are paid by the government to protect consumer interests.

City and county agencies such as the mayor's office, fire, police, and health departments, and welfare agencies are available to assist with consumer problems. Local media—newspapers and radio or television stations—will often give you information as to where you can get help.

Private Consumer Agencies

A number of private agencies, not affiliated with government, have been formed solely for the purpose of aiding consumers. In addition, there are some organizations that provide help to consumers as a sideline to their other activities. Some of these organizations are:

The *American Bankers Association* disseminates information about personal money management.

The *American Bar Association* offers material outlining steps to follow and pitfalls to avoid when purchasing a home.

The *Department of Community Services of the AFL-CIO* informs union members about consumer problems.

The *American Home Economics Association* improves the quality of individual and family life through education, cooperative programs, research, and public information.

The *American Medical Association* issues pamphlets that alert consumers to misleading advertisements and to the ineffectiveness of many health products and special remedies.

Associated Credit Bureaus is an international trade association serving the credit industry. Its local credit bureaus, besides providing credit evaluations, help customers maintain their credit records and assist consumers when they have credit difficulties.

The *Chamber of Commerce of the United States* is composed of over fifty local business and trade associations. Though directed primarily toward business, the chamber does issue publications and engage in activities of interest to consumers.

The *Consumer Bankers Association* provides information to consumers on installment lending and banking activities.

Consumer Research, Inc., conducts scientific tests of products that consumers buy and use.

The *Consumers Federation of America (CFA)* is dedicated to consumer action through legislation and education. It is a federation of national, state, regional, and local consumer organizations.

Consumers Union of the United States (CU) is the world's largest testing and information organization for consumers. It provides information on tested products and publishes *Consumer Reports* and a yearly buying guide. The organization participates in government hearings and acts as an advocate for consumer protection.

The *Council of Better Business Bureaus,* dedicated to building public confidence in the business system, is a fact-finding organization that investigates complaints of unfair and unethical business practices.

Ralph Nader, the famous consumer advocate, has organized five groups to report on various areas of consumer dissatisfaction. These are:

Center for Auto Safety
Center for Study of Responsive Law
Consumer Aviation Project

Project on Corporate Responsibility
Public Interest Research Group

The *National Consumer Finance Association* is involved in education and other programs in the field of consumer finance.

The *National Foundation for Consumer Credit* attempts to provide consumers with an understanding of credit through education, research, and counseling.

The *National Institute for Consumer Justice* was formed to improve grievance-solving mechanisms and find legal remedies for consumers.

All of the organizations listed are but representative of the many sources of consumer assistance. Only recently have consumers organized into cohesive and vocal groups to make their wishes known.

Class-Action Suits

A class-action lawsuit is one way in which consumers can attempt to resolve their grievances. Most consumers on their own cannot afford to take legal measures to obtain compensation for losses from dangerous or faulty products or practices. Many claims for damages arising from fraud or hazardous products are for amounts less than $1,000; for such small sums it is impractical for an individual to sustain the high cost of a lawsuit. Besides, the complex court system discourages the individual consumer who has a grievance against a retailer or manufacturer from seeking restitution. The process of restitution through the courts is too expensive, too time-consuming, and too technical for most people.

Class-action suits are a way of getting around these problems. In a class-action suit one consumer sues a retailer or corporation to obtain indemnity not only for himself but also for all other victims of the same offense. The other victims need not be identified until an advanced stage of the suit. One lawyer may handle the case for all claimants, and fees and expenses can be spread among all of the beneficiaries if they win. Such suits have the advantage of creating thousands of "private attorneys general" who serve as watchdogs over the consumer's interest and assist in enforcing consumer protection laws. An incentive to lawyers to initiate class-action suits on behalf of consumers is that they will be well compensated if they win. Damages in class-action suits run into many hundreds of thousands of dollars, and the courts award counsel fees of up to 30 percent of the sums recovered.

Only a few states permit class-action suits at this time. In many states the interpretation of existing law prevents class action. There is, however, considerable pressure from consumer groups for the right to act as a class in legal matters. In spite of strong opposition from manufacturers and retailers, there is congressional interest in legislation at the federal level to permit class-action suits. Class actions are making progress. Where class action has been permitted, it has demonstrated its value in obtaining consumer justice.

GLOSSARY OF NEW TERMS

Arbitration board   A group formed to hear both sides of a controversy in order to make a binding decision.

Class-action suit   A legal action in which the plaintiff is a representative of all persons injured by the same offense.

Disposable income   A person's income minus imposed personal taxes. "Take-home pay" approximates disposable income, although nontax items may have been deducted.

Ombudsman   A government official who investigates consumers' complaints against the government.

QUESTIONS FOR DISCUSSION

1. Discuss the basic causes or problems which have given rise to consumer movements in late nineteenth- and twentieth-century America.
2. Contrast consumers today and consumers at the time of earlier consumer movements.
3. Explain the provisions of the consumer "bill of rights" as proposed by President Kennedy in 1962.
4. Explain the general functions of the FDA, the FTC, and the Consumer Product Safety Commission.
5. Explain the role education has played in consumer movements.
6. Describe the functions of the adviser for consumer affairs and how this person's office was established.
7. Identify three issues of importance to consumers in the 1970s and explain why they are important.
8. List five important pieces of federal legislation that were enacted during the 1960s to benefit consumers. Can you describe the basic provisions of these laws? If not, where could you learn about them?
9. Discuss the kind of help consumers are asking the government to supply.
10. Define a "class-action suit" and explain how one is conducted.

SUGGESTED STUDENT ACTIVITIES

1. Prepare a chart of the consumer movements in America from the 1890s to the present. List factors that contributed to the movements, the periods of •time covered, and the major accomplishments.
2. Read one of the following books and summarize its contribution to consumerism:

   The Jungle, by Upton Sinclair
   Your Money's Worth, by Stuart Chase and F. J. Schlink
   100,000,000 Guinea Pigs, by Arthur Kallet and F. J. Schlink

3. Prepare a report on recent proposals and legislation for consumer protection. The areas of investigation could include tax reform, energy, national no-fault automobile insurance, national health insurance, credit reform, and consumer advocacy.

4. Investigate the recent actions of one of the following:

> Federal Trade Commission (FTC)
> Food and Drug Administration (FDA)
> Consumer Product Safety Commission (CPSC)
> Environmental Protection Agency (EPA)

Prepare a report of your findings.

5. Interview representatives of local groups concerned with consumer protection to find out the types of service rendered, the number of cases handled in the last month, and the procedures for securing service. Here are some suggestions:

> Better Business Bureau
> Chamber of Commerce
> Legal Aid Society
> Mayor's office
> Local or state office of consumer affairs

6. Select one law designed to protect the consumer that has been passed in the last ten years and investigate the ways in which it is being implemented and the benefits derived by local citizens. Explain whether you think the law is being enforced adequately.

FOR ADDITIONAL INFORMATION

Aaker, David A., and George S. Day, editors. *Consumerism: Search for the Consumer Interest.* New York: Free Press, 1974, pp. 5–93.
> This book is a compilation of articles written by well-known authors in the field of consumerism. The historical essays by Dameron and Herrmann present a thorough description of the consumer movements and how they have helped to generate change.

"Does Consumer Arbitration Really Work?" *Changing Times*, July 1973, pp. 19–21.
> Explains how arbitration courts could be located in neighborhoods to benefit consumers.

Garman, E. Thomas, and Sidney W. Eckert. *The Consumer's World: Buying, Money Management, and Issues.* New York: McGraw-Hill, 1974, pp. 3–56.
> The first three chapters focus on consumers, their dilemma, their functioning in the marketplace, and their changing role. The development of consumerism is traced and basic consumer problems are examined in depth.

"Got a Complaint? Call Your State Consumer Office." *Changing Times*, April 1975, pp. 43–48.
> Explains the general objectives of state consumer protection offices; suggests procedures for making a complaint; lists the principal powers and the names and telephone numbers of the state agencies.

A Guide to Sources of Consumer Information. Washington, D.C.: Information Resources Press, 1973.
> Lists sources of consumer services and information, including governmental agencies.

"How to Use Small Claims Court." *Consumer Reports*, October 1971, pp. 624–631.
  This article presents a good description of small claims courts and the ways they can serve consumers. The procedures for using a small claims court are explained.

"If You're Making a Complaint." *Consumers' Research*, May 1973, pp. 2, 43.
  Suggests steps to follow in making a complaint.

Jelley, Herbert M., and Robert O. Herrmann. *The American Consumer: Issues and Decisions.* New York: Gregg Division of McGraw-Hill, 1973, pp. 424–490. Part 6, "Consumer Assistance and Protection," is designed to inform the reader of the extent to which he or she is protected by existing laws and regulations. It also provides a historical account of consumer protection efforts.

"At Last They're Doing Something About Dangerous Products." *Changing Times*, February 1975, pp. 35–37.
  This article explains the broad powers of the Consumer Product Safety Commission and presents a sampling of actions the commission has taken.

Mead, William B. "Federal Regulation: The Price You Pay." *Money*, June 1975, pp. 38–41.
  Provides insight into the additional costs consumers are required to pay because of federal regulations. President Ford is quoted as saying that the average family may spend as much as $2,000 a year in higher prices that result from government regulations.

Miller, Roger Leroy. *Economic Issues for Consumers.* New York: West, 1975, pp. 415–451.
  Explains how the consumer can communicate his or her concerns. Consumer issues 14 and 15 describe consumer responsibilities and how to use a small claims court.

Shaw, Steven J., and Arch G. Woodside. "Consumerism and Corporate Responsibility: Viewpoints of Legislators." *Business and Economic Review*, Vol. 21, No. 3 (February 1975), pp. 8–14.
  This article provides background on consumer movements in America and presents findings from a study of how members of state legislative bodies felt about thirty-three issues of social concern. Representatives from ten different states were included in the survey, and the viewpoints varied substantially by state and by party affiliation. The journal in which this article is included is published by the Division of Research, College of Business Administration, University of South Carolina.

Udari, Stephen S. *Where to Go, Who to See, What to Do.* Austin, Texas: Steck Vaughn Company, 1973.
  This pamphlet is a fairly complete guide to both public and private consumer services. It provides sound advice on services in the areas of health and medicine, law, employment, recreation, and social activity.

15

You
and
Your
Taxes

15

As citizens we are all called upon to pay a share of the cost of government. Taxes levied upon you by federal, state, and local governments serve to provide a variety of services and protections. These taxes have a considerable effect on your spending plan, because they influence the amount of money you have available for other purposes.

In this chapter you will learn the kinds of taxes you pay, what you get for your taxes, and how to minimize your income taxes.

Kinds of Taxes

Taxes are levied at three levels of government: federal, state, and local (city and county). We pay taxes on the money we earn (income taxes), on what we spend (sales taxes, excise taxes, and utility taxes), and on what we own (personal property taxes and real estate taxes). We provide for old age and for illness through Social Security taxes and for the possibility of unemployment through unemployment insurance taxes. We even pay for those assets we leave behind when we depart this world through inheritance and estate taxes.

There are other, less obvious taxes that we pay, such as for automobile license plates, drivers' licenses, restaurant meals, movies and other entertainment, and motel and hotel rooms. Then, too, there are the taxes paid by professionals, such as lawyers, doctors, and barbers, that permit them to do business in their communities; manufacturers and retailers also pay taxes. These taxes affect the consumer indirectly, since their cost is reflected in the prices we pay for goods and services.

What You Get for Your Taxes

You receive a great variety of services and types of protection for the taxes you pay. At the local and state levels, taxes pay for such things as our educational systems (schools, teachers' salaries, and so on), help for the needy, water and sewage facilities, parks and recreation facilities, streets and roads, and police, fire, and health departments.

At the national level, taxes provide for our national defense and finance our relations with other nations through the United Nations, Peace Corps, and Agency for International Development. Taxes at the federal level also support highway systems, national parks, and educational systems. They pay for assistance for older people, those out of work, and those who can't pay medical bills. Federal taxes support research to improve our health, our education, the foods we eat, and the way we live. These are just some of the services our taxes provide.

There are many different opinions as to whether we get our money's worth for the taxes we pay. Lately, many people have been complaining that we do not. However, we can all agree that the ser-

vices provided at the state, local, and federal levels affect the way we
live and how we spend our money. Furthermore, it would be impossible for each of us to attempt to purchase, on our own, the services
we get from our government.

Controlling Your Taxes

As our society develops, demands are being made that government
provide us with more of the services and protection we want and need.
Better education for ourselves and our children, improved transportation facilities, greater environmental protection, and adequate health
and social programs are but a few of the services that are expected.
Taxes will be needed to pay for them.

Many taxpayers complain that they have no control over what
they are obliged to pay in taxes. Deductions are made from their earnings for Social Security and for federal and state income taxes. Sales
taxes and gasoline taxes must be paid at the point of sale. Excise taxes,
utility taxes, and other indirect taxes are included in the price of the
goods they buy. Under these circumstances how can taxpayers exercise
any control over how much they pay?

You can have a voice in tax decisions through your elected officials. You need to take an active part in selecting public officials who reflect your views about what services are needed and how these will be funded. You must take an interest in how your taxes are being spent, and make your opinions known to those officials who represent you. You should evaluate the cost of the services or protection you are seeking. Environmental controls to improve the quality of air and water are one example of measures that affect your taxes. How much are you willing to pay, in the form of increased prices for the gasoline you use, the car you drive, and the products you buy, in order to achieve the objective of better air and cleaner water? What priority should environmental control have compared to education and health services? Which is most important, and how much of our limited resources should be allocated to each? When you vote for services and protection with full knowledge of their cost, you are acting as a responsible citizen and you are exerting some control over the taxes you pay. You are also influencing your own money plan.

Reducing Your Tax Bill

Tax savings can best be accomplished with your federal income tax, since this represents the greatest of your tax obligations. In spite of the fact that your employer withholds federal income taxes from your earnings, you are obliged to file a federal income tax return each year. At that time you determine whether you owe additional taxes or whether you are entitled to a refund. The U.S. Treasury Department provides free, detailed information concerning how to prepare and file your federal income tax return. Inexpensive and informative material is also available from the other sources mentioned in the section "For Additional Information" at the end of this chapter.

Complete and adequate records are essential for calculating your tax liability. Do not trust to memory. Not only are you likely to overlook deductions to which you are entitled, but you will also lack proof to present to the Internal Revenue Service (IRS) to support the deductions you do claim. One way of keeping records is to use a notebook in which you itemize all your income and your expenditures day by day. Another way is to do all your spending by check and to record on the stub the purpose of each payment. Develop a method that meets your needs and that you find not too burdensome.

In order to minimize your tax obligation you need to understand:

1. What income is taxable and what is not taxable;
2. Which expenses are deductible from your taxable income.

Income, for tax purposes, includes payment you receive for labor (wages, salaries, commissions) and for capital investment (dividends,

Filling out your tax return is a tedious job, but good records make it easier.

interest). Profits from business or from the sale of property (real estate or investments) are also considered as income.

In addition, there are other types of taxable income that are sometimes overlooked. For example, if you receive tips as a waiter or waitress they are considered taxable income. Money won by participating in a contest is taxable; so is the fair market value of merchandise won. However, you do not pay taxes on educational awards in recognition of your past accomplishments.

Gifts or inheritances, Social Security benefits, employee death benefits up to $5,000, accident and health benefits, most life insurance proceeds, and interest payments from state and local governments are generally not taxable as income.

Deductions are divided into two classes:

1. *Money spent to earn income.* This includes the cost of business travel and entertainment, the depreciation of equipment used to produce income, management fees, and the price of uniforms and any other materials used in the performance of your job.
2. *Money spent for certain personal reasons.* You can deduct charitable contributions up to a specified limit, medical and dental expenses under certain conditions, alimony payments, interest and finance charges, certain taxes paid, and the value of personal possessions lost by casualty or theft.

Other savings in income taxes can be effected by taking advantage of the rules governing capital gains, joint returns, and gifts and trusts for children. There are ways to adjust your investment gains and losses. Before engaging in these legal but sophisticated means of tax savings, you should consult a knowledgeable tax accountant or attorney.

If you itemize your deductions instead of taking the standard deduction on your income tax return, you can often save money. Here are some suggestions:

1. Be certain to claim all the exemptions to which you are entitled.
2. Claim the dividend exemption of $100 on any dividend income you have received. On a joint return you may exclude up to $200.
3. Do not report as taxable income the stock dividends or stock rights you received on stock investments unless you had the choice of taking cash or stock.
4. If you use part of your home as an office, deduct the proportion of your home expenses that can be attributed to that section of the house. Include expenses for heat, lights, property taxes, mortgage interest, rent, telephone, insurance, and depreciation. Apportion these expenses on the basis of the number of rooms that you use for business purposes.
5. Be sure to deduct bad debts that have become worthless during the year for which your tax return is being prepared. Unless these are deducted in that year you lose the deduction.
6. Do not report gifts or bequests you have received as taxable income. *Income* from a gift or bequest is taxable, but not the gift itself.
7. Do not report as income any insurance proceeds that you receive as a beneficiary.
8. Deduct your contributions to religious, charitable, and educational institutions. A contribution need not be in cash. Any donation, such as clothing or furniture, entitles you to a deduction.
9. Small contributions can add up to many dollars, so list them all. Generally, up to 30 percent of your adjusted gross income may be deducted in this category.
10. You may not deduct the value of voluntary services donated to an organization as a charitable contribution, but you may deduct the cost of traveling to and from the place where the charity operates.
11. If you receive a large amount of income in one year, you may be able to take advantage of *income averaging*. This is applicable if your taxable income in the current year exceeds by more than $3,000 an amount that is one-third greater than the average of your taxable income in the four preceding years.
12. Deduct all interest paid on installment purchases. Sellers of goods on the installment plan are required to advise you of the total installment charges.

13. Deduct the interest you pay for all borrowings, including business, personal, and family debts.
14. Deduct all sales taxes paid to state and local governments. While there are tax tables to help you calculate this deduction, the tables do not include major purchases such as automobiles, so be sure to add them.
15. Include deductions for premiums on medical insurance. Be aware that there are limitations, but take the deductions to which you are entitled.
16. When itemizing medical expenses be sure to include transportation costs for trips to hospitals or doctors' offices, including parking and toll fees. Do not forget to include the medical expenses of all members of your family. Do not overlook bills paid for eyeglasses, hearing aids, and repairs to these items. Include all dental costs.
17. You may deduct expenses for home improvements that are made for medical purposes if your physician orders them. This would include the installation of air conditioners for medical purposes and of electric stairs for cardiac patients.
18. For education you engaged in to maintain your job skills, deduct the cost of courses taken, travel expenses, and living expenses while away from home. Regular courses leading to a degree may be deducted as an expense if these do not prepare you for a different occupation or profession.
19. Deduct expenses incurred to produce or collect income. This deduction would include investment counseling fees and rental of a safe-deposit box to hold securities. The services of an accountant you employ to keep track of your income are also deductible.
20. Deduct the cost of preparing your federal, state, and local tax returns, including duplications.
21. Be sure to include local or state income taxes, if you are required to pay such taxes, when you itemize your deductions.
22. Losses suffered from storm, fire, accident, or other casualty may be claimed on your return. If the loss is insured you must reduce your loss by the amount of any insurance benefit you receive. There is a $100 deductible for each casualty claim.
23. You may claim a loss of property for something that has been stolen from you, provided that you have reported the loss to the police and there is a police report on it. Here again there is a $100 deductible.
24. If you have worked for more than one employer and more than the maximum amount of Social Security tax has been deducted during the year, be sure to claim the overpayment when you file your income tax return.
25. If you pay a maid or sitter to watch your children or other dependents so you can go to work, you may be able to deduct all or part of these payments. There are limitations to this deduction.

26. The expenses of moving to a new location or to a new job may be deductible under certain conditions. Check these out when preparing your return.
27. The cost of work clothes may be deductible, as well as the cost of cleaning and repairing, if special attire is required for your job and cannot be worn on the street. Nurses' uniforms are an example of such clothes.
28. Tools and equipment you use on the job are also deductible. If the items last only one year, you can deduct their full cost in the year you buy them. Otherwise, you must depreciate them over their useful life spans.

In some instances it is to your advantage to take the standard deduction of 16 percent of adjusted gross income rather than itemizing deductions. It is well worth your time to calculate your tax obligation by both methods to ascertain which is best for you. If you are married it will probably be to your advantage to file a joint return for yourself and your spouse.

One way of preventing errors and maximizing savings on your tax return is to find a qualified person to help you. The Internal Revenue Service has a taxpayer-assistance service that can help answer your questions. Beware of "storefront" operators who promise to save you big money when you allow them to prepare your tax return for a fee. They may not be around to answer if your return is questioned. The errors will not be excused even though you paid for the service. If you must have help, seek an accountant or other qualified person who has been recommended to you because he is reliable.

While it is a legal obligation to pay taxes at all levels of government, there is nothing that requires you to pay more than your just responsibility. It is to your advantage, then, to take all legal measures to minimize your "tax bite," so that you are better able to meet your own goals or those of your family.

GLOSSARY OF NEW TERMS

Excise tax   A tax on the production, sale, or consumption of a commodity.
Income averaging   A process used in income tax preparation which permits you to spread large earnings in any one year over a five-year period if your taxable income for that year exceeds by more than $3,000 an amount that is one-third greater than the average of your taxable income in the four preceding years.
Itemized deductions   Deductions enumerated one by one on a person's income tax return. A taxpayer has a choice between itemizing deductions and taking the standard deduction.
Standard deduction   A stated amount (now 16 percent) that a person may deduct from his income when calculating his income tax obligations.

Taxable income   For income tax purposes, all payments you receive for labor, returns on capital investments, profits from business or property, and prizes won in contests.

QUESTIONS FOR DISCUSSION

1. Discuss the three levels of government at which taxes are levied and enumerate items on which consumers pay taxes at each level.
2. Explain how consumers are affected by taxes paid by business operators, manufacturers, and professionals.
3. List services that are provided by the federal government through taxation. Could these services be provided by private citizens?
4. Name some services that are paid for by taxes collected at the state level and local level.
5. Consumers frequently feel that they are the victims of taxation and there is little if anything they can do. Discuss ways in which consumers can have a voice in taxation.
6. Discuss the cost of environmental programs to improve the quality of life for all citizens. How much should consumers be willing to pay for such programs?
7. Identify items that are considered "income" by the Internal Revenue Service.
8. Suggest procedures for keeping track of your income and expenditures for income tax purposes.
9. Name the two major classifications of deductions permitted by the Internal Revenue Service.
10. Discuss ways in which to avoid paying more than your fair share of income tax.

SUGGESTED STUDENT ACTIVITIES

1. Visit an office of the Internal Revenue Service and find out what services and publications are available to help an individual taxpayer prepare a tax return.
2. Prepare a report on the services provided for by federal, state, and local taxes. Share your report with the class.
3. Collect newspaper articles and statements from legislators on the subject of taxes and the use of public monies. Evaluate the reasons given by politicians for voting "yes" or "no" on various tax issues.
4. Describe an imaginary family that pays federal income taxes. Include in your description all the information needed in filing a tax return. Then prepare the federal tax return for this family, using the appropriate forms. (If you prefer you may use your own family.)
5. Prepare a chart illustrating how the income of a wage earner affects the taxes he or she pays.
6. Investigate the outcomes of (a) failing to file an income tax return, (b) filing an incorrect or incomplete return, (c) submitting false information, and

(d) neglecting to keep records to verify the return. Report to the class on your findings.

7. Interview five adults who are paying taxes. Secure their opinions on whether local and state taxes are fair and justifiable. Summarize your findings and report to the class.

8. Write a short paper on why individuals should be willing to accept their responsibility for paying taxes.

9. Keep a list of all items that you purchase during a week. Determine how much you have spent for taxes. Does this amount seem reasonable? Why or why not?

10. Prepare a list of ways in which you can save on your income tax. Organize them under the major categories listed on the income tax form. Set up a record-keeping system so as to have information at hand when filling out your next income tax return.

FOR ADDITIONAL INFORMATION

Blodgett, Richard E. *The New York Times Book of Money*. New York: Quadrangle/ The New York Times Book Co., 1971, pp. 180–200.
Provides common-sense advice for saving on your federal tax bill.

Changing Times. *Your Income Tax: Do It Right and Save*. Washington, D.C.: The Kiplinger Magazine, 1972.
Contains information on where most taxpayers go wrong in preparing a tax return.

Commerce Clearing House. *Federal Tax Course*. New York: Commerce, published annually.
A complete overview of federal taxation.

"If Your Tax Return Is Audited." *Changing Times*, June 1973, pp. 21–23.
Tells how computers and people search for errors in tax returns. Explains what you can do if your return is challenged.

Internal Revenue Service. *Understanding Taxes*. Publication No. 21. Washington, D.C., 1971.
Helpful in learning how to prepare and file an income tax return. Various forms and examples are presented.

———. *Your Federal Income Tax: For Individuals*, Washington, D.C.: Government Printing Office. Published annually.
Provides information on filing your tax return. Available at most post offices for a small charge.

Lasser, J. K. *Your Income Tax*. New York: Simon and Schuster. Published annually.
This publication presents clear directions for filing your income tax return. It explains what to include as income and lists possible deductions.

Ochs, Jack. *Public Finance*. New York: Harper and Row, 1974.
This book explains tax theory as well as its application to preparing a tax return.

Peterson, George E., ed. *Property Tax Reform*. Publication No. URI-49000. Washington, D.C.: Urban Institute, n.d.
Excellent diversified discussion of current issues concerning property tax.

Phillips, E. Bryant, and Sylvia Lane. *Personal Finance: Text and Case Problems*. New York: John Wiley and Sons, 1974, pp. 373–410.
A comprehensive discussion of expenditures for government services.

Saalbach, William F. *Economics for the Consumer*. River Forest, Ill.: Laidlaw Brothers, 1974.

Discusses government spending and taxation. Contains charts, suggested activities, and a glossary of terms.

Stewart, Maxwell. *Money for Our Cities: Is Revenue Sharing the Answer?* Public Affairs Pamphlet No. 461. New York: Public Affairs Committee, 1971.

This twenty-four-page pamphlet, which presents easy-to-understand information on revenue sharing, can be obtained for 35 cents by writing to the Public Affairs Committee, 381 Park Avenue South, New York, N.Y. 10016.

"Tax Rulings That Could Affect You." *Changing Times*, July 1974, pp. 39–40.

This article explains the tax rulings and presents pertinent information for tax return preparers.

What Are Taxes? Be Informed Series. Unit 9, Part I. Syracuse, N.Y.: New Reader Press, 1973.

Interestingly written explanation of taxes and where the tax dollar goes. Simple, realistic examples are included.

16

Solving Your Money Problems

16

Now that you have read this text, you have the tools with which to build your own program of sound money management. You have the knowledge to increase the enjoyment you get from the money you earn and spend. But having knowledge is not the same as using it. Knowing is not doing. Only by using the information you have acquired will you be able to achieve a better standard of living for yourself or your family.

Putting into practice what you have learned in these pages means extra effort on your part—but effort that is rewarding. It's not easy to change your habits and practices. It takes time and the desire to succeed. But it will be well worth the time and effort when you see what happens once you start to use what you have learned about managing money.

The pages that follow will help you analyze the ways in which you have been spending your money and develop your own money-management plan. Follow the steps indicated. Think about your decisions. Be honest with yourself.

Identifying Your Money Problems

Take a sheet of paper and write down the three most important money problems that you face today. Think carefully. Is using your credit one of them? Do you have trouble planning your food expenses? List the problems in the order of importance to you.

Listed in Worksheet 16.1 are the areas of personal money management that we have considered in this text. Rank *all* of these now in their order of importance to you. Rank the most important item as number 1, the next as number 2, and so on until you have assigned a number to each item.

WORKSHEET 16.1
Ranking Your
Concerns

Item	Rank
Making a money plan	_____
Using credit	_____
Spending for household appliances	_____
Spending for housing	_____
Spending for transportation	_____
Spending for food	_____
Spending for clothes	_____
Spending for protection, including insurance	_____
Spending for health and recreation	_____
Saving, investing, and estate planning	_____
Paying taxes	_____

Are the items you have ranked 1, 2, and 3 in this list the same as the most important problems you identified to begin with? If they are not, go back and rethink the matter.

You have now identified the three most important money problems that you face. Once you have worked out your own way of taking care of these basic problems, the others will be much simpler to handle.

Five Steps to Solving Your Money Problems

The following five steps will help you find a solution to the three problems you have listed. You'll need more paper for this.

Take your most important problem first. Ask yourself, "What can I do about it?" What can you change in your current procedures? What new ways are there for you to confront this problem? You might want to change the ways you shop. Or you might want to find a new way to keep a record of your expenditures. Whatever you think needs to be done, enter it on your paper. Your sheet will look like Worksheet 16.2.

WORKSHEET 16.2
Beginning the Solution

Step 1.	What can I do about it?
a.	
b.	

SOLVING YOUR MONEY PROBLEMS

Once you have identified all of the possible approaches to your number one problem, you are ready for step 2. For each possible solution, ask yourself, "When will I do this?" Set a time for starting. Are you going to begin tomorrow? Next week? Or next payday? Set a time for finishing as well. Are you going to complete your program in one week, three months, six months, or one year? Be realistic about how much time you will need, but don't allow yourself to waste time. Your sheet will now look like Worksheet 16.3.

Step 3 asks you to identify those who can be of assistance to you in solving your problem. You have already identified the things you need to do and when you will do them. Now list the names of those who would be most likely to help you in achieving your goal. Can someone in your immediate family assist you? Can you turn to a good friend? Your banker? Also write down how these people would help you. What would you like them to do to help you with your solution? Your sheet will now look like Worksheet 16.4.

WORKSHEET 16.3
Second Step of
the Solution

Step 1.	What can I do about it?		
a. b.			
Step 2. *Begin*	**When will I do this?**		*Complete*
a. b.		a. b.	

Step 1.	What can I do about it?	
a. b.		

Step 2.	When will I do this?	
	Begin	*Complete*
a. b.		a. b.

Step 3.	What assistance will I need?	
	Who?	*How?*
a. b.		a. b.

WORKSHEET 16.4
Third Step of
the Solution

To take step 4, you identify the obstacles that might get in your way. What could keep you from achieving your goal? Are there bad habits that you think will be difficult to change? Will some members of your family interfere? When you have identified the obstacles that might get in your way, you are in a position to take steps to avoid them. Your sheet will now look like Worksheet 16.5.

The fifth and last step in the process of solving your problem is to recognize the rewards or satisfactions that will come to you if you succeed. They will give you the incentive you need to stick to the plan. Will you gain a better standard of living, or just plain "peace of mind"? You should also identify what will happen if you do not succeed in carrying out your plan and solving your problem. When you have identified both the rewards of success and the consequences of failure, your sheet will look like Worksheet 16.6.

You now have a plan of action to attack your most important money problem. Go on to problem number 2. In the same five steps develop a plan for solving it. Then go on to problem 3. Limit your

Step 1.	What can I do about it?	
a. b.		

Step 2.	When will I do this?	
Begin		*Complete*
a. b.	a. b.	

Step 3.	What assistance will I need?	
Who?		*How?*
a. b.	a. b.	

Step 4.	What might get in my way?
a. b.	

WORKSHEET 16.5
Fourth Step of
the Solution

efforts to these three problems. You will find that they interlock and that in solving one you are helping to solve the others.

From time to time you will want to check your progress. Use your five-step plan as a guide. Reread it to yourself and to your family.

Ask yourself how successful you have been in implementing the changes you listed in your plan. Are you meeting your time table? Are those from whom you sought assistance delivering the help you expected? If not, what do you need to know to get it from them? What have you done about the obstacles you thought might get in your way? How much closer are you to receiving the rewards you promised yourself when you made your plan? Or are you experiencing the consequences of failure?

The five steps to solving money problems will put you on the road to successful money management. Using the five steps will enable you to achieve the satisfactions you seek for the money you spend. You and your family will begin to live better. After all, isn't this what it's all about?

Step 1.	What can I do about it?
a.	
b.	

Step 2.		When will I do this?	
	Begin		*Complete*
a.		a.	
b.		b.	

Step 3.		What assistance will I need?	
	Who?		*How?*
a.		a.	
b.		b.	

Step 4.	What might get in my way?
a.	
b.	

Step 5.		What will happen?	
	If I fail		*If I succeed*
a.		a.	
b.		b.	

WORKSHEET 16.6
The Complete
Solution Plan

Index

References in **boldface** are to definitions of terms in glossaries.